Quincentennial Essays on St. Thomas More

Quincentennial Essays on St. Thomas More

Selected Papers from the Thomas More College Conference

Edited by Michael J. Moore

ALBION

Department of History
Appalachian State University
Boone, North Carolina

International Standard Book Number: 0-932530-00-1
Library of Congress Catalogue Card Number: 78-67288

Published by Albion, at the Department of
History, Appalachian State University,
Boone, North Carolina 28608

Printed in the United States of America.

Contents

Contributors

Frank Carpinelli, Associate Professor of English at Benedictine College, Atchison, Kansas, is continuing his study of the Thomas More family.

Dorothy (Dody) H. Donnelly, CSJ, Associate Professor of Historical Theology at the Graduate Theological Union, Berkeley, California, has edited and translated Thomas More's *Responsio ad Lutherum* (1962), and written widely on communication, and on the ministry.

Charles Clay Doyle, Assistant Professor of English at the University of Georgia, has published in *Moreana,* the *Journal of American Folklore,* and other journals. He is presently preparing a monograph on the popular nature of Thomas More's wit and humor.

Stephen Gresham, Assistant Professor of English at Auburn University, Alabama, received his Ph.D. in 1975 from the University of Missouri.

John A. Gueguen, Associate Professor of Political Science at Illinois State University, Normal, has published in *The Thomist,* and currently is writing about the relationship of classical and medieval thought to contemporary ideas.

J. H. Hexter is Distinguished Historian in Residence at Washington University, St. Louis, and Professor Emeritus of History at Yale University. He is well known as the author of *The Reign of King Pym* (1940), *More's UTOPIA: The Biography of an Idea* (1952), and for books on history and historiography, of which *On Historians* will be published in November, 1978. He is presently engaged with a study of the history of Anglo-American liberties.

Judith P. Jones, Assistant Professor of English at Auburn University, Montgomery, Alabama, has published articles in *Moreana* and has a bibliography of Thomas More forthcoming in *English Literary Renaissance.*

Lee Cullen Khanna, Assistant Professor of English at Montclair State College, Upper Montclair, N.J., has published articles in *Moreana,* and is presently writing a book on women in the work of Thomas More.

Richard C. Marius is Director of Expository Writing at Harvard University. He has edited *The Confutation of Tyndale's Answer* (1973) for the Yale edition of *The Complete Works of St. Thomas More,* edited *More's Dialogue Concerning Heresies and Matters of Religion* due in 1979, and written a study of Martin Luther (1974). An award winning novelist, he is also writing a biography of Thomas More to be published by Knopf.

Clarence H. Miller is Dorothy McBride Orthwein Professor of English Literature at St. Louis University. He has written extensively on More, Erasmus, and Renaissance literature, while editing Chaloner's *The Praise of Folie* (1965), and for Yale's *Complete Works of St. Thomas More,* the volume *De Tristitia Christi* (1976). He is presently editing More's *Answer to the first parte of the Poisoned Book* for the Yale *Complete Works,* and publishing (1979) a translation of Erasmus' *Praise of Folly* and *Letter to Dorp.*

Richard J. Schoeck is Professor of English and Humanities, and Chairman of the Department of Integrated Studies at the University of Colorado. He has written many books and articles on More and the Renaissance literary world, the most recent of which is *The Achievement of Thomas More* (1976). His current interests are with editing More's *Debellation,* and writing books on law and literature, and on justice in Shakespeare.

Sherianne Sellers Seibel was a student of Judith P. Jones who received her B.A. "With Honor" from Auburn University.

Thomas I. White, Assistant Professor of Philosophy and Religion at Upsala College, East Orange, N.J., has published articles on the *Utopia* in *Moreana* and *Renaissance Quarterly.* He is currently working on More's social and political thought and the influence of classical philosophy on More's *Utopia.*

Warren W. Wooden, Associate Professor of English at Marshall University, Huntington, West Va., has just published *The English Sermons of John Foxe* (1978), having written earlier articles on More and Renaissance literary figures. He has forthcoming an article on Roper's *Life of More* in *Moreana.*

Preface

A quincentennial conference honoring St. Thomas More took place at Thomas More College in Ft. Mitchell, Kentucky on February 9-11, 1978. Those days were known as the "Birthday Party," and the joyousness of the occasion focusing on the exchange of ideas between friends old and new provided for those attending a special blessing. Their gathering to commemorate the great Renaissance scholar and saint was fittingly sponsored by the only college in the world to bear his name, and helped to fulfill a goal of dedicated alumni, students, faculty, and friends when they moved Villa Madonna College from Covington, Kentucky, changed its name and purpose, and began in 1968 as Thomas More College to occupy a new campus in the countryside.

The guiding inspiration of this transformation was the Most Reverend Richard H. Ackerman, Bishop of Covington, who believed and sustained the idea that Catholic college education was a valuable and necessary part of the northern Kentucky academic world. The conference paid tribute to Bishop Ackerman's farsightedness and his dedication to education.

The conference was planned and organized by Dr. Raymond Hebert of the History faculty who chaired the coordinating committee. Every participant benefitted from his skill and judgment as plans for a major academic conference were developed. It was, of course, an enormous task, and its success testifies to the dedication of Hebert and his colleagues.

It is a pleasure for *Albion* to publish these essays, which with one exception were among the twenty-three papers read to the conference; and again, it has been due to the industry of Dr. Herbert that publication has been possible. He gathered the papers, consulted with their authors, and with the propitious intercession of Arthur J. Slavin initiated their joint publication by Thomas More College and *Albion*. The essay on images of women by Lee Cullen Khanna was solicited by Dr. Hebert to fill out a part of More studies that is of growing interest. It was not a conference paper, but its inclusion here is welcomed. The other papers, some of which have been revised since their delivery, have been selected as representative of the diverse and new scholarship presented at the conference.

An enjoyable summer has been spent in the preparation of this volume. To President Robert J. Giroux of Thomas More College, who authorized his college's commitment to publish these essays, Dr. Roy Carroll of Appalachian State University, and to the authors goes my thanks for their encouragement and assistance. Because of the restraints of time, imposed by the desire to publish during Thomas More's quincentennial year, it has not been possible for the authors to see proofs of their articles. They have reposed in me a trust that I hope has been adequately fulfilled. Yale University Press has given permission to use material from its publication of *De Tristitia Christi* in the essay by Professor Clarence Miller.

As this volume was being prepared occurred the death of Richard S. Sylvester (1926-1978), a man known to many who will read these pages. It was Richard Sylvester who originally gave his encouragement and blessing to the conference. It was Richard Sylvester who spoke at the dedication of the new Thomas More College campus. It is to Richard Sylvester that much of the scholarship presented here is indebted. As Executive Editor of the Yale edition of *The Complete Works of St. Thomas More* from 1958, he radiated a leadership and inspiration that was illumined by his deep knowledge of and love for Thomas More. In many ways, he touched and encouraged scholars and laymen to discover more about More and the Renaissance world. This volume of essays is a tribute to the memory of Richard Sylvester, and to his legacy.

Thomas More and The Daunce Family

Frank Carpinelli

The purposes of this paper are to offer some biographical data on Thomas More's son-in-law William Daunce, and his and Elizabeth More Daunce's descendants; and to consider the implications of Thomas More's statement—contained in his last letter to his daughter Margaret—that if his son John should inherit his property, then John should "breake not my will concerning his sister Daunce."

Most of the material I cover in the first part of this paper could fall under the title of "Thomas More's Son-In-Law William Daunce, and the *Other* William Dauntsey, Mercer and Alderman of London." This title should indicate that my first point is to identify More's son-in-law by distinguishing him from another man of practically the same name. Both men were prominent in London during the 1520s, 1530s, and 1540s. Unfortunately, some scholars have confused the two men, which is easy enough to do, since the spellings of their names vary in the contemporary documents. I will use the spelling of Daunce for More's son-in-law, and Dauntsey for the other man, who was a mercer and alderman. These seem to be the most common spellings of the family names for these two different men.

Let us start with the William Dauntsey. John Stow mentions him in his *Survey of London,* when he comments on Cordwainer Street ward, within which is "the fayre parish Church of Saint *Anthonies* in Budge Row. . . ." Stow provides the following entry for this parish: "*William Dauntsey* Mercer, one of the shiriffes, buried 1542."[1] The parish registers for St. Anthony's, or St. Antholin Budge Row, record the burial of "Mr. William Dauncy, alderman" on April 27, 1543. Interestingly, these same registers record the burial of "Mistris Dancy wife of Alderman Dancy," on June 16, 1542.[2] If the man mentioned in these parish registers were More's son-in-law, then we would know the burial date of not only this in-law of the More family, but also the burial date of Elizabeth More Daunce, Thomas More's second daughter.

---

[1]John Stow, *A Survey of London*, introd. and notes by C.L. Kingsford, 2 vols. (Oxford, 1971), I:250-52.
[2]J.L. Chester and George J. Armytage, eds., *The Parish Registers of St. Antholin, Budge Row . . .*, Publ. of Harleian Society Registers (London, 1883), VIII:3,4.

In addition to this information from parish registers, we also have extant the will of the William Dauntsey who was a mercer and an alderman. The contents of this will have been summarized in W.K. Jordan's *The Charities of London*, in which Jordan is concerned with the will since in 1542 it established a trust "for the founding of an almshouse and school" in Dauntsey's "native village of West Lavington, just to the south of Devizes in Wiltshire." Jordan notes: "This donor settled on his company as trustee properties then possessing a capital worth of £928, the income of which was to be employed in approximately even portions for the support of the two institutions"; and, "Dauntsey also left £200 to the Mercers' Company to be lent to four young men, each of whom would give, as interest, two loads of coal to the poor of St. Lawrence Jewry and the same to those of St. Antholin's." But Jordan adds some data on the mercer which is certainly not in his will: "He was a member (for Thetford) of the Reformation Parliament, had been an alderman for a long time, master of his company in 1532, and sheriff in 1530. His wife was a daughter of Sir Thomas More."[3]

In a 1961 article, Margaret Hastings produced a genealogical chart of the More family which identified the husband of Elizabeth More as "William Dauntsey/cit. and mercer/of London."[4] Also, in his 1966 edition of Stapleton's *Life* of More, E.E. Reynolds refers the reader to the Hastings article, noting that "there are several errors" in Stapleton's account of the More family; and, Reynolds himself includes a genealogical chart identifying Daunce as simply "mercer."[5] However, the facts indicate that this cannot be the case. In spite of the claims of Jordan, Hastings, and Reynolds, More's son-in-law was not the same man who was the mercer and alderman.

The William Daunce who was More's son-in-law did not die in April of 1543. Various commentators have noted that Daunce was implicated in the Plot of the Prebendaries against Cranmer in 1543, that he was imprisoned, and then pardoned "of all treasonable words against the King's supremacy" on April 24, 1544.[6] Also,

[3]W.K. Jordan, *The Charities of London, 1480-1660* (London, 1960), pp. 139, 224. 353.

[4]Margaret Hastings, "The Ancestry of Sir Thomas More," *Guildhall Miscellany*, II (1961):47-62.

[5]Thomas Stapleton, *The Life and Illustrious Martyrdom of Sir Thomas More*, ed. E.E. Reynolds (London, 1966), p. vi.

[6]William Roper, *The Lyfe of Sir Thomas Moore, Knighte*, ed. Elsie V. Hitchcock (London, 1935), p. 116.

several commentators have noted that the son-in-law of More was the son of Sir John Daunce, and that when Sir John died in December of 1545, William Daunce inherited his property. The *Letters and Papers of Henry VIII* calendars the warrant as follows:

> William Daunce. Warrant for livery of lands to him as s. and h. of Sir John Daunce who /by the office found 8 Dec. 37 Hen. VIII./ died seised of the late priory of Muresley, Bucks leaving the said William aged 45 years and more.[7]

Finally, I have determined when More's son-in-law did die. The date of his death is recorded in the *Calendar of the Patent Rolls* for Edward VI, in which we have an entry for February 20, 1549, on the inheritance of William Daunce's lands by his son and heir John:

> General livery to John Daunce, aged 23, as son and heir of William Daunce, gentleman, who died 28 May 2 Edward VI seised of the house and site of the late priory of Muresley *alias* St. Margaret's, Bucks, and its lands in Muresley, Ivinghoo, Wynleshorn, Eddesborough *alias* Edelborough, Northyll, Northetehyll, Pyghthethorne, Pytleshorne, Fresden, and Drayton, Bucks, held of the king in chief by the tenth part of one knight's fee and a rent of 32s. by the name of tenth.. . .[8]

Thus, More's son-in-law died on May 28, 1548. The inheritance of the Muresley property, passing to William Daunce from his father Sir John, and then to young John Daunce (grandson of Thomas More) from his father William, clearly establishes that we are here dealing with the correct line in the descent through the Daunces.

Further evidence distinguishing the mercer-alderman from More's son-in-law can be gathered from a brief examination of the careers of the two men. An outline of the early career of William Dauntsey can be obtained by glancing through the published records in the *Acts of Court of the Mercers' Company, 1453-1527*. We find that in 1505 Dauntsey was among a group "shewed to the assistens" to be considered to be of the livery; in 1507 he was taken into the livery; in 1509 he was chosen as one of the Auditors; in 1515 he was one of those taking part in the "General Courts of Merchauntes Adventerers"; and in 1516 he was elected a Master Warden. If we recall from the grant concerning inheritance of Sir John Daunce's property that More's son-in-law was about forty-five years old in 1545, then he

---

[7]Dated 26 May, 38 Hen. VIII. *Del.* Westm. 26 Nov. 38 Hen. VIII, *Letters and Papers, Foreign and Domestic, of the Reign of Henry VIII,* Vol. XXI, Part 2 (1546) (London, 1910), Item 476 (101). (Hereafter cited as *L & P Hen. VIII.*)

[8]*Calendar of the Patent Rolls, Edward VI* (London, 1926) V:334.

[9]*Acts of Court of the Mercers' Company, 1453-1527,* introd. Laetitia Lyell (Cambridge, Eng., 1936), pp. 271, 309-10, 352, 433, 440.

must have been born in about 1500, and would be too young to be assuming the offices just listed in the mercers' accounts. He would not have been taken into the company at age seven, chosen an Auditor at age nine, and made a Master Warden at age sixteen!

Just what did More's son-in-law do, if he was not a mercer? He seems to have been a minor government official following in his father's footsteps in the exchequer. His father had risen through the exchequer, and for William himself there is this grant in October 1528: "Wm. Daunce. To be one of the tellers of the Exchequer on a vacancy, with the usual fees."[10] By the time of his father's death in 1545, he seems to have been in line to succeed Sir John as general surveyor of the crown lands. According to W.C. Richardson, Sir John Daunce headed the Court of General Surveyors "until his death in December, 1545, when he was succeeded in that office by his son, William Daunce . . . ." Richardson then adds: "There is no evidence however, that William Daunce ever actually took over the duties of the office, for Walter Mildmay, the king's auditor, held the position by oral appointment from December, 1545, until January, 1547, when the court was merged with the augmentations."[11]

The final point distinguishing these two men is that their families came from different areas of England. References above, especially in his will, make it clear that the mercer came from West Lavington, Wiltshire. Dauntseys had been in this area for centuries; one need only consult the *Victoria County History of Wiltshire* to learn that various of them held manors in Wiltshire since the middle ages. Also, the family tree is widely available, and *Wiltshire Notes and Queries* is full of references to several Dauntseys, including our mercer.[12] On the other hand, the father of the More-related Daunce came from Thame, Oxfordshire, and most of Sir John's properties were in nearby parts of Buckinghamshire, while his first wife (William's mother) was from Berkshire. And, as we will note below, this William Daunce also acquired lands in Hertfordshire and Middlesex. Thus, the mercer is chiefly a Wessex or west country man, while More's son-in-law has his roots in counties surrounding London. But both men did live in London for several years.

I would like to turn again to the matter of the Daunce line. We

[10]*Del.* Westm. 7 Oct. 20 Hen. VIII, *L & P Hen. VIII*, IV, Item 4896 (7).

[11]W.C. Richardson, *Tudor Chamber Administration, 1485-1547* (Baton Rouge, 1952), pp. 365-66.

[12]See: *The Genealogist,* XII, n.s. (London, n.d.), pp. 23-24; *Victoria County History of Lancashire,* Vol. IV, p. 220n.; *Wiltshire Notes and Queries,* III (1899-1901):22, 23, 47-48, 85, 86, 124-26, 470.

have already seen that William Daunce's son and heir was named John, and that in 1549 he was twenty-three years old (since William Daunce and Elizabeth More were married on September 29, 1525, their son John must have been born within a year or so of their marriage).[13] The questions we may consider now are: Who were the other grandchildren of Thomas More in this Daunce line? And, who were Thomas More's descendants through William Daunce's son John? One sentence in Stapleton's *Life* is particularly valuable.

> Elizabeth, More's second daughter, married John [should be William] Dauncy and bore him five sons, John, Thomas, Bartholomew, William, and Germain, and two daughters, Alice and Elizabeth.[14]

With this statement in mind, and with the knowledge that the Daunces held land in Buckinghamshire, there are these comments in the *Victoria County History of Buckinghamshire,* on the Priory of St. Margaret or Muresley Priory:

> A lease of the site for twenty-one years was granted to John Verney in 1536, and two years after the reversion was granted in tail-male to Sir John Daunce, kt., who died seised of it in 1545, leaving a son William. Bartholomew Daunce died seised in 1593, having obtained a further grant; his heir was his son Richard, who held until his death in 1624, when his son, also called Richard, succeeded him.[15]

This entry does not mention John as heir to William; and it does not make clear whether the Bartholomew, who died in 1593, was a son of John, or, perhaps, the brother of John. Regardless, it seems to be the case that we have here some of Thomas More's descendents in the Daunce line.

William Daunce was granted a pardon in 1544 from his involvement in the plot against Cranmer which indicates where he held, or had held, lands: "Wm. Daunce, of Cayshobere, Herts, *alias* late of Cannons, Midd., *alias* of London."[16] Among the records for the Court of Request are documents concerning a "bill of compleynt" brought by two husbandmen, William Long and Thomas Lutt, against "Bartholomewe Dauntesey and Thomas Dauntesey" who were "ioyntlie possessed of the lease of a farm in Watford in the County of Herts called Caissobury."[17] Here, it seems likely, are two sons of William Daunce involved in a legal action (date: 1551) over

---

[13]Roper, *Life of More,* pp. 115-16.
[14]Stapleton, *Life,* p. 93.
[15]*The Victoria History of the County of Buckinghamshire,* ed. William Page, (London, 1925), III:382-283.
[16]*L & P Hen. VIII,* 1544, Pt. i, Item 444(5), quoted in Roper, *Life of More,* p. 116.
[17]Public Record Office, Requests 2, Bundle 16, No. 91.

land that had probably come down to them from their father.

The leads are numerous and enticing. Picking up on the reference to William Daunce holding land in "Cannons, Midd.," we note from the *Victoria County History of Middlesex,* in a section on Gore Hundred, Little Stanmore parish (also known as Whitchurch parish): "It was as the manor of Canons that the great manor-house and gardens were leased, separately from most of the estate, to William Daunce of Whitchurch in 1535." Little Stanmore reverted to the Crown in 1540, "and in 1543 the manor-house of Canons, as leased to William Daunce, was granted to the sitting tenant Hugh Losse and his heirs."[18] Did Daunce lose his land in Middlesex once he was implicated in the plot of 1543? And who was the Robert Dauncey who, according to ecclesiastical records, was a clerk and rector in parishes in the Mureseley area of Buckinghamshire, and also the parish of Whitchurch or Little Stanmore in Middlesex?[19] It will take considerable effort, and also some luck, to sort out the several Daunces we can discover in the sixteenth century records. To mention just one avenue that needs to be pursued: in the parish church of Blewbury, in Reading Hundred, Berkshire, is a "brass to Dame Alice Daunce, daughter of Thomas Latton, who died in 1527, containing the figures of herself and her husband Sir John Daunce, surveyor general to King Henry VIII." Below these two figures "are the figures of her five sons and two daughters."[20] So, if possible, we must get straightened out on the five sons and two daughters of Sir John Daunce, as well as the five sons and two daughters of William Daunce. The nephews and nieces and cousins may interact considerably, and they may be very close in age to one another.

I would like to pass now to another potentially dangerous, or at least difficult, endeavor: the conjecture over the possible meaning(s) of statements in a document without sufficient facts to conclusively establish the meaning of the statement. I am particularly interested in the meaning(s) of Thomas More's statement—contained in his last letter to his daughter Margaret—that if his son John should inherit

---

[18]*The Victoria County History of Middlesex,* Vol. V, ed. T.F.T. Baker (Oxford, 1976), pp. 114-15.

[19]See Richard Newcourt, *Repertorium Ecclesiasticum Parochiale Londinense* (London, 1708), and George Hennessy, compiler, *Novum Repertorium . . .*, (London, 1898).

[20]*The Victoria History of the County of Berkshire,* ed. William Page and Rev. P.H. Ditchfield (London, 1923), III:288. For more details on this tomb or memorial, see Elias Ashmole, *The Antiquities of Berkshire* (London, 1719), II:304-06. Ashmole gives the date of Dame Alice Daunce's death as 27 August 1523.

his property, then John should "breake not my will concerning his sister Daunce."

We don't know the contents of Thomas More's will, so we don't know what the will stipulated for "sister Daunce"; but I begin with the assumption that More meant for his daughter Elizabeth to share, in some way, in his estate. The overall tone of his last letter, written the day before he was beheaded, is extremely positive; the letter is full of blessings on "all my children, and all my godchildren and all our friends."[21] Towards the end of his letter, More comes to references to his son John, and to this sentence in particular: "Our Lord bless him and his good wife my loving daughter, to whom I pray him be good as he hath great cause: and that if the land of mine come to his hand he break not my will concerning his sister Dauncey."

If John thought of excluding Elizabeth from the will, what are the possible bases for tension between the Mores and the Daunces by July 1535? One is that shortly before More was executed, Sir John Daunce either took action to regain, or else was at least willing to accept, property that he had pledged in the marriage arrangements between the families ten years before, when his son William was to marry Thomas More's daughter Elizabeth. The calendaring of the grant to Sir John reads:

> Sir John Daunce of London, King's councillor. Grant of one part of an indenture made 26 Sept. 17 Hen. VIII., between Sir Thos. More of Chelsey, Middx., King's councillor, and the said Sir John, containing an agreement that Will. Daunce, s. and h. of the said Sir John, should marry Eliz. More, one of the ds. and hs. of the said Sir Thomas; and likewise a bond given by the said Sir John to the said Sir Thomas for the fulfilment of the said indenture; the said indenture and bond being confiscated to the King on account of certain contempts and misprisions committed by the said Sir Thomas.[22]

A slightly different rendering is given by James Gairdner: "Marriage articles of William Daunce, esq., son and heir of Sir John Daunce and Elizabeth daughter of Sir Thomas More, having been confiscated, were delivered up to Sir John Daunce."[23] So, Sir John was able to nullify his indenture and bond to More less than a month from the time of More's execution.

The two men had certainly known each other well since at least the early 1520s, and probably even before then. Daunce had been

[21]The text from the 1557 edition of More's *Works* is quoted in R.W. Chambers, *Thomas More* (Ann Arbor, Mich., 1958), p. 345.

[22]*Del.* Westm, 12 June 27 Hen. VIII, *L & P Hen. VIII,* Vol. VIII, Item 962 (10).

[23]James Gairdner, "Sir Thomas More's House at Chelsea," *Notes and Queries,* 2nd Series, No. 49 (Dec. 6, 1856):455.

receiver-general of revenues from wardship lands in 1509; treasurer of war during the campaign in France in 1513; chief butler of England in 1515; one of the general surveyors of crown lands in 1517; and he served during the early to mid 1520s with Sir John Heron, Treasurer of the Chamber, and then Heron's successor, Sir Henry Wyatt. While Wyatt served on special diplomatic missions abroad, the major financial transactions were delegated to Daunce.[24] More must have worked closely with Heron and Daunce, especially after 1521, when More was made Under-Treasurer of the Exchequer. Heron died on June 10, 1522, and the wardship of his son and heir Giles was granted to More on March 18, 1523.[25] The relationships among the three families must have been strongly cemented by the double wedding on September 29, 1525 of the son and heir of Sir John Heron, Giles, to Cecilia More, and the son and heir of Sir John Daunce, William, to Elizabeth More.

During the 1520s, we may chart the growing affluence of William Daunce—and also his growing dependence on the royal favor—by various grants he received. Under "Grants in April 1522": "Wm., son of Sir John Daunce, the King's councillor. Lease, for 60 years, of the manor of Whytechurche, Oxf., parcel of the duchy of Cornwall, in the honor of Wallyngford. . . ." Under "Grants in June 1527": "Wm. Daunce. Lease of the 1p. of Kennington, Surrey, part of the duchy of Cornwall, for 21 years. . . ." Under "Grants in October 1528": "Wm. Daunce. To be one of the tellers of the Exchequer on a vacancy, with the usual fees."[26] And, of course, he is elected to parliament in 1529.

Then comes the storm in the 1530s. Thomas More resigned the Great Seal in May 1532; was absent from the coronation of Anne Boleyn in June 1533; was imprisoned in Nov. 1534; and put to death in July 1535. What were the Daunces doing during this period? Sir John was on the list for "The King's New Year's Gifts" in January 1533; he was working closely with Cromwell on land deals, and seems to have been connected with plans for the suppression of monasteries; and, during the procession for the coronation of Anne Boleyn, the Chief Justices stopped at the home of Sir John Daunce "in Mark Lane," resting there for one half hour before going on to Tower Hill.[27] His continued good service to Henry VIII may be

---

[24] Richardson, *Tudor Chamber Administration*, pp. 239, 256-57, 283; C.G. Cruickshank, *Army Royal: Henry VIII's Invasion of France, 1513* (Oxford, 1969), p. 124.
[25] Roper, *Life of More*, p. 117.
[26] *L&P Hen. VIII*, Vol. III, Pt. II, Item 2214(19); Vol. IV, Items 3213(26), 4896(7).
[27] *L&P Hen. VIII*, Vol. VI, Items 32, 94, 95, 583; Vol. VII, Item 923 (xii).

measured by the grant he received in 1535, nullifying his indenture and bond to More; the grant he received in 1536, making perpetual his office as a general surveyor of crown lands; his grant in 1537 by which he received an annuity of £200, out of "customs in the ports of London, Exeter, and Dartmouth"; and his grant in 1538, whereby he received the lands of Muresley priory.[28] It is clear that Sir John remained the good and faithful servant of the king, and he certainly prospered from this course. What is not clear is just how much his general course of action, or his 1535 nullification of the indenture and bond he had made with More in 1525, contributed to tension between the More family and the Daunce family. I suspect that it contributed quite a bit.

What about William Daunce in the critical early 1530s? He evidently was concerned about those grants listed above. And someone else was interested in at least one of his grants, as this excerpt from a letter, written in 1533 and labeled "Sir Walter Stonore to Cromwell," shows: "Let me put you in remembrance of the fee-farm that young Dawnse has of the manor of Wychyrch in Oxfordshire, one of the four belonging to the honour of Wallingford, never let before."[29] As far as I have been able to tell, Daunce was able to retain this grant; and he picked up two more leases. One of these was the manor of Cassio, or Cassiobury which had belonged to the abbey of St. Albans, and then "at the Dissolution it was held by William Dauncey under a lease of 1532 for thirty-one years."[30] The other was the manor of Canons in Middlesex, which Daunce leased in 1535. (Cassiobury, Herts. and Canons, Middlesex, while in different counties are only about six or seven miles apart.) Because of all these grants he had received, or leases he had made, and because he was a member of the 1529-1535 parliament whose father was doing well working with Cromwell and Henry VIII, William Daunce must have felt tremendous pressure to cooperate with the king. On the other hand, his wife was the daughter of a man who was to lose his life because he would not cooperate with the king. Perhaps it was because of this dilemma faced by William Daunce that Thomas

[28]*L&P Hen. VIII,* Vol. X, 1015(6); XII, 1330(61); XIII, 887(20).
[29]*L&P Hen. VIII,* Vol. VI, 1689.
[30]*The Victoria History of the County of Hertfordshire,* ed. William Page (London, 1908), II:453.

More, in what seems to have been his last written request, beseeched that his son John "break not my will concerning his sister Daunce."[31]

[31]This final point on the meaning of Thomas More's statement about "sister Daunce" is certainly conjectural. While conceding this I don't wish to back off from my conjecture. In fact, I wish that time or space permitted a much more complete analysis of the details and the tone of More's last letter. For example, More explicitly sends his final blessings to each of his children and step-children and their spouses, *except* William and Elizabeth Daunce. I would argue that the omissions are glaringly obvious and significant.

The "Size" Of More (on His 500th Birthday)

Dorothy H. Donnelly, C.S.J.

"Size," according to Bernard Loomer,[1] has to do with the ability to synthesize one's life data into a somewhat harmonious whole that is one's self. Freedom emerges from such an effort. I see this "growth-mark-freedom" as somehow the very measure of the size of one's character and indicative of the shape of one's synthesis. This growth from freedom to more-nuanced freedom over a life-time seems closely related to the process that William James calls conversion:

> Wherein a self, hitherto divided, and consciously wrong, inferior and unhappy, becomes unified consciously right superior and happy in consequence of a firmer hold upon religious realities.[2]

Now conversions may be gradual or sudden. I prefer the gradual model for my enterprise of studying the size of the soul of Thomas More whose 500th birthday we celebrate. For if conversion is the essence of the Christian vocation, then More's life-story shows him following that call to grow through challenge after challenge all his life into the size that he called the imitation of Christ. For More was one of those saints whose *metanoia* takes place in the down-to-earthness of job, office, and family. He was one of those to whom Jesus spoke: "Stay in the city, until you are clothed with power from on high. . . . You are witnesses of these things . . . that repentance and forgiveness of sins should be preached in my name to all nations" (Luke 24:48-50). This call to grow, to change of heart, lured More on from freedom to freedom, and I'd like to consider highlights of that progress here. Conversion, as some of us see it today, may be four-fold, integrating the total "size" of persons: the intellectual (responsibility for one's beliefs, their consequences, and their revision), moral (responsibility for acting out the demands of one's enlightened beliefs), religious (assuming personal responsibility for responding in an appropriate manner to impulses of divine grace), and Donald Gelpi's addition to Bernard Lonergan: emotional or affective (balanced emotional growth; claiming responsibility for

[1]Bernard Loomer in "Bernie Loomer and the Size of God," *Graduate Theological Union Newsletter,* (Nov. 14, 1977):1.
[2]William James, *Varieties of Religious Experience* (New York, 1958), p. 157.

one's sexuality and emotions).[3]

Another name for this integral conversion is "holiness," proven by the constant faithful fulfillment of duty. Teilhard de Chardin said some forty years ago that we lacked a new definition of holiness. We still lack it. But a look at the forming shape and energies that molded the size of Thomas More might help us supply it.

No spirituality exists *in vacuo*. More's spiritual adventure had its cultural crucible; its historical, social, psychological, and theological moments. I have called a mélange of these formative factors More's See-Level,[4] his only way to see, to interpret, to judge, and to decide, the very human activities that ground the attitude called holiness.

Painful More's tale may be, but also pleasant:

> for the highest flights of charity, devotion, trust, patience, bravery to which the wings of human nature have spread themselves have been flown for religious ideals . . . , and the best fruits of religious experience are the best things that history has to show.[5]

First, let's look at the setting, time, place, and culture that helped ripen this rare fruit. More's time was the best of times—and the worst. It was Europe in the year of our Lord 1523, and the cast of characters was equal to the scenario. Michelangelo was 48; Raphael, 40. Hans Holbein the Younger, 26, was soon to paint the portrait of the new Speaker of the English House of Commons, Sir Thomas More, 45, then deep in theological diatribe defending his sovereign against Luther's scurrilous attack.

More's liege lord, Henry VIII, 32, lusty theologian turned King, had received the title, "Defender of the Faith," for the very Latin treatise Luther had attacked: Henry's "Assertio septem sacramentorum." Yet, in that same year (1521), Henry had also executed the greatest nobleman in England, the Duke of Buckingham, for "aspiring to his crown."

Martin Luther, 40, had also to deal with reactions from fellow-reformers, from Ulrich Zwingli, 39 (John Calvin was only 14 in 1523), and from the prince of Renaissance humanists, the acerbic, brilliant Erasmus of Rotterdam, 54, Thomas More's dearest friend.

Ignatius Loyola, 32, was off to the Holy Land. Miles Coverdale was working on his English translation of the Bible, while across the

[3]Donald Gelpi, *Charism and Sacrament: a Theology of Christian Conversion* (New York, 1976), p. 17.

[4]Dody H. Donnelly, *Team: Theory and Practice of Team Ministry* (New York, 1977), p. 5, where I refer to the culture, education, experience, environment, and expectation (C ÷ 4 E's = CE[4] = See-Level) out of which one judges, decides, and acts.

[5]James, *Varieties of Religious Experience*, p. 207.

Channel Lefèvre d'Etaples was publishing his French translation of the New Testament.

Hardly thirty years before, Columbus had taken an early "giant step for humankind," landing in San Salvador—ten years before Balboa had gazed in awe at the mighty sweep of the Pacific.

Now, for a brief, all too brief, moment (1522-1523), Christendom saw in the Dutchman, Adrian VI, a Pope who could tell his nuncio to the Diet of Worms:

> frankly confess that God permits this persecution *[Luther's]* to afflict His Church because of the sins of men, especially of the priests and prelates of the Church . . . , the illness has spread from the Supreme Pontiffs to the prelates below them.[6]

In words he represents an amazing contrast to the three popes preceding him: Alexander VI, Julius II, and Leo X, some of the worst figures of the Renaissance papacy. To the deep disappointment of More, Adrian VI died after one year's heroic effort to reform. He was followed by the Medici, Clement VII, who would play cat and mouse with Henry's divorce, a divorce that would free Henry to marry Anne Boleyn in order to secure a Tudor heir. But Henry would have to discard Catharine of Aragon, and antagonize Charles V, the Holy Roman Emperor, who just happened to be her nephew!

These were just some of the characters, as the curtain rose on the period for our consideration: More's "prime times" and conversions —his last twelve years on earth, 1523 to 1535. Besides these persons of the drama, other elements had conditioned his ripening, and helped shape the size of his spirituality.

First, his intellectual environment was propitious, for beneath the tangled intrigue of English and international politics, humanistic renaissance ideas flourished, flowering for England in More himself. His satiric *Utopia* signaled his membership in, and communication with, a Renaissance company of scholars headed by Desiderius Erasmus,. translator of five editions of the New Testament. It included Guillaume Budé, the most distinguished Greek scholar in Europe, and John Colet, founder of an innovative humanistic London school for boys.[7] Colet, influenced by the Florentine Platonists, breaking with medieval allegorical exegesis, preached his "new" historical sermons on St. Paul and Dionysius the Areopagite, sermons heard by the young More, who chose Colet as the guide of his life.

[6]Adrian VI, "Instruction to Chieregati," in John C. Olin, *The Catholic Reformation: Savonarola to Ignatius Loyola; Reform in the Church 1495-1540* (New York, 1969), p. 125.
[7]R.W. Chambers, *Thomas More* (Ann Arbor, 1958), p. 79.

Colet, tried and acquitted for heresy, died in 1519.

Basic to this humanistic flowering lay the recovery of the Greek and Latin texts of antiquity. From them radiated a new world of Renaissance values; such as the human person as sharer in the cosmos—as powerful to choose—as motivated to change history which now turned to analysis of times, places, and provenances of these very texts. But accurate texts must be made available from the sources in the original languages. Printing insured their captivity for posterity, and their incredibly wide dissemination, given the range of manuscripts at the time. It was the genius of Erasmus to recognize and capitalize on this.

Of course, for "devout humanists" like Erasmus, the texts of Scripture were paramount, for they would insure the reform of theology and church life. So the languages of the Bible became primary in the humanists' educational schemes. Yet rhetoric maintained its hold through memorizing of excerpts from these texts, classical or biblical. Massive collections of excerpts such as Erasmus's *Copia* and *Adagia*, and John Gerson's "Monotessaron" from the four gospels, were useful to More in his theological and spiritual writing, along with the "Catena aurea" of Thomas Aquinas, a collection of excerpts from the fathers.

This "education by excerpt," reminds that More was somewhat a self-made man, caught in an age deficient in self-help books. Oxford would only have given him the trivium, Latin, and perhaps elementary Greek. He later studied Greek in earnest with Thomas Linacre and William Grocin. In Grocin's church, St. Lawrence Jewry, More lectured on Augustine's *City of God*.[1] This says something about More's stature even at twenty three years of age: lecturing to London ecclesiastics on the fathers, and drawing bigger crowds than Grocin.

But this was a heavy and crucial conversion period for More. He had to decide on his vocation while immersed in activity: his law studies, life at the Carthusian Charterhouse trying out monastic life, study of the Fathers, study of Greek. Would it be law or the church, monastic or married life? Here his prayer and ascetical practices gave More the testing and self-knowledge he sought. He finally decided on marriage and the law. Yet, all his life he continued to wear his hair shirt—and ever deeper grew his prayer. In this life-decision, More combined intellectual and affective conversion through the mediation

[1]Nicholas Harpsfield, *The Life and Death of Sir Thomas More,* ed. Elsie V. Hitchcock (London, 1963), pp. 13-14.

of a religious conversion that impelled him to respond to what he discerned to be the impulse of God's grace leading him on.[9]

Twenty-four years and innumerable offices and exploits later, More was known as England's darling. Success seemed to dog his footsteps. His moral conversions shaped and "grew" him through decision after decision. He learned not to accept the rich cups, money prizes, gifts, and benefits that poured upon him as the King's counselor. As envoy and as judge, he tried to be humble, chaste, truthful, and yet kind.

Perhaps it was his common touch that led people to so identify with and trust him. For instance, More was a real estate operator who bought Crosby Hall in London and sold it for a good profit to an Italian businessman. He was a writer whose published works run to one and a quarter million English words, plus about 350,000 in Latin. And he had to do that writing moonlighting from his full-time public offices: Under-Sheriff (1510), envoy to Amiens and Cambrai (1527-1528), Speaker of the House (1523), and Lord Chancellor (1529). We're told he managed all of these by rising each morning at 2:00 A.M. and working till 7:00 A.M., when he would climb into his barge and be rowed off down the Thames to work.

Always, his life was grounded in the mundane, the real problems of his family, his associates, his countrymen. He was an expert on the construction and repair of sewers. He was a farmer with holdings in Glastonbury, Oxfordshire, Kent, and Middlesex.[10] He was a politician who was twice elected to Parliament where as Speaker he served as the "common mouth of the Commons," whose interests he truly cherished. He was a clever lawyer and, like his father, a judge. As a father, this twice-married man with four children, missed them so much when Henry embroiled him in business, that he claimed, "neither the mud, nor the rain nor the stumbling horse," could distract him from the thought of them. In his charming letters the lonesome father insisted the reason, "why I held you warmly in my arms, pelted you with cake, gave you round sweet ripe pears, dressed you in silks was because I could never bear to hear you cry."[11]

That same More loved tricks, games, and amateur theatrics, and supported in his own home the fool, Henry Patenson. He disliked

[9]Gelpi, *Charism and Sacrament*, p. 16.

[10]Frank Sullivan, "Thomas More, Knight, Martyr, Layman . . .," *Loyola University Alumnus* (1963). This commencement address made many choice allusions to More's commonality.

[11]See similar letters to his children and their school in Thomas More, *Selected Letters*, ed. Elizabeth F. Rogers (New Haven, 1961).

ball games, gambling and cards, but loved music, gaiety and song. He kept a private zoo, and had his favorite monkey painted into Holbein's famous More family portrait. This Renaissance man delighted in the humanistic coquetery that produced the *Utopia* as an exercise in ingenuity, so utterly rational that the babychicks in Utopia didn't trail around after their mothers, but behind the men who built the incubators! More was a man who could take care of himself. As he climbed the ladder of fame and fortune, of wealth and advancement, he grew rich, admired, and one of the most famous men in Europe. And he grew mortally afraid, afraid of the creeping disease he smelled all around him: the desire for "earthly glory," that great sire of spiritual malaise and death.

Coming as he did out of the late medieval tradition of spirituality, the Four Last Things, the Four Cardinal Virtues, and the Seven Deadly Sins were part of More's symbol-system. Among the deadly sins Pride danced closest to him; Pride, of all the seven, free and not deeply-tested or ever subdued. Through the daily prudent preparedness we shall see below, More stalked Pride as Pride stalked him. He fought it to a last stand in the Tower, using his gifts to mediate this phase of his religious and moral conversion.

Early on he was watchful not only for himself, but for his children and their tutors. He wrote to William Gonell, one of them:

> For as it becomes a good man to avoid infamy, so to *lay oneself out for renown* is the sign of a man who is not only arrogant, but ridiculous and miserable. A mind must be uneasy which ever wavers between joy and sadness because of other men's opinions . . . . Thus I have written at length on *not pursuing* glory, my dear Gonell . . . .[12]

Here was the truer, the deeply religious, pious More who had lived with the Carthusians, who had continued his monastic existence in his fine home in Chelsea trying to spend every Friday in prayer. More prayed with his household every night, attended Mass every morning, and had Scripture read during meals. He sang in his village choir (badly), and carried the processional cross in the local pilgrimages he loved to make.

This More gives us an index to the outward observance, the spiritual climate, and the popular worship of the period. Sixteenth century English religion was pietistic. People who could read favored the often legendary lives of saints, works on prayer, devotion, and spirituality; yet not of a deeply theological or scriptural kind. Scripture was neglected in England compared to the continent, perhaps due to the fear of Lollard influences.

[12]Ibid., To William Gonell, Letter 20, p. 104.

This pietistic religion failed to supply an intellectual understanding of one's faith. It led to theological anemia with the consequent divorce between religion and morality so deplored by More. It often led to patent self-deception.[13] Henry VIII could confess every day and receive communion at every feast while committing adultery with Anne Boleyn. Henry was not a-typical, but merely a most conspicuous exponent of a mentality that saw one's conscience and profit coinciding with no trouble to either, and with no harm to one's self-righteousness.

No wonder the harshness and violence of sixteenth century human relationships, whether in private or political life. No wonder, too, the anti-clericalism spawned from the cynicism of those who suffered from the coincidence of profit and conscience in clergy men like Wolsey, along with the monetary exactions, and the sometimes coercive jurisdiction, of churchmen who brought down the wrath of the Dean of St. Paul's, John Colet, in his stunning "Convocation Sermon."

Colet's sermons matter to More's spiritual background for they inaugurated a new era of scriptural exegesis and theological study. Colet adapted the approach of Italian humanism to the content of revelation, and used it for reform. Colet delivered this sermon at the clergy convocation in London in 1512. One can imagine the impact on the clerics assembled when Colet told them:

> I exhort you, reverend fathers, to endeavor to reform the condition of the church; because nothing has so disfigured the face of the church as the secular and wordly way of living on the part of the clergy . . . what a breathless race from benefice to benefice . . . priests give themselves to feasting . . . spend themselves in vain babbling, take part in sports and plays . . . hunting and hawking . . . every corruption, all the ruin of the church, all the scandals of the world come from the covetousness of priests . . . the laity themselves are scandalized and driven to ruin when those whose duty it is to draw men from this world teach men to love this world by their own devotion to worldly things . . . also their *spiritual weakness* and servile fear . . . makes them dare neither to do nor to say anything but what they know will be grateful and *pleasing to their princes.*[14]

Colet's preaching fed More's intellectual and religious growth. For Colet went on to describe his notion of a priest as embodying the moral and ethical, as well as the affective spirituality More espoused:

> For it is not, in my judgment, enough that a priest can construe a collect, propound a proposition, or reply to a sophism; but much more needful are a *good, pure, and holy life,* approved morals, moderate

[13]T.M. Parker, *The English Reformation to 1558,* (London, 1950), p. 17.
[14]Colet, John, "Convocation Sermon," in Olin, *Catholic Reformation,* p. 34.

knowledge of the Scriptures, some knowledge of the sacraments, above
all *fear of God and love of heavenly life.*[15]

This affective piety based on Paul and the Synoptics rather than
theological doctrines was a later development of the continental
"devotio moderna." Possibly, it was also the source of Colet's
preaching. More could have here gained his emphasis on the Passion
and the imitation of Christ for meditation. However, he rejected the
cruder manifestations of passion-centered piety found in some
English works of the time. Rather, More preferred to concentrate on
the "mind" of Christ, a meaningful choice that led to his use of
language that was biblical, dramatic, and devotional.[16] It also meant
Christ was arbiter of his values.

More further used his gifts as one of our earliest English comic
talents in those dialogues which so refresh the lengthy exposition of
his theological works. More often had to sacrifice this great comic
gift to the needs he was called on to meet in the Lutheran controversy, and in the super-activity of his daily schedule. But he went
through that ring, too. He decided that defending the church came
before perfecting his great literary gifts, and so gave us an interesting
translation of what asceticism can mean given each one's particular
gifts, lifestyle, and calling. Our English heritage, however, lost a
great comic genius, for as C.S. Lewis has observed, More's "merry
tales will bear comparison with anything of the kind in Chaucer or
Shakespeare."[17] Yet, our gallery of vital role-models gained "More"
who is so relevant to our needs in our present calls to conversion.

As More moved from choice to ever greater choice of freedoms,
England in its political, social, and moral choices rapidly deterior-
ated. For the Golden Age hailed by the humanists at Henry VIII's
accession, sabotaged by Cardinal Wolsey's ambitions and Henry's
schemes, produced an isolated England, and discarded the concept
of international Christendom. More had already suffered in close
contact with Wolsey's values as co-envoy and Speaker of the House.
Now, as Henry's "great matter" evolved, More formally declined to
give Henry the requested public opinion on the divorce. Gradually,
his influence with Henry VIII diminished. More chose again. This
time with portentous consequences, as the die was cast.

---

[15]Ibid. p. 36.

[16]*The Complete Works of St. Thomas More*, vol. 13, *A Treatise On the Passion; A
Treatise on the Blessed Body; Instructions and Prayers,* ed. Garry E. Haupt (New
Haven, 1976), pp. cxiii-cxv, (Hereafter cited as *CW.*)

[17]C.S. Lewis, *English Literature in the Sixteenth Century, Excluding Drama* (Oxford,
1954), p. 173.

A year later, in 1528, when Bishop Cuthbert Tunstall licensed More to refute the Lutheran heretics "as a holy work in the name of God," More was relieved to plunge into this service unrelated to the King's divorce, in spite of his reluctance to involve himself with theology. He put it cogently in the *Letter to Bugenhagen:*

> Since the thing had been thrust upon me, and perhaps, if I were silent, I would increase the wicked hope of the sender, I decided, rather, to answer your letter. I would thus prove to every man that, no matter how unskilled I may be in theology, still I am too constant a Christian to put up with being a Lutheran.[18]

The tone of this passage gives a hint of the lawyer More, whose wry wit could slay an opponent at the bar, or in a Renaissance dialogue. Yet, he tries to be honest about his own limitations as a trained theologian. It also hints at the sharpness, even the anger and bitterness that the "heretics" evoked in More. C.S. Lewis found that this desire to conquer at every moment on every issue stultified More's literary expression, for it made his controversial work monotonous and heavy, in spite of those welcome flashes of low comedy.[19] Again, More chose to use his talent in the service of conviction, not amusement, no matter how that hurt his Renaissance reputation as wit and scholar. Not an easy choice for the author of the *Utopia.* I believe More made it more readily because it delivered a broadside at temptations to pride and earthly glory that danced the slower as he rejected their allurements, and tried to use his gifts lamely, but honestly, for a cause beyond humanism.

More actually saw his writing as forestalling the triumph of those who would destroy his hopes for a reformed church through humanistic education, using the restored texts of Scripture. He felt that Lutheranism would spell the end of all those hopes and the end of civilization as Christians had known it for a thousand years.[20] So he took up his pen. Augustine, one of his models, won a similar battle; More would lose his, but this most learned layman in England, Privy-Councilor, High Steward of both Oxford and Cambridge, soon to be Lord Chancellor (1529), called upon by the hierarchy to defend the church theologically, said yes. Licensed in 1528, he wrote intensively, as if he felt the executioner's breath on his neck, and

---

[18]Letter 143 in *The Correspondence of Sir Thomas More,* ed. Elizabeth F. Rogers (Princeton 1947).

[19]Lewis, *English Literature,* p. 173. For Comments on More's style see *A Translation of St. Thomas More's "Responsio ad Lutherum,"* intro. Gertrude J. Donnelly (Washington, D.C., 1962).

[20]Philip Hughes, *The Reformation in England* (London, 1952), p. 147.

published his last book at Christmas in 1533. Four months later he again retired to a cell, not Carthusian this time, but his own in the Tower of London. The last act opened in his final phase of conversion: fifteen months of imprisonment—his graduate course in prayer, asceticism, abandonment, and surrender.

Briefly, More arrived back in a cell because Henry and history drove him into alienation from the crown. More, succeeding Wolsey as Chancellor, had to serve on a commission to study the divorce issue (1529). In that capacity, he gave Henry, privately, his negative opinion on the divorce. In 1530 he refused to sign a new appeal to the Pope for the divorce. In May of 1532, the clergy of England surrendered in fear to Henry, and More resigned as Chancellor, citing his declining health. More did not attend the çoronation of Anne Boleyn in June of 1533. In April of 1534 he was summoned to swear an oath of allegiance to the Act of Succession of Henry's heirs. But since he could not take the corollary oath making Henry head of the English church, he did not sign, and maintained discreet silence about his reason why.

Committed, finally, to that cell in the Tower (April, 1534), More felt death creep closer as Parliament, now Henry's tool, made denial of Henry's supremacy treason and punishable by death. Under the act of attainder passed against him, More lost all his property to the crown. His family suffered much, and More suffered more.

Between April and June of 1535 More was interrogated four times, but his legal skill parried every thrust. He never broke his silence and so came to Westminister as prisoner at the bar where once he sat as judge. Through the perjury of Richard Rich, More was sentenced to be "hanged, drawn, and quartered" (July 1, 1535). On July 6, however, through Henry's "clemency," he was merely beheaded at nine o'clock that morning on Tower Hill.

How did he pass through this agony and passion, this weariness, dread, and suffering of fifteen months of confinement? Actively and passively, More's soul grew martyr-size in those crucial months of final conversion. Characteristically, and all-of-a-piece with his whole life, More, in his common-sense piety and faith, literally *wrote* his way through them! He shored up his fear by presenting himself with the fruits of his fifty-six years of preparation for just this pass: years of working, observing, reflecting, meditating, listening to God's spirit, studying and writing.

By writing, More delivered his soul, integrated his images and emotions, and completed still deficient phases of his four-fold conversion. More prepared Thomas More to be neither over-bold nor over-fearful, but to soak his spirit in the living presence of His Lord that he might spring up to follow him when the signal came to go forth with Him carrying his cross to Tower Hill.

In the *De Tristitia,* studying the sadness of Jesus in the Garden, More talks about different kinds of martyrs, making room for himself, should he be called to this test:

> Is it not possible that God in His goodness removes fear from some persons not because He approves of . . . their boldness, but because *aware of their weakness,* he knows that they would not be equal to facing fear . . .? And *so God proportions the temperaments of His martyrs according to His own providence* in such a way that one rushes forth eagerly to his death, another creeps out hesitantly and fearfully, but for all that bears his death none the less bravely—unless someone imagines he ought to be thought less brave for *having fought down* not only his other enemies but also his own *weariness, sadness, and fear*—most strong feelings and mighty enemies indeed.[21]

It is fascinating to see More bring his negative emotions (dread, fear, sadness) into the light, and to exorcise and wrestle with More and God, about them. He will call them "temptations," and bring the living Christ to heal and expel them. C.G. Jung and Assogioli might well approve More's evoking his images in colorful prose, facing them, naming them, and smashing them against the rock which is Christ. In so doing he grew his soul to martyr-size in synergy with the Christ whose presence was his constant comfort and energizing experience.

He also seems to have worked through what we are told are the typical stages in facing news of one's death.

1. He *suspends belief* and parries pride in his possible martyr-status; he constantly avoids presumption.

2. He honestly *speaks out his anger* about the injustice of his case to his confidante, Meg Roper.

3. He suffers *sadness* and allows himself to *grieve* through the pages of the "Treatise on the Passion," "The Dialogue of Comfort . . ." and "The Sadness of Jesus."

4. Finally, we see those emotions orchestrated into the final *abandonment* and *surrender* that produced the heroic grey-beard climbing the scaffold needing help up, but able (he said wryly) to get down by himself!

More allowed himself to grieve, to act (write), to hope, to prophesy, and finally to be reconciled with himself and with the God who lured him on to final identification with the suffering Christ.

[21] *C.W.*. vol. 14, pt. 1, *De Tristitia Christi,* ed. Clarence Miller (New Haven, 1976), p. 245.

But More not only wrote his way through those savage periods of denial, sadness, and dread. He argued his way through as well, good lawyer to the end. It is this calm continuation of accustomed activities in the face of death that so often characterizes saints in their moment of final choice. Bishop John Fisher, More's co-martyr, wakened by his jailer at 5 A.M. with the news that he would die at ten, thanked and dismissed him in order to sleep four more hours! Death becomes another phase of their relationship with the God who in death calls them on to learn.

Continuation of usual activity in More has this same flavor as his faith blossomed into the hope, reconciliation, and reassurance that mark the integrally converted person. So his usual tools: humanistic dialogue-form, and his lawyer's seeing both sides of a case, undergird the "Dialogue of Comfort Against Tribulation" wherein More will call God his "Jailer and the Universal Hangman," but also, "Mother Hen" who protects those tempted to desert Christ through fear of persecution, torture, and death.[22] More argues with More in this dialogue, and quotes Psalm 90 to prove that God will protect from: 1) the fear of the night (danger and death); 2) the arrow that flies by day (prosperity that causes Pride); 3) the business that walks in the dark (wealth and fleshly pleasure); 4) the invasion of the noon-day devil (open persecution).[23]

More had felt the sting of each. He summarized his own life-long defense against them when he advised us to prepare for persecution:

> Many a time and oft *aforehand,* for then . . . reason can enter and with grace . . . *engender* and set sure not a sudden slight affection of sufferance for God's sake, but by a long continuánce, *a strong, deep-rooted habit.*[24]

More used Scripture to label these images of his fears: the night, the arrow, and the devil; he named and exorcised them, and they ceased to gnaw at his unconscious. His emotional conversion, thus, proceeded apace. For by resolving these emotions, he removed them as possible obstacles to his response to what God was offering through their pain and the events that caused them. More decided to come to terms with them, and did so as he wrote, argued,

---

[22]Thomas More, *A Dialogue of Comfort Against Tribulation,* ed. Leland Miles (Bloomington, 1965), II:10. Frank Manley calls More's "Dialogue" an intensely personal work of great power and a masterpiece of Renaissance devotional literature, see More, *C.W.,* Vol. 12, *A Dialogue of Comfort Against Tribulation,* ed. Louis L. Martz and Frank Manley, (New Haven, 1976), p. cxx.

[23]Ibid., pts. II and III.

[24]More, *A Dialogue,* ed. Miles, III:3.

recognized, named, and prayed his way through them, using Scripture and the presence of Christ. He thereby opened the door to the healing power of God's Spirit upon whom he called unceasingly. Gradually, his memories and fears were healed, for the More who climbed the scaffold was a liberated man.

In another conversion work, his "Treatise on the Passion," More shows how he brought about that healing. He always introduced Christ truly *with him* in every phase of this final fire-testing of their identification. To More, medieval-Renaissance product of the *devotio moderna,* the goal of all his striving was the imitation of Christ *in order* to identify with him, walk with him, and never to drop his eyes from that steady gaze. The "Dialogue" had ended with the contemplation of Christ on the cross. The English "Treatise" ended with Christ again with More, and this time through the Eucharist.

Finally, in the *De Tristitia* More brings it all together, entering into the psychology and mysticism of Christ's mental anguish in the Garden: his fear, sadness, weariness, and final surrender to the will of the Father.[25] For the garden was the breakthrough in Jesus' own conversion-experience, and More identified intensely with it. He resolved his own last struggle, and broke triumphantly through the ring carried in the arms of that Christ, his life-model and companion. More has Christ tell his fearful ones:

> My timorous and feeble little sheep . . . follow my leadership; if you do not trust yourself, place your trust in me. See, I am walking ahead of you along this fearful road.[26]

Lastly, this Jesus, More's model, being in an agony, *prayed* the longer. More now abandoned himself into the arms of this shepherd in hours of *prayerful* communion. This time prayer was one of their jokes, a piece of Renaissance paradox delighting the heart of More—and of the Christ who wrote the script. More, who had decided for the good of his soul to follow marriage and the law, leaving with regret the contemplative's cell, now had fifteen months of contemplative, solitary confinement! How wryly he must have smiled over that, thinking of the times he had prayed for "time-to-write" in his answering the heretics from two to seven each morning before his work-day began! It was their private joke, neither understood nor shared by family or friends, but More's delight. Finally he had both time to write and time to pray:

---

[25]See Miller's comments on this subject in *C. W.,* vol. 14, pt. 2, p. 776.
[26]Ibid., pt. 1, pp. 103-05.

> I believe, Meg, that they that have put me here ween they have done me a high displeasure. But I assure thee on my faith, my own good daughter, if it had not been for my wife and you that be my children, whom I account the chief part of my charge, I would not have failed long ere this to have closed myself in as straight a room, and straighter too. . . . Me thinketh God maketh me a wanton, and *setteth me on his lap and dandleth me.*[27]

It was this intense religious experience of Christ in prayer that mediated his emotional and moral conversions. His faith-dependence on Christ's presence gradually deepened, and completed his religious conversion, as More brought into subjection these emotional obstacles to the final surrender now called for.

The wisdom with which More navigated that last stretch of white water was truly phenomenal. Not only had he followed his own advice and so prepared his life-long for this enormous challenge, but he brought all his riches from a lifetime of discipline, order, patience, talent, and skill into gorgeous synergy as he rowed down those rapids with heart and pen.

He would write what he could, pray what he could, do what he could, and God would do the rest. More surrendered his life to Christ, for he said that with his hands "in the stormy seas he will hold me up from drowning. Mistrust him . . . will I not, though I feel me faint."[28] As he told his son-in-law, William Roper, as he was rowed down the Thames on the way to prison, kissing them all goodbye for the last time: "I thank God, Son Roper, *the field is won.*" More had entered the lists. The final jousting match had begun.

This battle More won, for as he wrote, prayed, and listened, he gave a foul fall to his two deadly enemies: presumption and despair, ancient sins against hope and the daughters of Pride, the "earthly glory" he so feared. More kept his lips sealed, never from stubbornness or superiority, but because along with his position in the reasonable Utopia, a man's conscience was the last citadel in Christendom. It would be stormed by neither King nor Parliament. Antigone and Socrates looked over More's shoulder as he held his ground for the right of the individual to choose his religious belief against the decision of the head of the state. As he told Mr. Secretary Cromwell:

> I am the King's true faithful subject and daily beadsman, and pray for his Highness and all the realm. I do noboby no harm, I say none harm, I think none harm, but wish everybody good. *And if this be not enough to keep a man alive, in good faith I long not to live.*[29]

[27]William Roper, *Life of Thomas More,* ed. Elsie V. Hitchcock (London, 1935), p. 76.
[28]R.W. Chambers, *Thomas More,* pp. 1434,43.
[29]Ibid., pp. 1451-52.

Skilled lawyer that he was More easily turned away the flimsy wording of the indictments at his trial, making his profound plea for the liberty of conscience that chooses to hold its tongue:

> Ye must understand that in things touching conscience, every true and good subject is more bound to have respect *to his conscience and to his soul than to any other thing in all the world beside;* namely when his conscience is in such sort as mine is . . . where the person giveth no occasion of slander, of tumult or sedition against his prince as it is with me; for I assure you that I have not to this hour disclosed and opened my conscience *to any person living in all the world.*[30]

Then, said More, all the more would he never have revealed his opinion to poor Richard Rich who now perjured himself to slay More. Of course, the kangaroo court condemned him, but also gave him his signal: "guilty." Now he could shoot this last rapid, go with the river, and it would not be proud and presumptious to witness to his conscience, his beliefs. He was already condemned! The die was cast, and he had not presumed to pull his life down around his head. More had used all his ability to avoid the presumption that he might be called to martyrdom. Now the gates clanged open and he was free. He had waited patiently and humbly for this trumpet call. Now he could rely on God's strength to carry him to shore with a mighty wind.

Once the sentence rang out, More, released, broke his silence, even correcting the judge who neglected to ask him why such judgment should not be given against him. More witnessed to what he saw happening in England and before his eyes at that moment; i.e., he truly prophesied, for he named it for what it was: the charge insufficient to condemn a man, the indictment, grounded upon an illegitimate Act of Parliament. He appealed to the general Council of Christendom and the cloud of witnesses of centuries against this one corrupt realm. Finally, he said with utmost clarity:

> Very and pure necessity for *the discharge of my conscience* enforceth me to speak so much. Wherein I call and appeal to God whose only sight pierceth into the very depths of man's heart to be my witness. Howbeit it is not for this supremacy that you seek my blood, as for that I would not condescend to the marriage.[31]

The Utopians have one criterion above all as to the success of one's life: how does a person die? More died well; he died willingly, merrily, full of good hope. For such, the Utopians rejoice and remember always. More was a man of patience, prudence, order,

---

[30]Harpsfield, *Life and Death,* p. 186.
[31]Ibid., pp. 193 ff.

and discipline, an ideal sixteenth-century official; he was no revolutionary in political terms. Yet, he was that most revolutionary of creatures: one who holds the last inviolable citadel, his individual conscience, as sacred and gives up his life rather than surrender it. It is this combination of conservative political stance toward authority, coupled with medieval-Renaissance spirituality, that led him to die for conscience' sake—one difficult of assessment for those who do not plunge deep into More's life of prayer, his values, and his final relationship with Christ.

Must each citizen listen to and be responsible for the shaping of his/her own conscience? A light answer does nothing to obviate the seriousness of the question. More's "yes" to it meant death. But because he took responsibility for his beliefs (intellectual conversion), he was freed to act them out with both joy and freedom (moral conversion), while the strengthening motivation of Christ's presence urged him to be true to his espoused values (religious conversion) after working through the emotional obstacles to liberty of heart and action (affective conversion).

Yet More was no plaster saint. This four-fold integration of life in responsible thought, feeling, decision, and action cost him no less than his life. Like every one of us, he went to death with a still-chipped edge,[32] parts of him that were never totally healed and transformed. That he accepted, too, for he had learned in prayer and converse in his Lord, as did his brother, Paul of Tarsus, that in his weakness was God's power made manifest. His task was not to emerge from the fire spotless, but surrendered, open, growing, laughing, and loving, because freed from self-concern. More made it to that place, and in so doing grew his soul saint-size.

---

[32]Donnelly, *Team.* By the "chipped edge" (p. 27) I mean some fault, habit, or attitude a bit twisted or in need of healing that allows us to know ourselves as needing conversion. Perhaps More's over-reaction to the "heretics" placed emotional blocks to his really hearing some of their better arguments.

Lenten Fare and the Language of Falsehood:
Pig and Pike, Fish and Fowl*

Charles Clay Doyle

Resounding throughout More's anti-Protestant works—antiphonally, as it were—are two specific complaints: the marriage of Lutheran priests, friars, monks, and nuns; and the Lutherans' disregard of prescribed fast-days on the calendar of the Roman Church. For More, these two points not only constituted abominable sacrileges in themselves, but also symbolized the entire range of heresy, blasphemy, and hypocrisy of which Luther, Tyndale, and the others partook. More missed no opportunity—and invented several—to rail at the "bestely bychery" of Luther with "cate his nunne," and the marriages of Huskyn, Bugenhagen, Bodenstein, Brunfels, Lambert, Bayfield, Joye, and other Reformed clergymen (in the *Confutation* alone, more than sixty instances of such railing occur, according to Louis Schuster's count).[1]

The second point, the flouting of fast-days, acutally belongs with a more pervasive system of metaphorical and literal references to food in More's polemical works: heretical books as poisons being ingested by the unwary populace; the devil swallowing corrupted souls; mouths "all out of taste" that judge "good and holsome" meats to be "bytter & peryllous"; the "vngracious frute" of "deceytful doctryne" (and the prototype of such fruit, Eve's apple as proffered by Satan); and, most important, the whole question of the Eucharist. There are several references also to regurgitation—as in the repeated allusion to the Biblical proverb of a dog returning to its vomit.

The two categories—sex and orality—are related in various complex ways, psychologically, theologically, and poetically. (Had More read Erik Erikson he might have added Luther's anality as a topic of abuse.) We think, for instance, of the practice of fasting to "tame the flesh," and the amusing absurdity to which More reduces Tyndale's recommendation of that practice ("then wolde many an

---

*The conference title of this paper was "Backgrounds and Foregrounds: Two Excursions into the Popular Aspects of More's Prose."
[1] *The Complete Works of St. Thomas More*, vol. 8 *The Confutation of Tyndale's Answer*, ed. Louis A. Schuster, et al (New Haven, 1973), pp. 1265 and 1477.

honest mayden be ashamed to faste any daye at all, lest she sholde seme therby to gyue yonge men warnynge that she were waxe warme and byd them yf they will speke, speke now"); or the portrait of the John the Baptist type of the good priest, who

> lyued in holy vowed chastyte and neuer wedded woman in hys dayes.. . .
> He lyued in . . . fastyng and forberynge meate. He dranke no wyne, but was content wyth water [or the immemorially obscure connection between the fruit of knowledge and carnal knowledge.][2]

I wish to focus upon a structural juncture in the *Confutation of Tyndale's Answer,* where More completes a thirty-five page "digression" on the sacraments. In the conclusion he lays the verbal groundwork for the passage that I shall examine:

> All the other heretyques hadde some pretexte of holynes in theyr lyuyng: these shamelesse heretiques lyue in open shamfull incestuouse lechery and call yt matrymony . . . these new heretyques be so farre fro shame/ that in the vnderstandynge of scrypture, and in the affyrmynge of all theyr heresyes/they wolde be byleued by theyr onely worde, agaynste all the old holy doctours that haue bene synnys the deth of Christe vnto this daye . . . neuer was there heretyque that durst for every shame so bold-ely barke agaynst them, tyll that now in these latter dayes the deuyll hath broke his chaynes, and of all extreme abomynacyon hathe set his poysoned barell a broche/from ye dreggy draught whereof god kepe euery good crysten man, and such as hath droken therof geue them grace to vomyte yt out agayne by tyme.[3]

Characteristically, this passage assails the Lutherans by mixing references to their sexual conduct with a description of their heresy as drink from the devil's own "poysoned barell," which for the victim's salvation must be quickly vomited. But another kind of orality is also at issue. Note the emphasis on *call* in "call yt matrymony" and on *worde* in "they wolde be byleued by theyr onely worde." More wishes to expose Tyndale as a neo-Scholastic who confounds things with words (at several points he calls Tyndale a juggler). The same theme is pursued when More commences what is nominally the next section of his argument. Here he lets fly at Tyndale with the sarcastic epithet *spiritual,* the quality by which the Reformers had sought to distinguish themselves from the Papists:

> Now that Tyndale hathe done with his owne spyrituall parte, & hath as ye haue herd holyly declared how hygh spyrytuall wysedome they use . . . now commeth he to the other parte/that is to all that are noe theretykes, whom he before called naturall and not borne agayne nor renewed with ye spyryt, all which folke he calleth here the worlde.. . . Here he meaneth that hym selfe and his felowes spyrytuall heuenly men/be not captyuate vnto the lawe of god, as we pore worldely men of mydle erth

---

[2]Ibid., pp. 64, 123.
[3]Ibid., p. 120.

be. For they be no ferther bounded to the law, but as the cause of the
law sought out by them selfe, leadeth them to and fro/and therefore
they be in an euangelycall and in manner angelycall lybertye to do what
they lyste/so yt they geue the lawe some cause that may serue theyr lust,
as they haue geuen to the law and commaundement of vowes/from
whych they haue set them self in such a spyrytuall lybertye, that munkes
and freres may lawfully lye with nunnes and lyue in lechery, and call yt
wedlocke.[4]

To amplify this point about the disingenuous juggling of words,
More gives condensed versions of two jokes, which I wish to allege
were popular at the time the book was written, and hence to the
English-speaking readership of the polemic it would have had the
appeal of the familiar rather than the novel—somewhat analogous to
the way in which proverbs appeal.

And in dede they may call yt wedlocke and they will as lollardes dyd of
late, that put a pygge in to the water, on good frydaye/and sayd go in
pygge and come oute pyke/and so when they had chaunged the name,
the toke yt for fyshe and ete yt. And so may these holy new spyrytuall
men, when munkes and freres wedde nunnes, they may call yt wedlocke & they will. But as the pore plough man sayd vnto the tauerner yt
gaue hym water in stede of wyne, god thank you mayster wyner for your
good wyne, but in good fayth sauynge for the worshypfull name of
wyne ich had as leue a dronken water: surely so may we well saye to
these new holy spyrytuall maryed munkes and freres/sauynge for the
worshypfull name of wedlocke, yt were as good they lyued in lecherye,
as in such byched bychery.[5]

For the first of those two episodes, the annotators of the Yale edition appropriately cite a close parallel to More's figure in John Skelton's *Why Come Ye Not To Court?* (1522/3), a protracted execra-
tion on Cardinal Wolsey. Skelton preserves the same alliterative antithesis of *pigs* and *pikes*. The self-indulgent Wolsey, the satirist
declares,

> hath suche a bull,
> He may take whom he wull,
> And as many as him lykys;
> May ete pigges in Lent for pikys,
> After the sectes of heretykis.... [6]

The lack of explicitness in this reference forces the inference that
Skelton was not originating such a story, but rather alluding to an
anecdote that his readers were expected to recognize. While it is not
possible to specify a precise prototype, there did exist a group of
related jests popular from the late middle ages which contain the

[4]Ibid., pp. 121-22.
[5]Ibid., p. 122.
[6]*Poetical Works,* ed. Alexander Dyce (London, 1843), II:59-60.

genetic proteins of the *pig-pike* incident, awaiting merely the proper recombinant catalyst.

We may begin by defining a broad category of jests concerning the foolish or willful, or lamely-rationalized violation of prescribed fasts. For example, the following is told (through probably not originated) by Poggio Bracciolini (d. 1459), and expanded in *Les Cent Nouvelles Nouvelles* (c. 1460). An inept pastor in the hinterlands failed to notice the arrival of Lent until Palm Sunday. He explained to his parishioners that, on account of an unusually hard winter, Lent had been forced to travel slowly and arrive belatedly.

The Priest Who Didn't Know About Palm Sunday

Aello is a very rustic town in our Apennine Mountains. There a priest lived, more provincial and ignorant than the natives. Time and the changes in the year were not understood, and he did not tell the people about Lent. The Saturday before Palm Sunday he came to market at Terra Nuova. Seeing the priests preparing olive branches and palms for the next day, he was surprised and wondered why. Then he realized his mistake—that Lent had passed without his noticing. He went back home and himself prepared branches and palms for the next day, when he told the assembled people, "Today it is the custom to display olive and palm branches. Penance must be done for only a week; we don't have a long fast this year. You should understand the reason: This year Carnival was very slow, unable to cross the mountains because of the cold weather and bad roads. Consequently Lent approached slowly with weary tread, able to bring with it no more than a single week, having left the others along the way. Therefore for the brief time that Lent will remain with you, everybody confess and do penance."[7]

---

[7]*De Sacerdote Qui Ignorabat Solennitatem Palmarum: [A]ellum oppidum est in nostris Apennini montibus admodum rusticanum in eo habitabat sace[r]dos rudior atque indoctior incolis, huic cum ignota essent tempora, annique uarietates, nequaquam indixit quadragesimam populo. Venit hic ad terram nouam ad mercatum sabbato ante solennitatem palmarum. Conspectis sacerdotibus oliuarum ramos ac palmulas in diem sequentem paratibus, admiratus quidnam id sibi uellet, cognouit tunc erratum suum, & quadragesimam iam nulla obseruatione suorum transisse. Reuersus in oppidum, & ipse ramos palmasque in posterum diem parauit, qui aduocata plebecula: Hodi inquit est dies quo rami oliuarum palmarumque dari ex consuetudine debent. Octaua die pascha erit, hac tamen hebdomada agenda est poenitentia, neque longius habemus hoc anno ieiunium. Cuius rei causam cognoscite: Carnispriuium hoc anno fuit tardum admodum & lentum, quod propter frigora & difficultatem itinerum hos montes nequiuit superare. Ideo ex quadragesima adeo tardo ac fesso gradu accessit, ut iam nil amplius quam hebdomadam unam secum ferat, reliquis in uia relictis. Hoc ergo modico tempore quo uobiscum mansura est confitemini, & poenitentiam agite omnes.* Quoted in *Opera* (Basel, 1538; reprinted Torino, 1964), I:425. Poggio also tells (ibid., p. 486) of an ignorant priest who informed his congregation of the coming Feast of Epiphany. (*Cras ait summa deuotione ueneremini Epiphaniam, maximum est enim & praecipuum festum*). "I'm not sure whether Epiphany was a man or a woman; but whatever the case, we must

Clearly, More's own Epigram 187, "On the Priest Who Foolishly Warned His Parishoners of a Fast Day When the Day Had Already Passed," belongs to the same category; it just carries the absurdity to a further degree:

> When our priest, as it happened, was advising his parishioners of the calendar for the coming week, he said, "The feast of St. Andrew the Martyr is a great and cherished feast; you know how dear to God Andrew was. Let austere fasting mortify the wayward flesh; this is the custom, established by the saints of old. Therefore I warn you all that in honor of this martyr you must fast—yesterday.[8]

Such jests typically satirize the ignorance of the clergy—a matter of great concern to the humanists.

More nearly immediate in their kinship to the *pig-pike* episode are several jests directed at the worldliness rather than the ignorance of ostensibly holy persons. These stories recount the outright serving or consumption of flesh as fish. From Caesarius of Heisterbach (c.1180-c. 1240) comes the following exemplum. A monk is entertaining visiting monks of the same order (*"non mihi constat utrum fuerint Cistercienses, vel Praemonstrateness"*), which is under the rule of perpetual abstinence. There is no fish in the house; so the monk surreptitiously commands the serving of a pork stew. When one of the guests discovers a pig's ear in the bottom of his bowl and protests, the host chides him for his finickiness, insisting that the fish had ears.

> One day he was hosting some religious persons, and there was no proper food or fish; so he told his cook, "We don't have any fish, and these monks are naive and hungry. Go make some stew, and remove the bones, and put in pepper, and then serve it and say, 'Have some of this nice fish.' "—When the bowl was nearly empty, one of the monks came upon a shoat's ear and showed a companion. The host saw this exchange and retorted with feigned indignation, "Eat up, for the glory of God; monks shouldn't be too curious. Besides, the fish had ears."[9]

---

observe the feast day with utmost devotion" (*nescio autem uir fuerit, an foemina, sed quisquis extiterit, a nobis est summo timore hic dies custodiendus*).

[8]*De Sacerdote Ridicvle Admonente Popvlvm De Ieivnio Cvm Dies Iam Praeterisset: Admonuit populum noster cum forte sacerdos Proxima quos fastos afferat hebdomada, Martyris Andreae magnum et memorabile festum est. Scitis, ait, charus quam fuit ille deo. Squalida lasciuam tenuent ieiunia carnem, Hoc suetum est, sancti hoc instituere patres. Praemoneo ergo omneis in martyris huius honorem Quod ieiunari debuit, inquit, heri.* Text and translation from *The Latin Epigrams of Thomas More*, ed. Leicester Bradner and Charles A. Lynch (Chicago, 1953), pp. 85 and 206-7.

[9]*Cum die quadam viros religiosos . . . hospitio suscepisset et cibi regulares deessent, piscesque non haberet, dicebat coco suo: Pisces non habemus, monachi simplices sunt et esuriunt, vade fac esicium, et ossibus eiectis, cum piperamentis praepara, sicque*

In Caesarius's examplum the unrigorous monk at least had the excuse of excessive zeal in hospitality. In a jest of Poggio's (retold in *Les Cents Nouvelles Nouvelles* and other places), the motive is purely and selfishly gluttonous. A Spanish bishop ordered for himself a meal of fish on Friday, but no fish were to be located. So he dined on two partridges that were being kept for Sunday. When the waiter remonstrated, the bishop declared that the was eating the birds *as* fish—that if a priest had the power to change mere bread into the very body of Christ, surely it was no great miracle for him to change partridges into fish [or *perdices* into *pices,* to keep the alliteration].

> #### The Spanish Bishop Who Consumed Partridges as Fish
> A Spanish bishop on a journey one Friday stopped at an inn. A servant went to procure fish, but none were to be had. However, he did locate a couple of partridges for his master, who ordered them bought, cooked, and set on the table. The amazed servant, who supposed the partridges were being purchased for Sunday, asked the bishop whether he would eat them on such a day of fasting from flesh. He answered, "I eat them as fish," an even more surprising response. He said, "Don't you know that I'm a priest? Which is greater—making the body of Christ from bread or fish from partridge?" And with the sign of the cross he commanded them turned into fish, and they were eaten as fish.[10]

Remarkably enough, a very similar joke occurs in our own time in America:

> A Jewish man who moved to an all Catholic neighborhood couldn't make a friend because of his religion. What's more, everybody hated him because on Friday night, when they were cooking fish, he would cook chicken, and the neighborhood would reek with its smell. The Jew finally decided to give in to the social pressures and become a Catholic. He told the priest that he wanted to convert, and the priest told him, "Fine. All you do is cross yourself every time you see someone and say, "Once a Jew, now a Catholic," and be sure to follow all the laws, and come to church, and eventually you'll become a Catholic." So he went

---

appones et dices: Comedite de bono rumbo. . . . Scutella pene evacuata, cum unus auriculam porcinam reperisset, et socio, vidente Decano, ostendisset, ille aliquid indignationis simulans intulit: Comedite pro Deo, monachi non debent esse tam curiosi; rumbus etiam aures habet. Dialogus Miraculorum (Ridgewood, N.J., 1966), I:438.

[10]*De Episcopo Hispano Qui Comedit Perdices Pro Piscibus: Episcopus Hispanus iter faciens die Veneris ad hospicium diuertit. Missoque seruo qui pisces emeret, non reperiri eos uenales, sed duas perdices patrono retulit. Ille eas emi, & simul coqui, ac in mensam ferri iussit. Admiratus seruus qui eas emptas pro die dominico crederet, quesiuit ab episcopo num eas esset esurus, cum tali die carnes essent prohibitae. Tum pro piscibus, inquit, utar. Multo id magis admiranti responsum. An nescis ait me sacerdotem esse? Quid est maius, inquit, ex pane corpus Christi facere, an ex perdicibus pisces? Factoque crucis signo cum eas in pices uerti imperasset, pro piscibus usus est. Opera,* I:476.

around crossing himself and repeating "Once a Jew, now a Catholic." Soon he had a lot of friends, but he still cooked chicken on Friday nights. So, the neighbors reported him to the priest who visited the ex-Jew and told him he had heard that he was still cooking chicken on Friday. The ex-Jew denied this. No matter how much proof the priest presented, he would not admit that he had cooked chicken on Friday, and so the priest relented. On the following Friday, the priest decided to go over to the new convert's house, and he could smell chicken cooking as he approached. Peeking in the kitchen window the priest saw the ex-Jew standing over a pot and crossing the chicken inside, while saying, "Once a chicken, now a fish."[11]

It should be noted that these jests about unholy transubstantiation tend to devolve upon some rival or outcast group. The Italian and French tellers attribute the sacriledge to a Spaniard, the American (and presumably Catholic) tellers to a Jew. It seems probable that a standard fifteenth or early-sixteenth century English form of the baptized-pig joke had similarly gotten attached to the Lollards, as in More's reference, with Skelton's *heretykis* being an approximate synonym (one that furnished a handy rhyme for *pikys*).

More's allusion to the jest is well calculated for satiric purposes. It points up the alleged "hocus pocus" of Tyndale's handling of language and truth, while indirectly, though unmistakably, placing Tyndale in the ranks of the disreputable Lollards—who, ironically, like Tyndale himself, rejected the doctrine of transubstantiation. More adroitly turned the tables on Tyndale by advancing against him and his colleagues the very allegation that the Reformers had consistently leveled against the Roman church: that they quibblingly adhered to the mere outward and verbal forms of faith with no regard for the genuine essence of faith. As he does pervasively in the *Confutation,* More symbolically substitutes blatantly illicit oral gratification for the sophistically rationalized fornication attributed to Luther and his followers. Were I to risk committing a Freudianism, I would note further the sexual import of the fact that the pig, having entered the (symbolically feminine) water, exits in the

[11]Alan Dundes, "A Study of Ethnic Slurs: The Jew and the Polack in the United States," *Journal of American Folklore,* 84 (1971): 196-97. Later in the *Confutation* More ventures a series of quips which may epitomize one or more other Firday-fasting jokes that the readers were supposed to recognize: The Lutherans "faste not, no not so myche as the .iii. golden frydayes/that is to wyt the frydaye nexte after Palme sondaye, and the frydaye nexte afore Easter daye, and good frydaye/but wyll eate flesshe vppon all thre, and vtterly loue no lenten faste nor lyghtly no faste ellys sauynge breke faste, and eate fast, and drynk fast, and slepe faste, and luske faste in theyr lecherye, & then come forth and rayle faste" (p. 653).

detumescent (and hence no longer forbidden) form of a pike. (The near identity imposed on the two species is reinforced by the phonetic similarity of the names—especially when we keep in mind that *pike* and *pick* were once variants of the same word; see Skelton's rhyming of *pike* and *heretic*.) *Pike* was a sixteenth-century slang designation for the phallus.[12] But enough of this Freudian *praeteritum*, which, if it has any validity, may suggest that More's use of the joke operates beneath, as well as on, the level of conscious analogy. In any case, the joke scores a satirical point for More's side.

Of the second jest, which follows immediately, many of the same things can be said. However, I want also to emphasize what I consider to be the popular province of it. More's presentation seems more like an allusion to a joke than a telling of one: "But as the pore plough man sayd vnto the tauerner yt gaue hym water in stead of wyne . . ., in good fayth sauynge for the worshypfull name of wyne ich had as leue a dronken water." Just three years after that was published, the following appeared in an English jest book:

> There came two homely men of the countreye in to a tauerne on a tyme to drinke a pynte of wine. So they satte stylle, and wyste not what wyne to calle for. At last, herynge euerye man call for white wyne as clere as water of the rocke, they bad the drawer brynge them a pynte of whyte wyne as clere as water of the rocke. The drawer, seyng and perceyuyng by their wordes that they were but blont felowes, he brought them a pinte of clere water. The one of them fylled the cuppe, and dranke to his felow, and sayd: "holde, neighbour, by masse, chadde as lefe drynke water, saue only for the name of wyne."[13]

I cannot prove it yet, but my hunch is that this fuller recounting derives not from More, but from a version antecedent to More's. That is, in each case More would be referring to a popular jest, one already known to his readers, for satiric effect—the aim of which, in the English polemics, was nothing less than winning the minds and souls of the Christian populace.

---

[12]Though generally it was so in its military sense rather than its metaphorical, piscatory one; see Eric Partridge, *Shakespeare's Bawdy* (New York, 1960), pp. 164 and 216. It may be noted that the modern slang *pecker*, which the *OED* demurely omits, is cognate with *pike*; the phallic *pecker* is recorded by John S. Farmer and William Ernest Henley in *Slang and Its Analogues* (New York, 1965), V:157.

[13]*Tales and quicke answeres, very mery, and pleasant to rede* (1535), no. 96.

The Dramaturgy of Tyranny: More's *Richard III* and Sackville's *Complaint of Buckingham*

Stephen Gresham

Tudor England was a unique culture in many respects, not least of which because it allowed, even encouraged, a man of politics to be as well a man of letters. Within certain limits, a man of letters could respond creatively to political issues of great concern to this culture. But the list of those who achieved a high degree of success in both politics and literature is brief because each of these endeavors demanded a special blend of imagination, command of language, dedication, courage, and sensitivity. Two men who epitomized this Tudor synthesis of politics and literature were Thomas More and Thomas Sackville, men whose careers offer some interesting parallels.

In addition to biographical parallels, there is a context in which we can compare the two as literary artists. That context is the handling of the theme of tyranny in More's *History of King Richard III* and Sackville's *Complaint of Henry, Duke of Buckingham*. In these works, More and Sackville create a dramatic vision of tyranny and its corrosive effects, and we can draw certain parallels between their treatments of this theme. Before demonstrating this literary commonality, however, I wish to trace briefly the similarities of their careers, and suggest that the environments in which they matured seem to have nurtured within them a profound concern for tyranny and civil disorder, a concern that may well have led them to dramatize such political evils.

The first parallel is that both attained political stature as young men and maintained it for several decades. Recall, for example, that More was a member of Parliament before he was twenty-five. Later, his public service included being undersheriff of London, member of a trade mission to Flanders, councillor and judge in the Court of Requests, and Under-treasurer. In 1523 he was elected speaker of the House of Commons, and, of course, in 1529 he was made Lord Chancellor of England. It was, in short, an enviable career, for More was as much devoted to his country and his king as his conscience would allow.[1]

[1]Richard J. Schoeck, *The Achievement of Thomas More: Aspects of His Life and Works,* (Victoria, B.C., 1976).

Although perhaps not as glittering as More's career, Sackville's experiences in the world of politics bear some resemblance. He, too, was a member of Parliament as a young man. His career included diplomatic missions for Queen Elizabeth. In 1572 Sackville was appointed commissioner at the state trial of Thomas Howard, Duke of Norfolk, whose communications with Mary, Queen of Scots led to an accusation of treason. The late 1580s found Sackville on a difficult diplomatic mission in the Low Countries. Finally, in 1599 he rose to the position of Lord High Treasurer of England, succeeding Lord Burghley, and two years later he sat as Lord High Steward of England at the trial of the Earl of Essex.[2]

One student of Sackville's political career has lauded him for his "impartiality, courage, and plain speaking."[3] Similar words, of course, could be used to characterize More in his public service. It is apparent that both men were intensely concerned with the best interests of the realm. Both saw the whole of political reality. More fully recognized that Henry VIII might exchange his head for a castle at any moment; Sackville knew likewise that politics was a precarious platform.[4] Yet despite the readily apparent uncertainties of the political world, both perceived a duty to serve, and to be ever watchful for abuses of power which might lead to tyranny and civil disorder.

We may take the parallel one additional step, for both More and Sackville received the benefits of the Inns of Court—more at Lincoln's Inn and Sackville at the Inner Temple. I extend Richard Schoeck's thesis that More's study of the law gave substance to his social and political concerns to Sackville as well.[5] Schoeck has demonstrated admirably that the ambient air of the Tudor Inns of Court also nurtured More's humanism.[6] The complete body of evidence cannot be presented here, but I believe that Sackville's humanism was also given impetus through the Inns of Court. Schoeck sharpens the focus of the parallel: "In the Tudor Inns of Court there would have been an atmosphere that fostered some, at least, of the emphases of humanism—rhetoric especially, for out of the Inns of Court were to come those fountain-heads of Elizabethan literary energy, the *Mirror for Magistrates* and *Gorboduc*. . . ."[7]

[2]See Normand Berlin, *Thomas Sackville* (New York, 1974).

[3]Charles Wilson, "Thomas Sackville: An Elizabethan Poet as Citizen," in Jan Van Dorsten, ed. *Ten Studies in Anglo-Dutch Relations* (London, 1974), p. 42.

[4]See Sackville's letter to Lord Burghley quoted in Berlin, *Sackville*, p. 20.

[5]Schoeck, *Thomas More*, p. 23.

[6]Ibid., pp. 23-24.

[7]Ibid.

Sackville, of course, had a hand in both of these works.

Let us turn to More's *Richard III* and Sackville's *Buckingham* for similarities in the treatment of the theme of tyranny and its attendant civil disorders.[8] Through careful attention to characterization, plot, and language, both artists dramatize this theme to heighten the reader's response. The common bonds of their characterization are that they create a vivid character who dominates the stage, retains many dimensions, and yet possesses a psychological unity.[9] The starting point is physical description. Acting upon their dramatic instincts, More and Sackville want their audiences to "see" their titular figure. We recall More's well-known description of Richard:

> little of stature, ill fetured of limmes, croke backed, his left shoulder much higher than his right, hard fauoured of visage. . . . He was malicious, wrathful, enuious, and from afore his birth, euer frowarde.[10]

This portrait is especially effective because More juxtaposes it against a flattering description of Edward IV:

> He was a goodly parsonage, and very Princely to behold, of hearte couragious, politique in counsaile, in aduersitie nothynge abashed . . . .He was of visage louelye; of bodye myghtie, stronge, and cleane made . . . .[11]

Edward thus becomes the visual antithesis of Richard.

For Sackville's visual introduction to Buckingham, we must turn to the final stanzas of the "Introduction," which serve as a preface to the narrative. In these stanzas, Sackville creates a dramatic intensity that transcends the conventional openings of tragic complaints:

> His cloke of black al pilde and quite forworne,
> Wringing his handes, and Fortune ofte doth blame,
> Which of a duke had made him nowe her skorne.
> With gastly lookes as one in maner lorne,
> Oft spred his armes, stretcht handes he ioynes as fast,
> With ruful chere, and vapored eyes vpcast.
>
> His cloke he rent, his manly breast he beat,
> His heare al thorne about the place it laye . . .
> His iyes they whurled about withouten staye,

---

[8] See *The Complete Works of St. Thomas More,* vol. 2, *The History of Richard III,* ed. Richard S. Sylvester (New Haven, 1963), (Hereafter cited as *CW*); and for Sackville, Lily B. Campbell, ed. *The Mirror for Magistrates, (New York, 1970).* On the subject of tyranny, see W.A. Armstrong, *"The Elizabethan Concept of the Tyrant,"* *Review of English Studies,* 22 (1946): 161-181.

[9] For my understanding of More's dramaturgy, I am much indebted to Arthur N. Kincaid, "The Dramatic Structure of Sir Thomas More's *History of King Richard III,"* *Studies in English Literature,* 12 (1972): 223-42.

[10] *CW, vol. 2, p. 7.*

[11] Ibid., p. 4.

> With stormy syghes the place dyd so complayne,
> As if his hart at eche had burst in twayne.[12]

On the one hand, More creates a vivid portrait of a tyrant; on the other, Sackville focuses on a character who unwisely put his trust in a tyrant and in turn suffered the tragic consequences.

Much has been said about the multi-faceted, yet unified character of Richard given to us by More.[13] In large part, this character unity stems from two qualities common to all tyrants—their dissimulation and their cruelty. Throughout More's prose account, these two qualities are shown with calculated repetition. Likewise, Sackville creates a sense of wholeness about Buckingham. We see Buckingham experience thoughts and emotions ranging from hope, pride, and power to despair, revenge, and fear.[14] However, the means whereby Sackville welds a psychological unity for Buckingham's character is through his carefully delineated relationship with the tyrant Richard. In fact, the center of Sackville's narrative is a unified drama of Buckingham's initial fascination with Richard's schemes, his loyalty to Richard's machinations, his growing awareness of Richard's tyrannical character, and his final realization that he must destroy the tyrant or be destroyed by him. Buckingham struts his time upon the stage in the shadow of a tyrant, and his gradual awakening to Richard's cruel and dissembling nature complements the wholeness of his character.

Through the theme of tyranny and its consequences, More and Sackville interweave characterization and plot. They trace the inevitable effects of tyranny with sensitivity, detail, and forcefulness; however, the dramatic appeal of these two works lies not just in the presentation of the external consequences of tyranny, but as well in the depiction of the internal troubles which plague tyrants and their followers. More captures this inward turmoil in his stage tyrant:

> Where he went abrode, his even whirled about, his body priuily fenced, his land euer on his dager, his countenance and maner like one always ready to strike againe, he toke ill rest a nightes, lay long wakyng and musing, sore weried with care and watch, rather slumbred then slept, troubled wyth fearful dreames, sodainly sommetyme sterte vp, leape out of his bed & runne about the chamber, so was his restles herte continually tossed & tumbled wt the tedious impression & stormy remembrance of his abominable dede.[15]

Such a passage clearly heightens More's dramatic vision of tyranny.

---

[12]Campbell, *Mirror,* p. 317.
[13]See Ibid., and *CW,* vol. 2, for detailed discussion.
[14]Berlin, *Sackville,* p. 61.
[15]*CW,* vol. 2, p. 87.

Sackville's description of tormented minds echoes More's, but he extends the psychological profile to include Buckingham. In this passage, Buckingham refers to the murder of the "royall babes" and the mental anguish it led to:

> These heauy burdens pressed vs vpon.
> Tormenting vs so by our selues alone,
> Muck like the felon that pursued by night,
> Startes at eche bushe as his foe were in sight.
>
> Nowe doubting state, nowe dreading loss of life,
> In feare of wrecke at euery blast of wynde,
> Now start in dreames through dread of murdrers knyfe,
> As though euen then revengement were assynde.
> With restles thought so is the guylty minde
> Turmoyled, and never feeleth ease or stay,
> But lives in feare of that which folowes aye.[16]

In these lines, Sackville reveals to us that tyranny had produced an inward chaos of the mind for both Richard and Buckingham.

We may also draw parallels between More and Sackville in their handling of language to dramatize their theme. For example, they share certain conventional images of Tudor literature, such as animal imagery—Richard aligned with "wolf," or "boar"; his victims with "lambs," or "deer." In addition, both picture Richard "thirsting" after power, and in keeping with their respective attempts to dramatize character and action, both rely on the conventional stage image to lend an element of tragic irony to their presentation. Here is More's well-known rendering of the image:

> And in a stage plaie, the people know right well that he that plaieth the sowdaine, in percase a souter, yet yf one of acquaintaunce perchaunce of litle nurture should call him by his name while he standeth in his miestie one of his tourmetours might fortune breke his hed for maryng the play. And so they saied, these matters by kynges games, as it were staige playes, and for the most part plaied vpon scaffoldes, in whiche poore menne bee but lookers on, and they that steppe vp with them when they cannot play their partes, they disorder the plaie and do theim selues no good.[17]

Focusing on Buckingham's demise, Sackville also chooses the transitory image of the stage:

> In place of whom, as it befel my lot,
> Like on a stage, so stept I in strayt waye,
> Enioying there but wofully god wot,
> As he that had a slender part to playe:
> To teache therby, in earth no state may stay,

[16]Campbell, *Mirror,* p. 325.
[17]*CW,* vol. 2, p. 81.

> But as our partes abridge or length our age
> So passe we all while others fyll the stage.[18]

Sackville's image succeeds because it is functional rather than decorative; indeed, in the narrative structure, it serves as a metaphor of moral conflict for the titular character. Does it not seem likely that the genius of More fostered Sackville's attempt to merge image and meaning?

This use of imagery signals that both More and Sackville would not allow their concern for political morality to overshadow their concern for language. This is apparent throughout *Richard III* and *Buckingham*. One specific instance might serve to solidify our view of this concern. What I am referring to is the use of the word *fear* by both More and Sackville. Remarkably, the word itself becomes a dramatic refrain, especially in Sackville's *Buckingham* where the word is repeated no fewer than twenty-seven times in the 777-line narrative. Language becomes inextricably bound with theme; fear and tyranny become virtually synonymous. Fear creates the mood of the presentation, it describes the reactions of others to Richard, and, more revealingly, it describes a prevalent aspect of the characters of both Richard and Buckingham.

More used the word *fear* to key us to the changes wrought by the tyrant Richard. Early in his narrative, More describes the final days of Edward IV's reign:

> In whych tyme of hys latter daies, thys Realm was in quyet and prosperous estate: no feare of outewarde enemyes, no warre in hande, nor none towarde, but such as no manne looked for: the people towarde the Prynce, not in a constrayned feare, but in a wyllynge and louynge obedyence. . . .[19]

Interestingly enough, however, it is Buckingham who calls our attention to the dramatic changes brought about by Richard. The shift in the mood of events is seen most clearly as Buckingham speculates on the Queen's reluctance to deliver the young Duke of York unto the care of Richard:

> Nowe then yf she refuse in the deliueraunce of hym, to folowe the counsaile of them whose wisdom she knoweth, whose trouth she wel trusteth: it is ethe to perceiue, that frowardnesse letteth her, and not feare. But goe to suppose that she feare (as who maye lette her to feare her own shadowe) the more she feareth to delyuer hym, the more oughte wee feare to leaue him in her handes. For if she caste suche fonde doubtes, that shee feare his hurte: then wyll she feare that hee shall be fette thence.[20]

---

[18]Campbell, *Mirror*, p. 319.
[19]*CW*, vol. 2, p. 4.
[20]Campbell, *Mirror*, p. 29.

Buckingham spins his diabolical logic into a web of fear that soon, with the direction of Richard, encompasses everyone of consequence in the realm. The word fear then echoes from moment to moment throughout the remainder of the work. As in the above passage, sometimes it appears as a noun, thus linking it with the nouns tyranny and tyrant; at other times it is a verb, identifying one of the main feelings common to those around Richard.

Whether as a direct borrowing or a similar artistic impulse, Sackville also concentrates on the word fear. Like More, he weaves the concept of fear into the core of his dramatic presentation. The word itself assumes such a significant part of the narrative that it heightens the dramatic effect of character and action. Sackville wishes us to see that fear characterizes the state of mind of both Richard and Buckingham, as well as those terrorized by this evil pair. Moreover, Sackville's narrative probes into the consequences of that fear:

> But what auaylde the terror and the fear,
> Wherewyth he kept his lieges vnder awe?
> It rather wan him hatred every where,
> And fayned faces forst by feare of lawe:
> That but while Fortune doth with fauour blaw
> Flatter through feare: for in theyr hart lurkes aye
> A secret hate that hopeth for a daye.[21]

In short, Sackville recognized the dramatic possibilities of the word fear and freely enlarged upon them.

There are some contrasts between More and Sackville and their handling of Richard III, Buckingham, and the theme of tyranny. Obviously, Sackville concentrates more heavily on Buckingham, and, unlike More, he does not include the episode in which Morton tempts Buckingham to revolt. It is also readily apparent that Sackville sees Buckingham's character in a less negative light. Finally, Sackville's narrative is less unified thematically, but we should bear in mind that the format of the *Mirror for Magistrates* essentially demanded that Sackville focus, at least briefly, on the conventional themes of mutability, fortune, and pride.

Two questions might concern us in conclusion. First, in their dramaturgy of tyranny, were More and Sackville suggesting contemporary parallels? For example, was More presenting a mirror image of Henry VIII? Was Sackville drawing parallels with mid-Tudor tyranny, perhaps specifically with Queen Mary's particular form of tyranny? It is tempting to say yes, but I sense that both men were too politically astute to draw contemporary parallels too precisely.

[21]Ibid., p. 327.

Furthermore, they were too much attuned to an artistic consciousness to allow a "mirroring" process to dominate their respective
creations.[22]

The second question is did More's *Richard III* directly influence
Sackville's *Buckingham?* Again, the temptation is to say yes. Beyond
question, More's work was well-respected during the 1550s[23] Of
greater significance, Sackville probably would have come into
contact with More's work through *Hall's Chronicle.* We know from
one of the prose links in the *Mirror for Magistrates* that its authors
consulted *Hall's Chronicle*[24] Hall printed a version of More's
Richard III in the *Chronicle,* but it would take a much longer study
to investigate fully the possible influence of More on Sackville. However, it would not be stretching the evidence too thinly to suggest
that More provided an attractive model of the way in which a timely
theme could be given a dramatic vision. Sackville was artist enough
to recognize More's achievement.

Comparing artists may not always lead to fruitful conclusions, but
in this case I believe that it does. Here we have seen that two great
Tudor artists shared a vision of the political world and molded that
vision in similar ways. Recognizing their commonality should
enhance our sensitivity to them, their works, and to the literary and
political consciousness of the Tudor period.

[22]See *CW,* vol. 2, p. ciii, for a discussion of whether More might be "mirroring"
Henry VIII. He also reminds that at the time of the composition of *Richard III,*
More's interest in the evils of tyranny was intense. Several of More's epigrams have
tyranny as their subject matter (see p. xcix).
[23]See R.W. Chambers, *The Place of St. Thomas More in English Literature and
History,* (New York, 1964), pp. 27-28 for discussion of the praise of More's *Richard
III* during the 1550s.
[24]Campbell, *Mirror,* p. 110.

Reading More's *Utopia* As A Criticism Of Plato*

John A. Gueguen

The works of St. Thomas More have provoked a wide variety of interpretive studies. As the centuries pass, the facets of his creative genius catch the rays of so many philosophical, social, and literary tendencies that observers still venture to offer a meaning hitherto undisclosed. Among these many facets, the one explored in this essay is his medieval outlook. It reveals More's formidable contribution to the history of philosophical criticism.

The medieval tendency of More's life and thought has been often noticed, but it is still commonly withheld from his best-known work.[1] Most of the *Utopia* scholarship has drawn attention to its humanistic and expansive outlook, and to the Renaissance intellectual milieu that seems to form its historical context. The More I have met in the *Utopia* and throughout his works is not, however, a representative of Renaissance or early modern thought—at least not as his friend Erasmus and other members of the More circle are representatives of it. More impresses me as a consistent contributor to the cultural, and especially the spiritual, heritage of medieval Christendom. Admittedly, Renaissance thought was based upon medieval assumptions. But its representative men were not at work, as was More, developing and extending those assumptions. While they were consumers of their heritage, More was still producing it.

More internalized the cosmopolitan spiritual universe of Christendom. He seems to stand at its apex peering with a hint of foreboding into the new world that is about to enfold Europe. The mind of Christendom was throughout his career the mind of Thomas More. It steeped him not only in a concern for the religious unity of

*Earlier versions have been delivered before the Second Conference of Utopian Studies at the University of Michigan, September 1977, and the Thirteenth Conference on Medieval Studies at Western Michigan University May 1978. I am grateful to the auditors of those presentations fortheir helpful comments, and especially to Professors Thomas White of Upsala College and Walter Nicgorski of the University of Notre Dame.
[1] A notable exception is P. Albert Duhamel, "Medievalism of More's *Utopia*," in R.S. Sylvester and G.P. Marc'hadour, eds., *Essential Articles for the Study of Thomas More*, (Hamden, Conn., 1977.) (Hereafter cited as *Essential Articles*.) While the author urges that the *Utopia* is "probably the most medieval of More's works" (p. 234), he has in mind mainly methodological resemblances to the medieval scholastics.

Europe, but in a like concern for his own spiritual integrity. More was well launched toward sainthood long before the fateful season for martyrdom in England. A commentary that I have found especially suggestive for this study asserts that in his spiritual formation and outlook More was superior to "the vast majority of his countrymen."[2] That "inner Catholicism," informing his dealings with the world and its inhabitants, would distinguish him not only from his own contemporaries, but from most of ours as well.

Looking at More and his *Utopia* against that medieval universality and spirituality, I find him engaged more with matters of theology than of law or statecraft, education or economics, as we secularized moderns tend to view those disciplines. Further, I see the *Utopia* as a part of a theological controversy, not with any of More's contemporaries, but with Plato whom More deemed "so wise" as to merit esteem as "the great philosopher."[3] Accordingly, it is my thesis that More's *Utopia* pursues a fundamental reformation of Platonic theology. It seeks in characteristically Platonic fashion, in dialogue, to disclose a new Plato, a corrected Plato. As he engages the ancient Athenian in theological controversy by means of discourse on an ideal commonwealth, More both acknowledges Plato's excellence in the order of reason, and shows its limitations in the light of revelation.[4]

[2]Marshall Smelser, "The Political Philosophy of Sir Thomas More as Expressed in His Theological Controversies," in *St. Louis University Studies in Honor of St. Thomas Aquinas* (St. Louis, 1943), I:19. Thus, Duhamel ("Medievalism," p. 238), can say that "the *Utopia* can be read . . . by anyone familiar with only 'profane' learning. Its full significance, however, cannot be grasped without some knowledge of the implied 'divine' knowledge."

[3]More's *Dialogue Concerning Heresies,* in the section "On Translating Scripture into the Vernacular." Duhamel ("'Medievalism," p. 249), paraphrases another significant passage from More's *Dialogue of Comfort:* "We shall therefore neither fully accept the philosophers in political theory, nor utterly reject them, but correct their theories according to the prescriptions of revelation." But he finds Aristotle's *Politics* and Aquinas' *Commentary* more congruent with the *Utopia* than Plato's works. Although More alludes to other ancients besides Plato (Aristotle, Cicero, Seneca, Plutarch, Epicurus), with none of them does he bear so strong a spiritual kinship as with Plato. They surely did impress More as worthy teachers, but it is in the Platonic philosophical family where he is to be located.

[4]Rainer Pineas, "Thomas More's Use of the Dialogue Form as a Weapon of Religious Controversy," *Studies in the Renaissance,* 7 (1960): 193-206, does not cite Plato; he goes back no further than to Augustine for a precedent. Martin Fleisher, (*Radical Reform and Political Persuasion in the Life of Thomas More* [Genève, 1973]) alludes to Platonic parallels, and contrasts the *Utopia* and the *Republic* (pp. 130 ff). Fleisher quotes the prefatory "rival" passage, but asserts that "*Utopia* is superior because it portrays a living commonwealth while the *Republic* merely inquires into the philoso-

Before examining this critique and its implications, it is necessary to establish the Platonic tradition as More found it, especially its bearing upon theological matters of concern to him.[5]

The moral objective. What matters most to Plato is the soul and its salvation through personal moral reformation. All are engaged in a lifetime struggle between the good and evil forces which pull toward virtue and vice. Ultimately, happiness depends upon the successful outcome of that struggle: Plato continually persuades men to take cognizance of their moral condition and to correct its imperfections. Since men live together in cities, this effort implicates the formational and deformational influences of political institutions. Vigilance must be maintained against legal and educational ignorance disguised as wisdom, for if unchecked such wisdom will lead to the worst condition of cities and souls.

Since men can also be reformed by those same institutions when they are based on right principles, it is the task of political philosophy to discover those principles. In the actual world of our experience, they can never entirely remove the defects of soul, but they can reduce or confine them. The search for the right principles leads to constructing, in speech, the best arrangement of a city. For although the best must always be a stranger in our world it can serve each man as a model or standard of what is possible in his own life, according as he is blessed by chance and favorable opportunities.

The educational means. Plato is a critic of existing laws and educa-

---

phical principles of such a society." His major thesis is that More is engaged in "radical criticism of society" (p. 172), that like his fellow humanists More advocates "the reformation of society according to the principle of radical equality" (p. 131), and provides in the *Utopia* a "program of social reform" intended to "revive the Christian commonwealth" (pp. 146, 172; cf. pp. 68, 124, 129, 141). In thus reading More's intentions almost exclusively from a worldly point of view, he sees the *Utopia*'s chief significance along socio-economic and institutional lines. More is made out to be a radical reformer of his own *society,* and not of the Platonic or any other philosophical or theological orientation. When he deals with Christian humanism Fleisher places the emphasis on humanism rather than on Christian. This may be correct in the case of Erasmus and others, but they were not martyrs and saints. A more extreme lack of theological awareness is in the notes and commentary of Robert M. Adams' critical edition of the *Utopia* (New York, 1975).

[5] My study of the platonic tradition has been informed most persuasively by Professors Leo Strauss and Eric Voegelin. I read *Republic, Statesman,* and *Laws* as essentially in agreement with each other and with the whole body of the dialogues and epistles of Plato. Accordingly, what follows is an attempt to view his teaching as a composite whole, as I believe More viewed it. In particular, he would find Plato's theological orientation especially evident in Book X of *Laws,* as read in the context of that whole dialogue and of the second half of *Republic* X.

tional systems because invariably they incorporate wrong principles to which the old educators and legislators are blind or indifferent. Since Plato aims at the moral improvement of men who must dwell in more or less disordered cities, he is not a reformer who seeks to alter or abolish defective political institutions. Indeed, he refuses even to take political action seriously. The only things worth serious attention are the origin and the end of the soul. Everything in between, that is, everything in this world, constitutes a playground for philosophical education which leads souls little by little to discover how they deviate from their origins, how they fall short of their ends, and what they must do to correct themselves. In that broad tactical space, the Platonic philosopher-educator conducts persuasive discourses calculated to lead people—especially the young—to form right opinions about the serious things.

In view of its objective, this conversation is most serious. But in view of the twists and turns it must take in order to keep securing agreement, it is a kind of game. While the Platonic discourse preserves loyalty to a fundamental insight which informs the whole enterprise, it stays loose and flexible. Guided by an essentially incommunicable vision of what is good, beautiful, and true in itself, the philosophical educator practices the "charms" of dialectical argument which spiritually "seduce" the innocent participants by means of conversational tactics designed to "compel" assent. The success of the enterprise demands openness to the quest, hence the docility and absence of fixed opinions characteristic of those who are young in spirit. The key to the invincibility of Platonic education is its employment of word-disquises which veil the conviction and the intention. These are needed because ordinary language is ill-equipped to convey the deepest insights, because those following the argument are spiritually immature and inexperienced, and because the argument's implications are usually subversive of the city's disordered regime.

The theological core. Ultimately, Plato's teaching is about the divine things which supply right principles and the fundamental orientation of human life. The philosophy which Plato practiced was really a theological orientation which sought to purge, and even replace, the old errors and superstitions about the universe. This new theology required a priesthood of philosopher-educators who could expound the Platonic "revelation" about God and its implications for human life in private and public. The salvation of souls would require the ministry of Plato's followers since only they could understand, safeguard, and transmit so precious a legacy. It is this theological dimension of Plato's philosophy which I will argue required Thomas More to engage in a correction, and not a rejection, of the Platonic tradition.

More shared with St. Augustine, and perhaps even learned from him as well as Cicero, admiration for Plato's moral and educational genius. But if that genius was to be of service to Christendom in its coming time of trial, someone would need to complete what Augustine had begun by performing upon Plato the kind of criticism Aquinas had performed upon Aristotle 250 years earlier. That other St. Thomas had made use of Aristotelian methodology—the demonstrative treatise—to complete Aristotle. Now More would employ the characteristic mode of Platonic discourse—the dialectical conversation—to complete, or correct, Plato. This criticism would be constructive, aimed at building upon an essentially correct, but incomplete, insight about what is right and good. More's work forms an interesting contrast to the criticism of a later chancellor of England whose *New Atlantis* and *Wisdom of the Ancients* would aim at the destruction and replacement of the classical wisdom.

Having reviewed the fundamentals of the Platonic tradition, we are ready now to inquire how More argued with Plato, to what purpose, and with what effect. In what follows, I do not mean to give the impression that More depreciates the classical learning so much valued by the members of his circle. He only notes how and why it falls short of the whole truth, which is to be found in Christian life and learning. Thus, as a Christian humanist, More would feel a remoteness from Plato as well as an affinity with him.

Utopia scholarship, I believe, has insufficiently understood this dual association. It has often been noticed that More engaged in a positive commentary on Plato. In this introduction to the Yale edition, Father Surtz finds More citing Plato "because his republic was considered as best able to furnish ideas to any builder of an ideal commonwealth."[6] The affinity is appreciated, while the remoteness is overlooked.

It was not so among More's fellow humanists. In the parerga, for example, one letter calls it to our attention: "The *Utopia* contains principles of such a sort as it is not possible to find in Plato . . . . Its lessons are less philosophical perhaps . . . , but more Christian."[7]

[6]*The Complete Works of St. Thomas More,* vol. 4, *Utopia,* ed. Edward Surtz, S.J. and J.H. Hexter (New Haven, 1965), p. clvi. In their Commentary the editors call *Utopia* "a tribute to Plato" (note 100, p. 375). (Hereafter cited as *CW*.)
[7]Beatus Rhenanus to Willibald Pirckheimer, Basel, Feb. 23, 1518; Ibid., p. 253.

More's friend, Peter Giles, has Anemolius, Utopia's poet laureate, declare: "I am a rival (*aemula*) of Plato's republic (*civitas*), perhaps even a victor (*victrix*) over it."[8] It seems clear that More wanted to show in the encounter with Raphael Hythloday that an accommodation with his own theology would require a radical revision of Plato's. Through Raphael, a Utopian stranger of his own creation and a kind of contemporary Plato, More is able to dialogue with the master himself.[9] He can have no doubt about its outcome since the argument is now informed by the superior revelation of Christian faith.

Attention has been drawn to the dual nature of the association between More and Plato in the *Utopia*. It is "common knowledge," James Steintrager writes, "that More's *Utopia* is patterned after Plato's *Republic*." But, "it is equally evident that More did not merely repeat the teaching of the *Republic*. There are significant differences between the two works."[10] Yet, after so promising an observation the author is content to examine the *Utopia's* merely descriptive elements (almost entirely in Book II) rather than undertaking an analysis of More's intention. He deals with the decorative furnishings of the two dialogues without examining the intellectual homes in which these furnishings are placed.[11]

[8]Ibid., p. 21. Unfortunately most paperback versions omit this poem, together with the entire parerga.

[9]When Peter Giles introduces Raphael to More at the beginning of Book I, he emphasizes that the "sailing" of this "stranger . . . advanced in years," "learned in Greek," and "mainly interested in philosophy, . . . has been like . . . Plato."

[10]"Plato and More's *Utopia,*" *Social Research*, 36 (Autumn, 1969): 357-372. This is a critique of J.H. Hexter's comparisons of the *Republic* and *Utopia* in *More's Utopia: The Biography of an Idea* (Princeton, N.J., 1952). I share enthusiastically Steintrager's insistence that the *Utopia* "is a masterpiece of the highest order which, accordingly, demands the most careful attention" (p. 372).

[11]For Steintrager (ibid.), the "crucial points are the corresponding treatments of war and international relations, communism, elitism, educational systems, and religious-moral teachings. Like many other comparative studies, this one focuses on the *Utopia's* more "realistic," less austere political principles without going into the reasons for More's need to engage in Platonic criticism. The author barely hints at these (n. 28, p. 367): In the *Republic*, which begins in the evening, Socrates is detained in order to witness a new and alien religious festival (which in fact he never attends), while in the *Utopia*, which begins in the morning, More is just coming from church, an old and familiar religious service which he has willingly attended. In contrast, Harry Neumann, "On the Platonism of More's *Utopia*," *Social Research* 33 (Winter 1966): 495-512 (based entirely on Book I) maintains that "More intended his arguments as a refutation of Raphael's views," but he does not associate Raphael with Plato, and he fundamentally misunderstands the *Republic* by overlooking its irony (see p. 504).

A more promising comparison of More and Plato is in Eva Brann's commentary on the *Utopia*.[12] Beginning with Peter Giles' prefatory poem, she suggests that of all More's friends, Giles best understood that a full treatment of Plato would have to employ the Platonic arts of discourse. In part, this was necessary because it allowed More to disguise his own thoughts about the most important things—precisely those things cited in Guillaume Budé's assertion that *Utopia* possesses "the true wisdom *of Christianity* for public and private life."[13]

More importantly, Brann recognizes More's use of the Platonic "spirit of irony" with its "serene playfulness."[14] A memorable example is the flashback in Book I to a scene in the household of Cardinal Morton where More has Raphael tease us about "jesting in earnest," about the serious and the playful, the grave and the merry, and ultimately about wisdom and folly. The reader's problem—what to ponder carefully and what to enjoy as a joke—was evidently as intentional with More as with Plato. Yet, nearly all commentators persist in treating seriously what Plato and More surely regarded as comical about life in their two commonwealths. This is especially clear in matters having to do with the body, since Plato and More are evidently seeking to abstract from the body, the better to focus attention on the soul.

As in Plato's *Republic* and *Laws,* the detailed regulations of Utopian life are means and not ends. They serve only to bring us into contact with what is truly serious—the state of character these regulations are meant to form. Neither Plato nor More take seriously (as ends) this world and its furnishings—especially those things their contemporaries valued most. In the Platonic tradition the world's importance lies only in its serving as the stage on which man's struggle is played out, and eventually won or lost. What is most real is always what is most unseen and unheard in the world. As most commentators devote themselves to the comic aspects of the *Utopia,* they tend to pass over the truly serious level of the dialogue where More is intent, among other things, upon reforming Plato's notions of what really is right and wrong about life and death.

Brann's study suggests other ideas for a fuller consideration of

[12]She adopts the words of Harpsfield in titling her article, " 'An Exquisite Platform': *Utopia,*" *Interpretation,* 3 (Autumn, 1972): 1-26.
[13]Ibid., p. 5.
[14]Ibid., pp. 11, 23ff. G. K. Chesterton's famous appreciation of More correctly identifies the *Utopia* as a "playground," in "The Fame of Blessed Thomas More," in *Essential Articles,* p. 501.

More's criticism of Plato (a reference, for instance, to his opening assertion that the *Republic* is his "defeated rival"). But it does not explore the reasons for, and the extent of, More's revision of the theological fundamentals of Plato's teaching.

One final instance of a scholarly treatment of More's intentions with respect to Plato finds it significant that the Utopian discussion occurs in a garden, the traditional setting for important transformations of orientation.[15] In the *Critias,* Harry Berger writes that Plato had converted Heraclitus and shifted the emphasis in philosophy from body to soul, "from object to image, from perception to thought, from history to myth, from nature to spirit, from the beginning of experience to its end."[16] Carrying this analogy further, I suggest that More, while approving of that shift, saw its insufficiency in light of the Christian revelation and undertook—also in a garden—to "convert" Plato by shifting the emphasis again: from image and myth to direct experience and possession. In the *Utopia* More accomplishes this by drawing us into the Platonic universe, the better to send us beyond it.[17] He is at first attracted by what seems familiar and congenial about Raphael, but eventually he challenges and even opposes him, and all with Platonic irony.

In view of these suggestions about the lofty aim of the *Utopia,* we can begin to understand why More's Christianity, and his identity with medieval civilization, necessitated a fundamental reformation of the Platonic tradition. More intended to alert his fellow humanists to the shortcomings, even more than to the strengths, of the ancient wisdom as an intellectual framework within which to deal with contemporary threats to virtue and salvation. He preceded Bacon and other moderns as a critic, and unlike their rejection of the ancient wisdom, More sought to save it for posterity by transforming it into a more potent account, because a truer and a more complete one, of man's spiritual condition and destiny. Without such a correction by Christian wisdom, the Platonic insight would be able to survive in the new Europe only as an antiquarian, not an operational, one.

It will suffice for the present to trace this intention in outline. From his theological vantage point, More is able to see that the *soul* is worth more, and capable of more, than Plato knew, that the *best* and the *happiest* lies not merely in respecting and venerating human-

---

[15]Harry Berger, Jr., "The Renaissance Imagination: Second World and Green World," *The Centennial Review,* 9 (Winter, 1965): 63-74.
[16]Ibid., p. 73.
[17]See, ibid., p.70.

ity and its natural perfections, but in respecting and venerating—and eventually experiencing—the divine Persons in God, loving and serving Him as He has shown that He desires to be loved and served. Likewise, the *worst* bondage is not summarized in Platonic-Utopian slavery, punishment, law, marriage, war, sickness, and death, any more than the greatest freedom is achieved through their travel, pleasure, industry, harmony, peace, health, and life.

Ultimately, this life and all of its goods are for the sake of The Life and its supreme Good. The well-being and happiness of dwellers in the simply Platonic Utopia is based upon reason and nature. Utopian virtues are the natural ones of prudence, moderation, courage, and justice. Utopian pleasures are the natural ones, those of mind and of body in subjection to mind. The vices and the pains spurned in Utopia are likewise natural: folly, immoderation, cowardice, injustice, and the inevitable consequences of excess—especially avarice.

For the Christian humanist there is much more in life than all of that. Reason and nature can be reliable guides, but they are inadequate norms for the organization of a satisfactory life in the more spacious Christian universe. Although they are indispensable prerequisites, one has to advance beyond the natural virtues to faith, hope, and charity—a wisdom and love far dearer to More than the classical *sophia* and *eros*.[18] Yet the higher virtues are even easier to attain, for one need only open himself through humble admission of his nothingness in order for God to enter with His enabling grace.

Hence, too, a Christian advances beyond the natural vices (the initial obstacles), and goes on to reject the supernatural folly, vanity, and ignorance of pride, the root cause of disorder in souls, and consequently in cities. In so doing he escapes the true pains of eternal punishment. It seems that More wants to call attention to the qualitative difference between the spiritual disease afflicting his contemporaries (who regarded themselves as Christians), and the *amatheia* and *hubris* of the pre-Christian moral universe.[19] *Utopia*'s instruction in humility shows that like all the supernatural virtues it

---

[18]See R. W. Chambers, *Thomas More* (London, 1953), pp. 127 ff., and C. S. Lewis' commentary thereon in *English Literature in the Sixteenth Century* (Oxford, 1954). Chambers did not carry this point on to a complete examination of More's reform of the Platonic tradition, and Lewis professed to see only fun and merriment in *Utopia*.

[19]Hexter (*More's Utopia*, pp. 73, 77, 79), recognized that "More's Christian faith . . . provided him with a basic insight into the underlying pattern of evil," and especially with the knowledge that the sin of pride is "the most disastrous infection of man's soul," and 'the cancer of the commonwealth.''

presupposes nature. But while our knowledge of humility proceeds first from reason, it goes much further. Reason is a kind of black-and-white portal to the marvellous world of color which More finds in faith. In the scholastic tradition which formed More's philosophy and theology, right reason (reason informed by faith) is the constant point of reference. Thus what is sometimes read in *Utopia* as an attachment to, or preference for, reason is better described as an appreciation for its instrumental role in coming to the truth. More praises the virtues of classical moral philosophy because they are necessary conditions for salvation. He is surely no advocate of *sola virtus*. For More the highest order of virtue requires not only a well-trained intellect and even temperament, but a pure heart and, above all, a living faith. More always follows the medieval scholastics in seeing the moral as preparatory to the theological virtues, a differentiation basic to his Christian ethic.

In the next place, we should consider what the *Utopia* tells us about natural religion grounded in reasonable experience, and the yearning for "a better revelation." It is here that More makes his strongest case for the reform of Plato's teaching about the highest things. It is significant that he places the name of Christ entirely in capital letters.[20] The Utopian religion (and Plato's) certainly aims in the right direction. It is theistic and even monotheistic; it is cultic, placing emphasis upon the worship of the Deity; it is ascetical, transcending in the purest cases even the good pleasures; it is moral, recognizing in religion the most powerful incitement to virtue; and it is eschatological, placing true happiness beyond this life. As religion arrived at through reason and experience, More stands in admiration of this achievement of Platonic theology. And yet, he would say, it is open to, and even presses toward something further—the very possession of a personal God who has walked with men and spoken with them about His creation and about Himself, about the rewards promised His followers for their faithfulness to the difficult and yet easy way of love, and about the punishments in store for those who deliberately reject that way.

The section on religion is a more obvious place where More is at work doing something more than *Utopia's* commentators usually see

[20]In the original Latin text, reprinted in the Yale edition, the only words capitalized are Christ and Christianity. Martin Fleisher, (*Radical Reform*, p. 123) has noticed that "the good news Hythloday brings back from Utopia . . . does not clash with the Gospel. On the contrary, evangelism represents its completion and perfection." But since his study aims at More's presumed primary, or even exclusive, interest in social reform, he does not pursue the point.

in it—partly because they have not sufficiently reflected on the depth of More's Christianity, and partly because they accept too readily the conventional or textbook presentation of Plato's political philosophy. Throughout the *Utopia* More is showing that while this island has a happy social order, it nonetheless falls short of what it could have. Though Utopia is far superior to England, More does not offer it as a model or blueprint. Not only does he have reservations whether he *shall* ever see it come to pass, but also whether he or anyone *should* ever see it. Utopia is only a rudimentary society representing reason at its best, and is thus ready for the improvements which Christ's teachings alone could make.

It seems clear that the *Utopia* can be read as an intentional correction, or reformation, of Plato's theology. Inasmuch as More still wanted to acknowledge the suprisingly clear insights of his ancient friend, it may be better to say that in *Utopia* he attempts to reveal a new, fairer and younger Plato, just as Plato himself had claimed to do with Socrates.[21]

Like the Platonic tradition which it renovates and enriches, the *Utopia* is so open, wide, and deep that it surely takes an overly bold commentator to insist that he has found its one and only meaning. As More's friends observed in their humorous exchange of letters, Utopia is indeed difficult to locate. The interpretation I am suggesting, however, enables other facets of More's achievement to come more clearly into view. It becomes easier, for instance, to understand the disagreement among *Utopia* scholars, between those who find it simply a playful work intending nothing serious and those who regard it as an earnest proposal for social reorganization. Like any good Platonic work it reveals both messages, for it is serious and playful at the same time. Yet this combination leaves both interpretations somewhere short of More's full intention. Moreover, as a Christian work the *Utopia*'s seriousness is made all the graver by the elevated stakes, in life and in death, while the playfulness is the joyful—or as More would say it—the merry pursuit of both life and death.

Finally, this reading of *Utopia* also opens avenues for further interpretation of More's whole career. To indicate only one of these by way of conclusion, I believe a case can be made that he already divines the social and political aberrations—even disasters—which would shortly come to be, through utopian attempts to mold civil communities according to some theological prescription. Still, in his

[21]Epistle II, 314c.

own lifetime, the same Christian impulse which led him to a utopian reformation of Plato would require him to react against a utopian reformation of Christianity by Luther.[22] Such is the wondrous ambiguity of the Platonic dialect when it discovers the utopian genre in the literature of political philosophy.

[22]See John Headley, "More Against Luther," *Moreana*, 15 (November, 1967): 211-223.

Thomas More and the Problem of Counsel

J. H. Hexter

A couple of days back it was, quite likely, the five hundredth anniversary of the birth of Thomas More.[1] The occasion here today is one of many this year that will celebrate that anniversary in the United States, in Britain, and perhaps at Rome and in Russia. A demimillenial anniversary is a thing all men have had or will have in common with Thomas More; few, indeed, are the men who have had or will have their five hundredth birthday remembered at all, much less in the U.S., Britain, Rome, and Moscow as Thomas More's will be.

Who was Thomas More that so many should celebrate his birthday half a thousand years later?

There are several answers to that question, but only one correct one. More was a martyr, done to death for refusing to renounce beliefs that he profoundly held. But in the past 1900 years thousands of Christians, both Roman and Protestant, have been done to death for standing by their faith, and few of them have their 500th or 1,000th or 1,500th birthday commemorated. More was also one who held high office in the government of the English realm, ultimately that of Lord Chancellor, the highest office in dignity under the King. But neither outside nor inside the realm of England do people celebrate the birthday anniversary of any other dead Lord Chancellor. No, this year we do not celebrate the birth of a mere official or even of a mere martyr; but a martyr and an official who wrote a particular book, *Utopia*. More was to write many books, but outside a constricted circle he is remembered only as the author of one. Had he not been the author of *Utopia*, I doubt that we would be celebrating the 500th anniversary of More's birth today.

What I want to do now is to take you back 462 years to 1516, to another birthday of Thomas More's, his thirty-eighth. That is to take you truly *in medias res* (into the midst of affairs) in two ways. First, into the midst of Thomas More's adult life, just about at midpoint

[1]Professor Hexter read his paper on February 10, 1978. It was the principle address to the conference, and commentaries on it were delivered by Professors Richard Marius, Clarence Miller, Richard Schoeck, Susan K. Shapiro, and Arthur J. Slavin.

between his attainment of his majority and his attainment of martyrdom. Second, into the midst of the book, *Utopia,* for which he is remembered, with one part of it finished, the other part barely underway.

In February 1516, on his thirty-eighth birthday, who was Thomas More? He was a Londoner, undersheriff of the City. He was a cultivated lawyer and a successful one, who nevertheless was darkly distrustful of the common law, his sole means of livelihood. He was a devoted father with four young daughters and a young son to see established in life. He was a wit, and a man of some literary pretensions and promise.[2] By his thirty-eighth birthday it is not unlikely that malicious men were beginning to say about him the sort of thing an academic curmudgeon I once knew said of a man described to him as "a promising scholar."

Yes, indeed. Oh, yes. John James was a promising scholar twenty years ago, and at forty he is still—promising.

In the case of More it would have been a misplaced sneer, however. During the past year, he had spent many months of enforced idleness as a member of a mission sent by the King of England to negotiate a trade treaty with the Netherlands, a mission superseded but not recalled. He whiled away some of his idle time with a visit to a friend of his friend Erasmus, Peter Giles of Antwerp. There it seems likely the two new friends hit on a pastime, a rather odd one, especially suited to literati with a taste for politics. The question they tossed back and forth was probably of this order: given men as they are by nature, what would be the *optimum status reipublicae,* the best state of a commonwealth, the best public ordering of human life? Emancipated from humdrum, free to distance himself from the world of everyday, in this partly playful, partly serious exercise, More let his imagination take flight and soar. He achieved a vision of a social world where men might live together in peace and justice, a world that never had been, but still conceivably might be. He called that imagined world Utopia, and probably before he left the Netherlands in October 1515 he had written down and elaborated what stuck in his mind from his conversations with Peter Giles. What he had written is now the introduction to the book *Utopia,* and the second part of that book, the Discourse on the Utopian commonwealth.

[2]More's recently written *History of Richard III* did not suffice to fulfill that promise. In the 1510s, no work of English prose could make good a man's claim to literary excellence. It was no accident that More's previous work in verse and the current one in prose, *Utopia,* by which he set literary store, were in Latin, the language appropriate for use by those who sought literary glory.

In February 1516 he was back home doing at least three complicated things. He was ruefully facing the financial damage that his
mission to the Netherlands had inflicted on his personal and family
affairs; he was weighing up the possible costs and benefits of a
change in his career line; and he was reflecting on a political question
that in the past half-century had elicited an extraordinary amount of
tough thinking, the problem of counsel. The three things were
convergent for Thomas More at that moment in February 1516. We
will approach the convergence from the direction of the problem of
counsel.

In the previous fifty-odd years, four hard-headed statesmen-
writers—Sir John Fortescue, Philippe de Commines, Niccolo Machiavelli, and Claude de Seyssel—had put their minds to the problem
raised by the need of rulers for good advice. The sum of their in-
dependent efforts probably constitutes a weighty a mass of sharp
thinking on the subject of how a ruler could get good and avoid bad
advice as has ever been accumulated in an equivalent time.

And now, quite possibly unaware of the reflections of any of his
four recent predecessors, quite surely unaware of two of them,
Thomas More turned his thought to the problem of counsel. In one
way his angle of vision was the opposite of theirs. All of the others
wrote about counsel during or after a career that they had given over
to counselling rulers—Fortescue, Henry VI of England; Commines,
Louis XI of France; Seyssel, Charles VIII and Louis XII of France;
and Machiavelli, the Florentine Signoria. Of the counselling of rulers
Thomas More by contrast had had no previous direct experience. He
had, however, had some indirect experience: he had known more or
less intimately several men who held considerable places in the councils of Henry VIII or his father—Richard Pace, Cuthbert Tunstall,
William Warham, Archbishop of Canterbury and until recently Lord
Chancellor, and most closely in his youth, the late John Cardinal
Morton, formerly Archbishop of Canterbury and Lord Chancellor to
Henry VII, in whose household More had once served.

In February 1516 at the age of thirty-eight, quite possibly for the
first time in his life, Thomas More began to think hard and seriously
about the counselling of rulers. What led him, a private man, at his
age to focus his attention on the matter, to reflect on it as fruitfully,
perhaps, as any man in history has ever done? It was the offer, un-
expected and unsought, of a place in the King's service that forced
the dilemmas of counsel on his attention. Henry VIII's first minister,
Thomas Cardinal Wolsey, and the young King himself had been

seeking to persuade More to accept a pension of the King along with what that implied: giving the King a first claim on his services.

This was the career choice that More had to face at an age when most men no longer have any such choice: should he continue with his law practice, or should he move in the direction that promised a career at court as advisor to Henry VIII? The signpost that pointed toward court may have appeared all the more attractive to him at the moment because of the impact of his mission to the Netherlands on his domestic economy. He had, in effect lost a half year's income from legal services while he dawdled at the King's command in the Netherlands.

Given the difficult financial straits that More saw he would have to navigate, given his aversion to committing to the practice of law the time and effort that would see him through those straits, what was complicated about his career choice? Why should he hesitate even for a moment to seize the chance to advance himself in the government's service that Henry and Wolsey were offering him? He himself characterized the offer as one "very much not to be despised whether one considers the honor or the profit of it." Centuries earlier, Henry II had described justice as *magnum emolumentum* (a great emolument); in the reign of Henry VIII office was clearly *maximum emolumentum,* the greatest source of reward of all, both in honor and in profit. Moreover, a good many of More's old coterie of friends devoted to literature had already entered the King's service. Why should he not follow them?

I suspect that had that question been put to More a year earlier he might have replied, "Indeed, why not?" and embarked on a court career without much hesitation. Except for the aversion to government service often expressed by his dear friend Erasmus, little in his own experience at the time would have led More to pause long on the threshold of the court, while within lay the means to serve his prince and his country with both honor and profit, to escape the practice of law, and to find his way out of his current economic squeeze. Yet the one thing we are sure of about Thomas More's response to the opportunity offered him to serve as an advisor to his King early in 1516 is that he did not immediately grasp at it. He hesitated; he even considered declining the pension offered him. He may have held out against the solicitations of Henry, Wolsey, and his own friends at court for about two years. We know very little about those solicitations, or about how More dealt with them.

We are, however, pretty sure about one thing he did—a rather odd thing—that was occasioned by the invitation to counsel he received.

Rather soon after he had received it, he altered the Discourse on the Utopian commonwealth that he had written during his enforced leisure in the Netherlands. Between the introduction and the Discourse itself, he opened a seam, and into the opening he inserted a dialogue among the three characters he had already brought forward in the introduction—the traveller Raphael Hythloday, who in the Discourse describes the Utopian commonwealth, and Peter Giles and Thomas More, the silent auditors of Hythloday's account. So workman-like a literary job did More do in smoothing the joins between the introduction and the Dialogue, the Dialogue and the Discourse, that it was four hundred years before anyone noticed them.[3]

The dialogue that More inserted in his little work on Utopia is a dialogue about counsel, about advising the first magistrate, the prince. It owes its originality to the odd conjuncture of events in which More found himself at the moment. He was not precommitted to a career as counsellor to a ruler, but he was under pressure so to commit himself. On the other hand, he had recently written a book of whose meaning he was bound at the moment to be conscious, a book that bore indirectly, but in a peculiarly powerful way, on the matter of counsel. The discourse on Utopia had come into being just at the moment of More's life when it was certain decisively to shape its author's reflections on the career choice he faced.

The discourse on Utopia that More had written in 1515 is many kinds of book, a work in several genres: it is a fanciful *jeu d'esprit,* a witty satire, a moral tract, an imaginary travellers' tale, a political pamphlet, and—a genre of which it is the earliest member—a utopia. It is also in an unmistakable and quite literal sense a radical work: it goes to the very roots of the central issues about the right ordering of human affairs; and, although in playful guise, it deals with those issues seriously. The Utopian commonwealth that the Discourse describes is tranquil, internally peaceful, without brawls and disorders. The citizens live frugally, but well, in friendly, not hostile, intercourse with their neighbors. Crime is rare, education universal, poverty non-existent. All adults work, none too hard, and all are cared for in illness and old age. There are few priests, no lawyers, and no professional soldiers, but many scholars. These conditions are achieved by the utter abolition of markets, money, and private

[3]To the best of my knowledge the first writer to suggest that More had inserted a dialogue in a finished text was Hermann Oncken in 1922. The suggestion appears to have been forgotten. I independently "discovered" the break in 1950. See *More's UTOPIA: The Biography of an Idea* (Princeton, 1952), pp. 13, n.5, and 18-21.

property, by the enforcement of the utmost equality, not only in wealth, but in housing, political right, and work. Utopia is a communal society all the way down to common dress and common meals. The ligature that binds together everything that is not casual in the Utopian commonwealth, and playful in the description of it, is the utter supression of the dominion of man over man, of the emulation and striving for superiority that the quest for dominion generates, and of all the means for feeding the insatiable maw of human pride which riches, private property, and inequality create. In the Utopian Commonwealth this eradication of pride, the most destructive of all sins, is the work of the institutional structure of communal equality so briefly described above.

Even as More, at leisure in the Netherlands, set down his description of the best ordering of human life, and of the conditions under which it might be possible, he was aware of how hideously the world he lived in differed from the world he had conceived. Time after time he wrote in a way that made stark the contrast between the decent, truly Christian, life of the Utopians and the abomination that was life in the Europe of his day, a Europe Christian by self-proclamation only, with its frivolous wars of conquest, its vainglorious pomps, its idle rich, its grinding poverty, and its grinders of the faces of the poor—the kings, the great lords and their armed hirelings, the churchmen, and the depopulators of plowlands who drove the weak and powerless from their small holdings.

This anti-Utopian world of Christian Europe lived by rules utterly antithetic to those that made Utopia the best human society—private property, a money economy, selling what one has to sell and buying what one can afford to buy, instead of giving what one can spare and taking only what one needs. In 1515 More may have started to construct in his imagination a society opposite to the one he knew, and then found that society good. Or he may have started to construct a society that he deemed good, and found it the opposite to the one he knew. Whichever way it was (and surely by the time he got around to setting down his fantasy it was a bit of both), the fanciful traveller's discourse on Utopia also comes out as a serious, radical, and systematic onslaught on the institutional foundations and practices of the society More lived in.

Scarcely had he laid down his pen from writing his intellectually coherent indictment of his own society—an indictment for theft, robbery, and murder, among other crimes—than More found himself pressed to serve his native prince, a man who by the very nature of his office was called upon to preserve the iniquitous ordering of affairs of which in fact he was a chief beneficiary.

Little wonder, then, that in February 1516 the counselling of a ruler presented a difficult dilemma for Thomas More; little wonder that in the Dialogue of Council he examined it from a point of view from which no writer had deeply explored the questions of counsel before, and from which no one was ever to explore them more shrewdly again. For in the Dialogue More does not deal with the old question: How can a ruler ensure that he gets the best advice? Rather he wrestles with the question from the side of the potential counsellor: Why should a man become a counsellor to a ruler? What good is it likely to do him, to do the ruler who makes him a counsellor, to do the commonwealth on behalf of which he offers counsel? Little wonder that in the Dialogue he wrestled hard with these questions concerning counsel, because in February 1516 for Thomas More these questions merge into the one he was asking himself: "Should a man *like me,* Thomas More, enter the council of my King, Henry VIII of England?" It is hard to believe that when we read the Dialogue of Counsel which makes up most of the first book of More's *Utopia* we are not listening in on an internal dialogue that the author was having with himself as he weighed the pluses against the minuses of entry into the King's service. What was there about the life of a counsellor that could persuade a man like More to surrender the freedom of a happy private and literary life to swarm with the multitude that is always drawn to that center of power and honor, the ruler? What proper considerations might draw a man like More to court?

At the crux of the Dialogue of Counsel in Utopia lies an exchange between the fictitious Raphael Hythloday and the semifictitious Thomas More. In the Dialogue More argues that a man like Hythloday, learned, experienced, and committed to the improvement of the ordering of society—a man like Thomas More, too, please note—should become the councillor of a ruler. Hythloday resists the suggestion. In the argument that follows the author unintentionally proves that despite his revulsion from it, his training in the common law had its uses. It enables him to eliminate by a sort of tacit stipulation all peripheral matters and thus quickly join the issue. On the one side in the Dialogue More does not press the gains in wealth, power, and honor that the position of counsellor to a ruler would afford to clever men like Hythloday and himself, if they merely sought their own advantage. When Hythloday rejects those considerations, More does not press the point. On the other side, Hythloday does not immediately insist that men like More and he must reject a place in the councils of rulers in Europe because no European country is soundly based on community of property as is Utopia. Those peripheral matters set aside, then, what are the central issues bearing on whether men like Hythloday and More, concerned to better the world and knowing how it can be bettered, shall put their talents at the disposal of a ruler? In the Dialogue, More says, men of "truly generous and philosophic spirit" should apply both "industry and talent to the public interest." And the place to do that is the council of a ruler, for from there Hythloday could persuade the ruler to "straight-forward and honorable courses." That rulers should be so persuaded is most important, for from such as they, "as from a never-failing spring, flows a stream of all that is good or evil over a whole nation."

Hythloday demurs. He would get nowhere with his advice, he says, in the atmosphere surrounding a ruler. Everybody else will bad-mouth any proposal *he* makes, because he will be jealous of any proposal that *they* do not make themselves. It will be that way because that is the way it always is around princes.

More persists. It is only in the courts of great rulers, giving them sound advice, that men can do the greatest good to the commonweal, and to do that is Hythloday's most important duty, as it is the most important duty of every good man when the opportunity offers. How can a philosopher like him expect kings to rule like philosophers when he will not even condescend to advise them?

Again Hythloday demurs. Of course philosophers would be glad to advise rulers if they thought there was a chance that rulers would take their advice. But from their youth the minds of kings are corrupted by evil notions. If by his advice he (Hythloday) were to try to uproot the weeds of evil from a ruler's soul, he would incur contempt or be banished from the ruler's presence. Suppose him to be at a secret session of the council when foreign affairs are being discussed in the ruler's presence. All the cleverest councillors are there. Each seeks to overreach the others in proposing bribery, ruses, frauds, skullduggery, violence, and war in order to enable the ruler to do down his neighbors, lay hands on some of their territory, and thus cover himself with glory. Suppose, then, Hythloday continues, that after all that I were to say

> that all this war-mongering, by which so many different nations were kept in social turmoil as a result of royal connivings and schemings, would certainly exhaust his treasury and demoralize his people, and yet very probably in the end come to nothing . . . /that/ rather than that he should love his people and be loved by them; he should live among them, and govern them kindly, and let other kingdoms alone, since his own is big enough, if not too big for him.

How welcome, Hythloday asks, would such advice be? How welcome would it be if he felt obliged to advise the ruler to stop taxing the poor for the benefit of the rich and to maintain his costly wars?

At this point in the Dialogue More reaches the end of his patience. Of course, he says, such advice so given would not be welcome. Nor indeed should Hythloday give such advice, at least not in such a day. The way, More grumbles, of a soft-headed academic pedant, suitable perhaps, as we might say, for private chit-chat at the Faculty Club, but not for blurting out at a serious gathering of advisors to a ruler. To win one's way in the councils of rulers one must play a careful game. One must cut the pattern of advice to fit the cloth of feasability.

> I don't think you should offer advice or thrust on people ideas of this sort which you know will not be listened to. What good will it do? When your listeners are already prepossessed against you and firmly convinced of opposite opinions, what good can you do with your rhapsody of newfangled ideas? This academic philosophy is quite agreeable in the private conversation of close friends, but in the councils of kings, where grave matters are being authoritatively decided, there is no place for it.

So More makes the key politician's point. Politics is the art of the possible; the way to win is not the way of declamation but the way of calculation, of timing. This is just as true of the good man who would lead the ruler in the right way for the common welfare as it is of the bad man who would lead him in the wrong way for the bad man's welfare. Therefore let the wise enter into public life at as high a level as they can, not in the foolish hope of remaking the world to fit their fancies, but with the sensible purpose of counterposing the wicked advice that comes to the powerful from all quarters, and with the reasonable aim of making bad policies less bad.

But Hythloday, too, loses patience. What, he counters, is so fantastic about the advice he proposed? Is an adviser not to discourage the ruler from wicked wars and the exploitative taxing of men's goods?

> If we dismiss as out of the question and absurd everything which the perverse custom of men have made to seem unusual, we shall have to set aside most of the commandments of Christ.

All that the sort of politic prudence proposed by More will accomplish, he goes on, "is to make men feel a little more secure in their consciences about doing evil." As to handling situations tactfully in counselling a ruler so that what cannot be made good will be made as little bad as possible, that is *really* academic pedantry. What chance would a counsellor have of getting away with that kind of footdragging? For such a one

there is no way to dissemble, no way to shut your eyes to things. You
must openly approve the worst proposals, and consent to the most
vicious decisions.

In such circumstances how could anyone hope to do good, sur-
rounded, as he is sure to be, by colleagues far more likely to corrupt
the best of men than to lapse into decency themselves.

So ended for practical purposes the Dialogue of Counsel that
Thomas More, its author, then slipped between the introduction to
his little "treatise" on the Utopian commonwealth and the Discourse
on Utopia itself. As we have just seen, in that Dialogue the pros and
cons of the entry of a free intellectual and literary man into service
of a ruler are deeply probed. Who won the argument—Hythloday or
More? What was the author's own view in the end? Let us try to
imagine the general point of view of an intellectual in private life
who recognizes a duty to serve the commonwealth. From that point
of view look at the arguments of More (for public service in office)
on the one hand and those of Hythloday (against public service in office) on the other. It is hard to choose between them, to feel that the
author was clearly pointing one way or the other. It looks like a
draw.

If one accepts the notion that the Dialogue of Counsel is the report
of an internal dialogue that Thomas More was having with himself,
as he wrote, or had just recently gone through with himself, one can
safely abandon the notion that, as some argue, the Dialogue was
merely a bit of jolly whimsy, a *jeu d'esprit* from the outcome of
which the author was wholly detached. Thomas More simply could
not have been neutral in a matter that so closely touched him, a
matter on which shortly he would have to make a decision that might
change his whole course and way of life. Since with respect to counsel Thomas More, our oracle, *speaks* in riddles, we are driven to observing his *actions* in hope that some features among them will limn
his convictions or at least drop a few legible hints as to their nature.
But alas, More's actions are as ambiguous as the outcome of the
Dialogue itself. At first he declines to accept the pension offered by
the King, then later he accepts the pension, and later, perhaps as
much as a year and a half later, receives office. He slowly rises to the
chief office of all in dignity: he becomes Lord Chancellor. Then, for
being silent, refusing even faint praise to what he deems a wicked
course, Thomas More lives out to the letter the prediction of Hythloday about the fate of such as he in a ruler's council: at the instance
of his prince he dies a traitor's death.

If the Dialogue of Counsel failed to solve the problem of him who raised it about the rule for entering the service of the state, what sense is there to that Dialogue, what use is it to us? Thomas More, the man who first thought through the question of counsel from the point of view of one who felt bound to dedicate his talents to the commonwelfare, *thought all the way through it, but did not solve his own problem.* Therefore we may do well to suppose that his question of counsel does not resolve itself into the form of inquiry particularly attractive to a scientistic and pragmatic era like ours—the form of problem and solution. For example, problem: Does a serious man do best to serve the common welfare in public office? Solution: on investigation of the evidence, such a man serves the public welfare best in public office. The first thing we can learn from the Dialogue of Counsel is that the question of counsel defeats this straight-forward problem-solving approach. To the question of Thomas More and his like in every era, must I seek and accept high office in order to do what I ought with my talents, the answer of the Dialogue is not a solution but the horns of a dilemma. First, if you do not take high office, you will be able to do for the people none of the multitude of things which require the decision, support, and action of the ruler. Second, if you do gain high office, far from your winning the ruler to all the good things you propose, your own good name will be used to mask the evil courses other counsellors intend, courses to which they will have no trouble cajoling the ruler. Paradoxically, whichever choice you make—private life, public life—you will be defiled with pride—the pride of the active reformer who thinks he can immerse himself in the slough of public life and come up clean, smelling like roses; the pride of a non-participant in his own purity, too utterly precious to be lowered into contact with dirty reality.

For those who think they are in the world for the good of their fellow men, to know that such are indeed the conditions both of participation in public life and of abstention from it is to know that the inherent paradox cannot be resolved. It is also to know it can and must be accepted and lived with, and above all that it must be kept in mind. Then whatever one's choice as between public service and private endeavor, one lives alert to the perils of both, and especially to the perils of one's own choice. That is the value to us of Thomas More's struggle with the question of counsel—not a problem solved, but a dilemma made explicit, and a paradox identified. When it is solved a problem goes away: it ceases to be a problem and an obstacle; it becomes a process or a procedure. When we discover a dilemma, it does not go away, and when we lay bare the paradox that generates the dilemma, it just sits there staring back at us.

As we have seen, confronted with the dilemma of counsel that his own inquiry had laid bare, Thomas More acted ambiguously, with an ambiguity that lasted the rest of his life. Yet perhaps in the matter of counsel his conduct is as exemplary as his words are illuminating. It will be a sad day when men who wish well to their fellows avoid the opportunity to serve them in public places, lest their own virtue be sullied by the dirty peddlers who will always haunt such places. But having entered public service such men must be ready for the day when their master-in-office requires them to do such things as in conscience and decency they cannot do. It will be a sad day, too, when in the face of such a dilemma they do as they are ordered. A political structure that makes neither of these courses—participation, withdrawal—impossible is in some measure tolerable, salvageable, however deeply mired it may be. When we think of the issue of counsel as Thomas More dealt with it, we may also thing of our country in the reign of Richard Nixon. We may think of those faithful servants of the people and of their chief, Elliot Richardson and William Ruckleshaus. There came a point where their boss demanded that they "subscribe to the most ruinous devices," when their mere continuance in office made them "a screen for the wickedness and folly of others." At that point they refused to subscribe and refused to be used as a screen, and so reluctantly became hero-victims in a chain of events we all know. The dilemma of counsel was rightly played out in the "Saturday Night Massacre."

Thomas More's Feminism: To Reform or Re-Form

Judith P. Jones and Sherianne Sellers Seibel

In 1973 we began a study of Thomas More's polemical works. We were looking for ways in which the polemical element reasserted itself in More's prison writings, but soon found ourselves marking the numerous references to women. These comments and anecdotes were very different from those in the *Utopia* and in More's letters to his children. We were of course familiar with other paradoxical elements in More's life and thought; his dichotomous attitude toward women merely strengthened our image of him standing like a wobbly colossus with one foot set firmly in the Middle Ages and the other trying to find a stable spot in the modern world.

Professors R.W. Chambers and J.H. Hexter have best described the philosophical poles that drew More in opposite directions. Chambers sees More's life and works in terms of an essential conservatism, the conservatism of the medieval church. For him, both More's household and the societal structure of the *Utopia* are expressions of a medieval heritage characteristically patriarchal, monastic, and hierarchical.[1] Apparently, Chambers sees no conflict between More's patriarchal conservatism and the unusual way in which he raised his daughters, giving them the classical education reserved at that time for boys and young men.[2]

According to Hexter, Chambers overstates the extent to which More's orientation is a medieval one. Hexter sees the thought in *Utopia* as radical in its attempt to transcend aristocratic and hierarchical forms with the essentially modern concept of communism: the Utopian society is "on the margins of modernity" not because of the details of its institutions, but because the spirit responsible for the creation of those institutions attempts to eliminate disorders which the medieval mind accepted as the deserved and inevitable condition of human life. Hexter's commentary on the *Utopia* indicates that there was something in Renaissance humanism that made it possible for More to conceive of improving society by the application of human effort and human reason. More's modernity enables

[1]R.W. Chambers, *Thomas More* (Ann Arbor, Mich., 1958), pp. 131-44, 178, 256-67.
[2]Ibid., pp. 175-91.

him to imagine the elimination, not just the amelioration, of the conditions responsible for evil in the world. He is radical for his time in thinking that humanity can be changed by changing the environment.[3] But I believe that More's commitment to medieval social structures limited the modernity of his vision.

Sixteenth century humanists emphasized the importance of the individual, committed themselves to the cultural and moral advantages they felt to be inherent in an understanding of classical literature, and opened doors to facets of human character in Western culture which had seldom been explored.[4] But they tried to keep their potentially revolutionary ideas within the boundaries of a society defined by the Catholic church. The possibility of conflict was perhaps inherent in the relationship between the potentially revolutionary nature of humanism and the innate conservation of the church. Tragically, it was a conflict which men like Thomas More could not resolve. Although More could advocate altering the institutions of society, as he did in *Utopia*, he could not tolerate changing the structure of the church which for him defined the world. He remained true to his medieval heritage in seeing the church as the whole, not part, of society.

The attitude toward women which appears in his personal letters, and in the *Utopia*, reflects More's humanistic belief in the importance of the individual and the validity of human resourcefulness. But hostile medieval stereotypes permeate the presentation of women in much of More's writing, especially in the polemical books. Also, there is a conflict between what he did with his daughters and what he often said about women in general. Although More was proud of his daughters' academic achievements and committed to their education, the women in his books are likely to be lazy, garrulous, and foolish.

Thomas More provided humanist tutors for the children of his household and insisted that the girls and boys be educated alike. The students in his home included his own children, Margaret, Elizabeth, Cecily, and John, as well as a number of other young people, most of them girls. Because his students were predominantly female, his letters to them reflect his opinions concerning the education of

[3] J. H. Hexter, "Utopia and its Historical Milieu," in *The Complete Works of St. Thomas More*, Vol. 4, *Utopia*, ed. Edward Surtz, S.J. and J.H. Hexter (New Haven, 1965), pp. xlv-cxxiv. (Hereafter cited as *CW*.)
[4] See Paul Oskar Kristeller, *Renaissance Thought, the Classic, Scholastic, and Humanist Strains* (New York, 1961), pp. 3-23.

women. They reiterate his commitment to classical learning and to the skills of speaking and writing well. More's insistence upon advanced education for women derives from his devotion to the broad objectives of humanistic education, objectives which were designed to produce persons of moral, intellectual, and cultural superiority.

But the conflict between old and new is apparent even in More's letters to his family. They are modern in the sense that Professor Hexter considers the philosophy of *Utopia* to be modern; in them, More asserts the rational nature of humanity as a source of human salvation and perfection. But the opinions they contain about women are traditional in emphasizing the importance of female obedience and virtue.

In a letter to William Gonell, one of the tutors to his school, More makes plain the elements in his philosophy of education. He praises Gonell for the progress his students are making and insists, as he often does in the letters of this period, that, as valuable as learning is for its own sake, its ultimate purpose lies in the fact that it produces the wisdom which leads to virtue. He then directs Gonell to encourage all of the children "to put virtue in the first place among goods, learning in the second; and in their studies to esteem most whatever may teach them piety towards God, charity to all, and modesty and Christian humility in themselves."[5] This letter is a succinct statement of the humanist philosophy of education and includes More's justification for extending this philosophy to women— because women are as well suited to learning as men. Still, in praising Elizabeth's behavior, More gives special emphasis to virtue in a woman: "Let her understand that such conduct delights me more than all the learning in the world. Though I prefer learning joined with virtue to all the treasurers of kings, yet renown for learning, if you take away moral probity, brings nothing else but notorious and noteworthy infamy, especially in a woman."[6]

Erasmus, in a letter to William Budé, stressed the superiority of the literary accomplishments of the young women of More's household and noticed that the women were neither idle, nor "busied in feminine trifles."[7] But according to another humanist, Luis Vives, a

---

[5]Thomas More, *Selected Letters,* ed. Elizabeth F. Rogers (New Haven, 1961), p. 105. (Hereafter cited as *Letters.)*
[6]Ibid., p. 103.
[7]Desiderius Erasmus, *Opus epistolarum Des. Erasmi Roterodami,* ed. P.S. Allen and H.M. Allen (London, 1906-47), IV: 575-80. Rev. T.E. Bridgett, *Life and Writings of Sir Thomas More* (London, 1891), pp. 114-16.

woman is educated primarily to insure her honesty and chastity, and to mitigate her natural inclinations to idleness and disobedience. In fact, Vives insists that More's sole motive in educating his daughters was to increase their virtue.[8] He further emphasized the utilitarian aspects of a woman's education: it should teach her to handle wool and flax and provide such intellectual training as she will need to raise children. But the intellectual benefits of her education should never be displayed outside her own home.[9]

There is little evidence in More's letters of the attitude that dominates Vives' philosophy. His main concern is with the progress of his children in classical learning and literary skills. It is particularly significant that in two letters to Margaret, one written shortly after her marriage, and one shortly before the birth of her first child, More insists that his daughter pursue her studies and in no way associates them with domestic skills.[10] Nor did More share Vives' insistence that the learning of women be kept in the home, out of the sight of men. In letters written in 1522 and 1523, More told of showing Margaret's letters to John Veysey, Bishop of Exeter, and to Reginald Pole. When Pole expressed surprise that Margaret could have written such a letter without the help of a tutor, More praised her scholarship extravagantly and assured Pole that it would indeed have been hard to find a man who did not need Margaret's help.[11]

The letters make it clear that More was proud of the accomplishments of his daughters, that he demanded a high level of performance from them, and that he was at least as interested in their intellectual development as he was in their moral development. In the letter written to Margaret after her marriage to William Roper, More encourages his daughter to continue her studies with the distinguished mathematician and astronomer, Nicholas Kratzer. He ignores the feminine virtues of chastity and obedience, but expresses a broad, individualized, attitude toward the development of the human mind and soul:

> Though I earnestly hope that you will devote the rest of your life to medical science and sacred literature, so that you may be well furnished for the whole scope of human life, (which is to have a sound mind in a sound body), and I know that you have already laid the foundations of these studies, and there will be always opportunity to continue the

---

[8]Juan Luis Vives, "The Instruction of a Christian Woman," in *Vives and the Renaissance Education of Women,* ed. Foster Watson (London, 1912), p. 53.
[9]Ibid., pp. 43-49, 55-62.
[10]*Letters,* pp. 147-149, 154-55.
[11]Ibid., p. 154.

building; yet I am of Opinion that you may with great advantage give some years of your yet flourishing youth to humane letters and so-called liberal studies. And this both because youth is more fitted for a struggle with difficulties and because it is uncertain whether you will ever in the future have the benefit of so sedulous, affectionate, and learned a teacher. I need not say that by such studies a good judgment is formed or perfected.[12]

Although More's letter to Gonell makes clear his commitment to the ideal of virtue acquired through education, especially for women, most of the letters to his school are predominantly concerned with the other major element in the educational philosophy of the humanists —the training of reasonable, intelligent individuals capable of thinking, judging, writing, and speaking well. The letters emphasize the importance of the work itself and the diligence necessary to accomplish it.

In the letters to his children and their tutors, More defends the education of women in terms of Hexter's definition of modernity: human progress is possible even for women, a truly revolutionary notion at that time. The modern belief in progress also pervades the *Utopia* where society is improved by the removal of some of tradition's senseless sexual distinctions: men and women have similar opportunities in education and in occupational choice, and the laws governing marriage and divorce are applied equally to men and women. But although More shows women in the unconventional roles of farmer, scholar, and priest, he always subjects them to the authority of men. In theory women have equality of opportunity, but all the officials are men; and the hierarchical and patriarchal nature of Utopian society is, as Chambers suggests, pervasive: brides go to the household of their husbands, wives wait on their husbands, males govern, control the conversation at meals, and even get the best food. Though females are not barred from the priesthood, "only a widow advanced in years is ever chosen, and that rather rarely."[13] Just how rarely quickly becomes evident since all the other references to priests in the *Utopia* indicate that they are male. For example, in describing dining habits, More says that the priest *and his wife* sit with the governor *and his wife* to preside.[14]

Although there are no radical notions about changing the structure of authority in Utopia, a spirit of real reform pervades the economic system. One of the appealing aspects of Utopian society is that no

[12]Ibid., p. 149.
[13]*CW*, vol. 4, p. 229.
[14]*CW*, vol. 4, p. 143.

one needs to work more than six hours a day. The reason for this is that women share the work equally with men. More's spokesman, Hythloday, says, "This phenomenon you too will understand if you consider how large a part of the population in other countries exists without working. First, there are almost all the women, who constitute half the whole. . . ."[15] Here More reveals a telling unconscious bias. He defines work as those occupations which are traditionally male, ignoring the labor women normally do in a society. By exclusion, he represents women's work as insignificant, not important enough to be considered work. Nowhere is the bias against women's work more evident than in the kitchens of Utopia. In the discussion of occupations Hythloday says that besides agriculture "each is taught one particular craft as his own. This is generally either wool-making or linen-making or masonry or metal-working or carpentry. There is no other pursuit which *occupies any number worth mentioning.*"[16] Yet every woman in Utopia is involved in another occupation, that of preparing and organizing the meals for the communities which eat together in large dining halls. Even in Utopia working women have two jobs.

The *Utopia* demonstrates More's ability to respond to problems with novel solutions—but only so long as the solutions leave the traditional organization of authority intact. More works into what Chambers sees as a monastic patriarchy the spirit of reform which Hexter calls modern. It is because of the modernity of his attitudes toward women in the letters and in some aspects of the society he describes in *Utopia* that scholars have often hailed More as a feminist. But the "feminism" we see in his letters and in parts of the Utopia represents only one facet of More's concept of womanhood. His later writings show something very different.

Beginning in 1528, Thomas More accepted the task of defending the doctrines of the Catholic church against the attacks of the Lutherans; he wrote hard for six years, repeatedly exhorting the common people to remain loyal to Church traditions. He attacked the Lutherans with a malevolence and hostility that often surprises readers who know More only as the Catholic saint who wrote a clever book of reform. His polemical books also present a stereotypical medieval view of women and their place in society, openly displaying the prejudices suggested in *Utopia,* and contradicting the modern orientation of the letters. They replace the limited feminism

[15]Ibid., p. 129.
[16]Ibid., pp. 125-27.

of the early works with the antifeminism of the medieval sermon, which portrays women as seductive, proud, immoral, idle, extravagant, gluttonous, greedy, hypocritical, envious, foolish, and intellectually inferior to men. Now More is, for the first time, writing to unsophisticated readers for whom caricature and personal abuse have all the appeal of the familiar. He never forgets that this audience responds best to the rhetoric of the pulpit. Perhaps both More's scurrilous treatment of his opponents and his abusive treatment of women spring from a motive deeper than the simple, conscious desire to attract and interest an audience. They may, in fact, be related expressions of an innate conservatism. More wanted to reform the church and society from *within* the medieval framework. When he saw the Lutheran reformers destroying the structure itself and altering not only church practices, but the whole of human relatedness to authority, he responded with the determination of one who thinks that everything of value is about to fall into chaos. The church had created a God-centered and male-centered universe. For More, the destruction of the system meant simply the end of the world, the destruction of reality itself. Not surprisingly, he reverted to the familiar forms he had once tried to change.

In *The Confutation of Tyndale's Answer,* More mocks William Tyndale's proposal that women be allowed to become priests and asserts the essential inferiority of women. Later, he adds to his argument the idea that it would be irreverent to the sacrament of Christ's body for a woman to preside at the Mass.[17] Here More affirms two elements in the medieval image of woman—her inferiority and her impurity. He implies that it is the quality of femaleness itself that makes it a desecration for a woman to administer Holy Communion. In tone and intent, More's position in the *Confutation* is the opposite of the one he takes in the *Utopia* where he accepts the possibility of women serving as priests, although only under the most limited circumstances. A comparison of the two treatments of the ordination of women suggests that by the time More wrote the *Confutation,* his commitment to the authority of the church had surpassed his commitment to the humanist ideals of reform.

In his Reformation writings, More frequently depicts Eve in the language of the medieval pulpit, and attributes her destructive qualities to women in general. The medieval churchman was inclined to compare all women to Eve in her boldness, foolishness, garrulity,

---

[17]*CW,* vol. 8, *The Confutation of Tyndale's Answer,* ed. Louis A. Schuster, et al (New Haven, 1973), pp. 92, 190-91, 261, 594-95.

and pride and to warn against the daughters of Eve as seductive obstacles to salvation. In his unfinished *Four Last Things,* written some five or six years after the *Utopia* and a few years before the first of the polemical books, More admonished against the sin of gluttony with the example of Eve whose greed and pride led her to desire the apple, and thus to destroy the innocence that God had first allotted the human race.[18] In the same book, he depicts Eve as the instrument of the Devil who drew Adam into the temptation that was the damnation of them both.[19] Later, in the *Confutation of Tyndale's Answer,* More describes Eve as one inspired by the Devil.[20] The medieval characterization of Eve describes all women as archtemptresses, as stumbling blocks to men who desire salvation. More's use of this stereotype implies his acceptance of it. In the *Dialogue Concerning Tyndale,* More tells of ten "dubious" women who accuse an innocent young friar of letting them lie with him for a penance. More reminds the friend to whom he tells the story that the accusation against the friar had to be taken lightly since the accusers were "only" women and less worthy of belief than men. The tale displays elements common to the medieval conception of Eve and all women as temptresses, gossips, and liars.[21] Another, and more surprising, use of the traditional characterization of Eve appears in More's treatment of her desire for knowledge, which the church had often interpreted to be a combination of greed and pride. In the *Four Last Things,* Eve takes the apple because her pride makes her want the knowledge that will make her "in manner a goddess."[22] And in the *Tyndale,* More uses the evil result of Eve's "inordinate appetite of Knowledge" as an argument against laypersons reading and interpreting the Bible for themselves.[23] More is modern when he admonishes female students to pursue knowledge for its own sake and for the good it can do them intellectually and spiritually. Yet, in the polemical works, he affirms the tradition that a desire of knowledge is the source of Eve's sinful pride. His dual attitude toward knowledge, particularly in women, emphasizes his paradoxical philosophical position. He is typically humanistic in his desire to improve men and women through learning, but medieval in his fear of the power

[18]Thomas More, *The English Works of Sir Thomas More,* ed. W.E. Campbell and A.W. Reed, 2 vol. (London, 1931), I:493.

[19]Ibid., I:469-70.

[20]*CW*, vol. 8, p. 50.

[21]More, *The English Works,* II:49.

[22]Ibid., I:493.

[23]Ibid., II:243-44.

of knowledge. In his letters, and in the *Utopia,* More praises and encourages scholarship in women, but in other contexts, he perpetuates the traditional view that knowledge in a woman, and even in the average man, is an evil that threatens the authority of God and society.

The most common medieval complaint against women, however, was not that they were seductive and greedy, but that they were foolish and garrulous. Here again, More takes advantage of, and apparently accepts, the view of the medieval clergy.[24] Indeed, there are few pages written after the *Utopia* in which More does not suggest the fatuousness and general intellectual inferiority of women. In *Tyndale,* he comments that the words of women are to be taken less seriously than those of men, and uses dramatic examples to show women to be foolish and frivolous, as well as superstitious.[25] Similarly, in the *Confutation* women appear as contrary, illogical, and unlearned.[26] More's *Apologye* further assumes the general inferiority of women, and offers a long tale which delineates the medieval preacher's idle, gossipy, extravagant, and shrewish female.[27] The phrases "but a woman," "even a women," "but an unlearned woman," and "only a woman" dominate the descriptions of women throughout the polemical works. Also, like the medieval preacher, More links general female silliness with garrulity.[28] One of the major faults of the wife in the *Apologye* is that she is too conversant with her gossips.[29] Even the *Dialogue of Comfort,* which is so much mellower in tone than the controversial books which precede it, evokes the image of the talkative woman when Anthony, More's spokesman, tells his nephew that a "fond old man is often so full of wordes as a woman."[30] But More's most caustic use of the type of the gossipy woman appears in the *Tyndale* in his argument against women in the priesthood, when he argues that it would be unwise for anyone to go to confession to a woman because she would be sure to gossip everything she heard: neither God nor the Devil can hold a

[24]G.R. Owst, *Literature and Pulpit in Medieval England* (New York, 1961), p. 386.
[25]More, *The English Works,* II:49, 161, 185, 248.
[26]*CW,* vol. 8, pp. 604-06, 775.
[27]Thomas More, *The Apologye of Syr Thomas More, Knyght,* ed. Arthur Irving Taft (London, 1971), pp. 63-66.
[28]Owst, *Literature and Pulpit,* pp. 386-89, 492.
[29]More, *The Apologye,* p. 65.
[30]*CW,* vol. 12, *A Dialogue of Comfort Against Tribulation,* ed. Louis L. Martz and Frank Manley (New Haven, 1976), p. 78.

woman's tongue.[31]

Yet More sometimes enriches his later works with portraits of admirable women. By far his most attractive women are the earthy, practical ones who, despite their natural limitations, usually outwit the men with whom they deal. The best example is the Wife of the Bottle of Botolphs Wharf, whose story appears in the *Confutation,* who enters into a debate, and outwits, the reformer Robert Barnes. With her great energy and wisdom she is the opposite of the idle, foolish women who dominate the satire of the medieval pulpit and much of More's polemical writing. Her earthly language and tales, even her simplicity, bawdiness, and garrulity become assets to the church. Still, however, More insists upon female inferiority when he adds that the Wife is only a woman "vsynge no reason but suche as a woman myght fynd."[32] The case for the church is so strong that even a woman can win against the men who would deny it! In his use of the common woman as a figure to be admired, More is still drawing on the tradition of the medieval sermon where examples often derive their humor from the incongruous image of a mere woman outwitting her male superiors.[33]

Diverse and conflicting attitudes toward women clash in More's writing. The more modern of them conform to Hexter's definition of modernity, and the more conventional to Chambers' explanation of More's conservative roots in the traditions of the medieval church. Hexter''s definition limits itself to the level of modernity that More was able to achieve; he was modern in his desire to improve the world he found himself in, yet he could not allow change to go beyond the boundaries society had already established. More's modernity, like his feminism, is limited by his commitment to the societal structure of the church-centered middle ages. He was, to use Hexter's phrase, on the "margins" of modernity. He did not approach the level of modernness which Carl Jung describes in *Modern Man in Search of a Soul* when he says:

> The man we call modern . . . is . . . the man who stands upon a peak, or at the very edge of the world, the abyss of the future before him . . . He alone is modern who is fully conscious of the present. The man whom we can with justice call "modern" is solitary. He is so of necessity and at all times, for every step towards a fuller consciousness of the present removes him further from his original *"participation mystique"* with the mass of men—from submersion in a common unconsciousness. Every

[31]More, *The English Works,* II:257-59.
[32]*CW,* vol. 8, p. 905.
[33]Owst, *Literature and Pulpit,* pp. 163-64.

step forward means an act of tearing himself loose from that all-embracing, pristine unconsciousness which claims the bulk of mankind almost entirely. . . . Indeed, he is completely modern only when he has come to the very edge of the world, leaving behind him all that has been discarded and outgrown, and acknowledging that he stands before a void out of which all things may grow.[34]

More could advocate change from within the organization of the "bulk of mankind," but he could not take the radically modern position of one who stands outside the traditions of the past and continuously recreates his future and his world.

One thing can be said of many of his contemporaries: he had an intense interest in the roles and potential of women. Although this interest pervades his life and his works, his later writings seem to contradict his youthful faith in the possibility of improving women through education. What appears to be a change in his attitude may not, however, have been merely a result of his growing older. More lived in an age of transition. The mingling of contradictory elements in his thought may be an expression of tendencies that were inextricably intertwined in the minds of most Renaissance thinkers. Even so, the young man who sought improvements in his church became the older man frightened by the Reformation; he was afraid of restructuring the church because to change its basic concepts was to alter the reality by which medieval society functioned. It is with the movement from reforming to re-forming that More's modernity stops and turns him back to the safety of medieval values.

[34]C.G. Jung, *Modern Man in Search of a Soul* (New York, 1933), pp. 196-97.

Images of Women in Thomas More's Poetry

Lee Cullen Khanna

Although Thomas More's influence on women's education has been recognized, women in his writings have been too long neglected.[1] The images of women in More's Latin and English poems deserve special attention because they suggest the range of More's literary approaches to women, and because they can serve as a guide to both the seriousness and importance of these differing approaches.

In More's canon women play many parts. Wise queens, utopian priests, innkeepers, vicious wives, teachers, and temptresses are among those to amaze and amuse readers. More's attitude toward these actresses varies from admiring to patronizing, from courtly compliment to empathetic understanding. The sheer number of female characters, and anecdotes about women, testifies to his interest in women; and his modulations of tone suggest a complexity characteristic of the man.

Both the empathetic view of women and satiric attacks on their sex can be seen in the *Epigrammata*. Among the two hundred and fifty epigrams, about twenty mock women. Several of them are translations from the Greek Anthology that was More's primary source and so reflect traditional satire on female vanity, greed, and lust. One epigram, for example, treats the young woman who resisted her rapist until he drew his sword and threatened to leave her. "Terrified by so dire a threat she lay down at once and said, 'Go ahead, but it is an act of violence.' "[2] Another, more typical, satirizes the unfaithful wife:

> My friend Aratus has a fruitful wife—yes, very fruitful wife. No doubt about it, for three times she has conceived children without any assistance from her husband.[3]

[1] I recently suggested that More's respect for women was expressed in his work as well as in the education of his daughters: "No Less Real than Ideal: Images of Women in More's Work," *Moreana*, 15 (December, 1977), 35-51. In *Richard III*, for example, he created female characters of intelligence and moral force. For a modern discussion of the extent of More's influence on women's education see Pearl Hogrefe, *Tudor Women: Commoners and Queens* (Ames, Iowa, 1975), pp. 98-102.

[2] Leicester Bradner and Charles Arthur Lynch, *The Latin Epigrams of Thomas More* (Chicago, 1953), No. 149. (Hereafter cited as *Epigrams.)*

[3] Ibid., No. 147.

In such epigrams More appeals to a stock response, adding only his pointed Latin phrasing to the ancient stereotypes. But these jokes aim only at a quick laugh and never seem to have fully engaged More's imagination. One can measure the difference in both the quality of the poetry and More's relative involvement in his subject by comparing the satiric epigrams to the longer original poems added to the 1520 edition of the *Epigrammata.* The work of More's maturity, two of these poems center on women and are elegant, subtle, and memorable.

The first is an apology to a "certain noble lady" whom More had unwittingly slighted. The fact that the slight was unwitting is an important point in the poem, and More stresses it by setting up polarities between himself and the lady. She had entered his house when he was conversing with a prominent cleric who was so eloquent that More never noticed the lady's arrival. His obtuseness becomes the immediate point of contrast with her. "My eyes," he says, "failed to observe even so brilliant a beauty as hers."[4] The contrast is even more pointed in the Latin where the last word of each line balances the lady's "lumen" against More's "stupor."[5] Looking back at the incident, More is horrified at the failure of his eyes *("O oculos")* which used to be able to spot a radiant girl even at a distance. He wonders whether his eyes are now dimmed through age, the workings of some evil spirit, or the power of the cleric's eloquence. He seems to settle on the latter explanation, for this "mighty prelate" has the power of Orpheus to charm wild beasts. Thus More labels himself a beast by implication, even as he condemned his blindness and stupidity before. The final self-accusation is his own speechlessness, for he failed to acknowledge the lady's presence *("Ut miserum est non posse loqui!").* Certainly to be dumb at the wrong moment would have been barbarian *(barbaries)* for a humanist, trained in both the moral and aesthetic value of eloquence.

But the lady, although given no opportunity to speak, seems nevertheless to be graced with attributes respected by humanists. She is cultured *("matrona . . . cultu spectanda superbo"),* beautiful, and virtuous. When she enters the drawing room, she proceeds to examine "some choice coins of ancient beauty and, famous herself, enjoyed the famous portraits thereon." Like Budé, like More himself, she values and seems informed about classical coins. Indeed the

[4]Ibid., No. 249.
[5]"Nostra nec in tantum uertuntur lumina lumen, / O mihi plus ipso nate stupore / stupor." (Ibid., No. 249.)

use of the word *"cultu"* seems to bespeak education as much as elegance. She is cultivated where More is beastly, bright where he is obtuse, graceful and considerate where he is rude or even, he fears, "brutal." She is obviously able to appreciate the eloquence, the learned conversation so valued by humanists because More beseeches the eloquent prelate to apologize in his behalf, assuming of course that she will respond, as More himself did, to his "gift of charming speech."

One of the delights of this charming poem is the exquisite irony of its central opposition. For in the process of opposing his rude, silent, obtuse self to the cultured lady, More reveals his own graciousness, eloquence, and sensitivity. The poem is as elegant as the lady herself, and was perhaps intended for her perusal as well as that of the "mighty prelate." In fact, one of the greatest tributes this poem makes to the lady in question is not finally the courtly elevation of the beautiful woman, but the implicit suggestion that the cleric, the speaker, and the lady are in some sense equals.[6] They may not speak the same language literally ("I have no command of French /my lady speaks only her native French./") but they share the humanist values of virtue, knowledge of the classics (as the coins suggest), and eloquence. It is the latter, in fact, that is both the "object and the wit" of this deceptively slight poem.

This stylistic grace, or *sprezzatura,* also distinguishes another occasional poem added to the 1520 edition, "He Expresses Joy at Finding . . . Her Whom He Had Loved as a Mere Boy."[7] It too is inspired by a woman and is a graceful recollection of youthful infatuation, prompted by a chance meeting many years later. Proust's taste of the madeleine opened a vaster floodgate of memory, but, given the relative brevity of More's poem, its subtlety and delicacy of feeling is hardly less effective. In contrast to the "noble lady" epigram where More did not see the Frenchwoman, the speaker here begins by exclaiming that Elizabeth is "restored to his sight." Indeed the entire poem is about seeing, the various ways of seeing prompted by this woman. "When I was just a boy," the speaker exclaims, "I saw you first; now on the threshold of old age, I see you again." The two kinds of vision are juxtaposed throughout the poem: the remarkably vivid vision of the beautiful young girl, seen through the eyes of a smitten boy, and the mature vision of a man meditating on the fleet-

[6]It is related irony that the process of polarizing the speaker and the lady (the elegant verse itself) actually suggests their similarity.

[7]Ibid., No. 247.

ing quality of beauty, the strange twists of destiny.

The mature, realistic vision comes first in the poem. Once, he says, "your face inspired me with innocent devotion." But now, he insists with a startling realism:

> that face is no part of your appearance; where has it gone? When the vision I once loved comes before me, I see, alas, how utterly your actual appearance fails to resemble it. The years, always envious of young beauty, have robbed you of yourself. . . .

The careful courtesy that marked the tribute to the French lady has disappeared. But the very harshness of this confrontation with aging seems to free the speaker for the fullness of memory which follows. Although the lady has been robbed of herself, the speaker has not lost her. "That beauty of countenance," he continues,

> to which my eyes so often clung now occupies my heart. . . . There comes now to my mind that distant day which first revealed you to me as you played amid a group of girls; this was a time when your yellow hair enhanced the pure white of your neck; your lips by contrast with your face were like roses in the snow; your eyes, like stars, held my eyes fast and through them made their way into my heart: I was helpless, as though stunned by a lightningstroke, when I gazed and continued to gaze upon your face.

This romantic scene is unusual in More's canon, as is his use of Petrarchan imagery. Although such imagery becomes all too familiar in later English sonnets, its handling here is startling and effective.

Throughout the poem the emphasis falls on two isolated moments in time—"that distant day" of the Petrarchan vision, and "that notable day" that brings them together after so many years. The joy of the second finally seems to equal the joy of the first, and the two are deliberately confused by the end of the poem.[8] The speaker says, "Our love was blameless; if duty could not keep it so, that day itself *(ipsa dies)* would be enough to keep love blameless still." Does *"ipsa dies"* refer to the original vision or to the meeting that occasioned the poem? The ambiguity is, I believe, deliberate.

The merging of the two days eliminates the unessential to reveal the enduring. Although the speaker confronts the changes wrought by time, his imagination can recreate, and thus perpetuate, the dream of first love. It is ultimately the enduring vision of the heart he celebrates ("That beauty of countenance to which my eyes so often clung now occupies my heart.")

---

[8]The reader can see the joy of that moment in time *(ista dies)* and the beginning of the ambiguity about "that day" even more clearly in the Latin: *"Ergo ita disiunctos diuersaque fata secutos / Tot nunc post hyemes reddidit* ista dies */ Ista dies* qua rara meo mihi laetior aeuo / Contigit occursu sospitis alma tui."* (Emphasis mine).

The speaker closes with a hearty good wish for another meeting twenty-five years hence. But in the spirit of the poem it is as much a promise as a fitting farewell, because their innocent love, intensely experienced, has achieved a kind of perpetuity through the power of More's art. The ambiguous *"ipsa dies"* comes close to the emotional triumph over time realized near the end of Shakespeare's sonnets.

The feminine presence in this poem is clearly a positive, even an inspirational one. It is perhaps as romantic as anything in More's work. But we learn little about Elizabeth apart from her Laura-like beauty and its lasting effect.

Another epigram, "To Candidus: How to Choose A Wife," is more informative.[9] Although it has none of the warmth or elusive charm of the recollection of first love, its didacticism affords a clearer view of More's respect for women. In fact, this poem, one of the most popular and, hopefully, most influential of More's epigrams, praises the intellectual and outspoken woman. The heart of the speaker's recommendation to Candidus deals with the value of a learned wife. In fact, forms of the verb to teach (*doceo*) ring through its central lines culminating in the image of Candidus leaving the company of men to return home to his learned wife (*"doctaeque coniugis"*).[10] In effect, More applies to a woman his own most dearly held humanist values. Like his friends Colet, Erasmus, and Vives, More believed in the moral and rhetorical value of studying the "oldest and best books" (the best Greek and Latin texts.) But even Colet's school, St. Paul's, did not admit women. In contrast, Thomas More's school at Chelsea did, and, perhaps even more importantly, so did his art.

"Let her be either educated or capable of being educated" (*Instructa literis/Vel talis ut modo/Sit apta literis*), the speaker exclaims after describing the desirable modesty of the ideal woman's behavior. The value of such education is the sound judgment it confers:

> Happy is the woman whose education permits her to derive from the best of ancient works the principles which confer a blessing on life. Armed with this learning, she would not yield to pride in prosperity, nor to grief in distress—even though misfortune strike her down . . . If she is well instructed herself, then some day she will teach your little grand-

[9]Ibid., No. 125.
[10]The section on learning is the heart of the poem and is followed by the appeal to classical models: Ovid's daughter rivalled her father in the composition of poetry, Tullia must have been learned to earn the love of Cicero, and Cornelia was as much a teacher as mother to her famous sons.

sons, at an early age, to read. . . . By her comments she would restrain you if ever vain success should exalt you or speechless grief should cast you down. When she speaks, it will be difficult to judge between her extraordinary ability to say what she thinks and her thoughtful understanding of all kinds of affairs.

In this passage one clearly sees More's belief that learning fosters wisdom and eloquence.[11] The "extraordinary ability to say what one thinks and thoughtful understanding of all kinds of affairs" (*summa eloquentia/Iam cum omnium graui/Rerum scientia*) are the goals of humanist education in the Renaissance. But More's application of this new faith in education to a woman is unusual.

It is important to recognize the centrality of humanist values in the poem. Even before the passage on learning, More emphasizes "virtue" as the major attribute of the ideal woman.[12] The speaker urges Candidus to be guided by reason in the selection of a wife, and so dismiss such mundane attractions as beauty and money in favor of *"virtutis inclytae"* (renowed virtue). The standard translation of "chastity" is misleading here, I think, because it does not include the intellectual, moral, and rhetorical strengths of the woman so important to More's description.[13] Although the speaker goes on to describe

[11]One finds evidence of this conviction in More's correspondence. In the letter to Oxford University, he defends secular education and says, "No one has ever claimed that a man needed Greek and Latin, or indeed any education to be saved. Still, this education which he (a foolish preacher) calls secular *does train the soul in virtue" (Itaque quod ad seculares literas pertinet, quanquam nemo negat saluum esse quemquam sine literis, non illis modo, sed prorsus vllis posse,* doctrina *tamen, etiam secularis, ut ille vocat,* animam ad virtutem praeparat . . . .) Emphasis mine, *The Correspondence of Sir Thomas More,* ed. Elizabeth F. Rogers (Princeton, N.J., 1947), p. 115.

[12]In the 1518 letter to Gonell More links learning (*doctrina*) and virtue (*virtus*) consistently throughout. Virtue of mind will be worth more to a woman than the beauty of Helen or riches of Croesus, "not because that learning will be a glory to her, though learning will accompany virtue as a shadow does a body, but because the reward of wisdom is too solid to be lost with riches or to perish with beauty, since it depends on the inner knowledge of what is right. . . ." *(Non quod ea res gloriae futura sit, quanquam ea quoque virtutem velut umbra corpus comitabitur, sed quod solidius est Sapientiae praemium, quam vt vel cum diuitiis auferri vel cum forma deperire queat: vtpote quod a recti conscientia non ab aliorum sermone pendeat. . . .)* Ibid., p. 121. In this case More seems to mean self-knowledge, or conscience, by *virtus* and says that such wisdom is fostered by learning.

[13]Neither the subsequent description of the woman's intellectual strength nor More's common use of *virtus* justifies this translation. In the *Utopia,* for example, the word *virtus* appears some forty times (see Thomas I. White, "Index Verborum to *Utopia," Moreana,* 52 (November, 1976): 17), and refers to moral probity, intellectual skill, and spiritual eminence, but never to chastity. On the other hand, when More does mean chastity, he seems to prefer the words *pudor* or *castus.* One good example can be

the sweetness (*"dulcis"*), serenity (*"serenitas"*), and modest restraint of her behavior, these traits have less to do with chastity than with the *"modestia"* that is appropriate humility, good, judgment, and moderation in all things.[14] In her speech, for example, there should be neither "pointless garrulity" nor "boorish taciturnity." Surely this golden mean would be desirable for man or woman.

At the end of the poem the speaker returns to the notion of "virtue" once again as the essence of the ideal woman's desirability. The Latin is *"virtutis indole,"* and is repeated twice in the closing lines, again in contrast to beauty and money. Here Bradner and Lynch choose, more accurately I believe, the translation "inborn gift of virtue."

> If nature has denied the gift of beauty to a girl . . . if she has this inborn
> gift of virtue, she would be in my eyes fairer than the swan. If elusive
> fortune has denied her a dowry . . . if she has this inborn gift of virtue,
> she would be in my eyes richer, Croesus, than you.

Although More's poem is cast in the framework of an appeal to the prospective husband, the virtue he describes goes far beyond chastity. The detailed central passages on education and its effects, and the language chosen (*virtus/scientia/eloquentia*), demand a broader interpretation of virtue in a woman. Indeed it goes well beyond feminine stereotypes insofar as it incorporates learning and eloquence. Because these attributes apply equally to man or woman this poem clearly demonstrates More's respect for the female mind, a

found in an epigram to Busleyden on his muse *(Epigrams,* No. 235). More urges Busleyden to publish and not to fear for the chastity of his muse: "Does it seem to you that the chaste band of maidens ought to be kept far from the society of men . . .? Have no fear; publish your Muse—she has an unyielding chastity.. . ." *(An tibi casta procul coetu cohibenda uirili / Cohors uidetur uirginum . . .? Ede tuam intrepidus, pudor est inflexilis illi . . . .)* Emphasis mine. For evidence of More's frequent connection of virtue (*virtus*) and learning, see note 12. In a verse epistle to his children (Ibid., No. 248), More commends them for their eloquence and judgment and calls these accomplishments their virtues (*virtutibus*) twice in the last four lines of the poem.

[14]This interpretation of *modestia* was reinforced for me by Abbé Germain Marc'hadour when he read an earlier version of this paper. Certainly the understanding of moderation or humility, rather than maidenly bashfulness, is reinforced by More's use of the concept in the 1518 letter to Gonell where he says, "warn my children to avoid as it were the precipices of pride and haughtiness, and to walk in the pleasant meadows of modesty . . . to esteem most whatever may teach them piety towards God, charity to all, and modesty and Christian humility in themselves" (*vti liberos meos subinde admonerent vitatis vt fastus et superbiae praecipitiis, per amaena modestiae prata graderentur . . . ex his eas maxime e quibus maxime possint pietatem in Deum, charitatem in omnes, in se modestiam et Christianam humilitatem discere).* *The Correspondence of Sir Thomas More,* p. 122.

respect unusual for the time.

Although the three Latin poems discussed here are different from one another in style and tone, they are alike in being among the best poems in the *Epigrammata*. They are alike also in presenting positive images of women. There is a similar connection to be noticed when one turns to the English poems.

Among the relatively few English verses, one stands out as exceptionally effective. "A Ruful Lamentacion," an elegy in rhyme royal occasioned by the death of Elizabeth of York (1503), is spoken by Elizabeth herself.[15] She reflects on her untimely death and bids farewell to her family. Such elegies were typically based on a *contemptus mundi* theme, but More's poem is unique, as Frederic Tromly has shown, in its sympathy for the speaker. In fact the elegaic genre is modified, because a sensitive and eloquent woman talks.[16] In this poem a woman is not just the occasion for compliment or meditation, but becomes a model of wisdom.

In the fullness of her character and relationships, however, she goes beyond the ideal but abstract wife of Candidus. We can identify with Elizabeth in her tenderness towards her children as she remembers each in turn. We are moved by her obvious pain at the necessary parting with them, and the many others she still cares for —her husband, her sisters, her subjects. Her solicitude puts her well beyond earlier speakers in the elegaic tradition who were merely sinners bemoaning their own vice and pride. Elizabeth leaves her family reluctantly, but comes to accept the truth of her own mortality, and acquires the wisdom to turn her address to God. She is not a

---

[15]"A Ruful Lamentacion," in Thomas More, *History of King Richard III and Selections from the English and Latin Poems,* ed. Richard S. Sylvester (New Haven, 1976), pp. 119-122, (Hereafter cited as *Lamentacion*.) Several critics have praised this poem including A.F. Pollard and C.S. Lewis. Recently it has attracted more careful attention. See: Sister Thea Bowman's "A Ruful Lamentacion," M.A. Thesis, The Catholic University of America, 1969, Sister Mary Edith Willow, *An Analysis of the English Poems of St. Thomas More* (Nieuwkoop, 1974), pp. 139-73, and Frederic B. Tromly, "More's Transformation of Didactic Lament," *Moreana,* 53 (March, 1977): 45-56. Tromly's study is a particularly sensitive reading and most useful in generically placing the poem.

[16]Ibid. It is interesting that some of the most effective passages in More's prose also involve a female speaker. Queen Elizabeth Woodville's dialogue in *Richard III* is a good example (see Khanna, "No Less than Ideal.") And in the *Confutation of Tyndale's Answer* More puts some of his own best arguments againt the reformers in the mouths of two "simple" women: See *The Complete Works of St. Thomas More,* vol. 8, *The Confutation of Tyndale's Answer,* ed. Louis A. Schuster, *et al* (New Haven, 1973), pp. 883-905. My longer study of women in More's work will include a discussion of female characters in the polemical literature.

figure to be condemned by the reader for her folly, but to be embraced for her humanity and, finally, her wisdom.

It is especially significant that Thomas More creates a female figure for whom the reader feels such empathy, that he casts his finest English verse in the voice of a female speaker, that through a woman he moves the English elegy from the condemnation of vice to the admiration of virtue.

Modern readers might still ask, however, if Elizabeth is not yet another stereotype. So clearly seen in relation to her husband and children, is she simply the traditional ideal of the chaste good wife? I think not. Although one could hardly doubt Elizabeth of York's chastity, More does not mention it. She is surely the good wife and mother, but her domestic affections do not encompass her. She is a woman of authority and position, and her "wit" as well as her wealth is mentioned in the poem.

The reader sees evidence of wisdom in her ability to properly evaluate the things of this world. She moves quickly from a reliance on her royal blood and enthusiasm over her husband's "castles and towers" to a recognition of other kinds of "edification." In the sixth stanza she exclaims "that costly worke of yours, Myne owne dere lorde, now shall I never see." But the self pity is transformed as she continues to speak to Henry:

> Almighty god vouchsafe to graunt that ye,
> For you and your children well may edefy.
> My palace bylded is, and lo now here I ly.[17]

Her growing insight can almost be traced in these lines as Elizabeth moves beyond worldly claims. Both mundane and spiritual values are included in her witty pun on "edefy." Whereas formerly she had been content with Henry's magnificent buildings, Elizabeth suggests a new kind of edification with the stress on "well" and "edefy" in the second line. Surely she hopes for the intellectual and moral edification of her family here. The fact that her "palace" is now her tomb underscores the need for a new kind of edification. (Modern readers might remember the vanity of building in stone in Shelley's "ozymandias.")

Finally, there is particular poignancy in her reference to her children. As the embodiment of the ideal wife, Elizabeth was probably moral teacher as well as mother. In hoping that Henry will take up this important task, she demonstrates her continued concern for them, here as elsewhere in the poem. These few lines illustrate the

---

[17]*Lamentacion*, 11. 40-42.

warmth and intelligence of the queen, and the fine play of her mind seen throughout the poem.

Her understanding of the irony of life's unpredictability is visible again in her farewell to her daughter, Margaret. She recalls her dread of Margaret's departure to Scotland after her impending marriage to James IV:

> Now as I gone, and have left you behynde.
> O mortall folke that we be very blynde.
> That we least feare, full oft it is most nye,
> From you depart I fyrst, and lo now here I lye.[18]

Further irony, wisdom, and eloquence are apparent in the final stanza of the poem:

> Adew my lordes, adew my ladies all,
> Adew my faithfull servauntes every chone,
> Adew my commons whom I never shall,
> See in this world, wherefore to the alone,
> Immortal god verely three and one,
> I me commende, thy infinite mercy,
> Shew to thy servant, for lo now here I ly.[19]

In this stanza she turns her attention from members of her court, to her servants, to her people (the commons), and then to God.[20] The movement reflects her painfully acquired wisdom, for she bids farewell to her servants in order to recognize her true role as God's servant. The earlier references to "servants" becomes ironic in terms of the final line, and again reinforces the discrepancy between worldly and spiritual values, the recognition of which constitutes true wisdom. It is not "only a woman's" wisdom here, for it represents Thomas More's interpretation of what wisdom was—for man or woman.

---

[18]Ibid., 11. 53-56.

[19]Ibid., 11. 78-84.

[20]Much of the dramatic effect of More's poem is achieved by his device of changing auditors for his speaker. Elizabeth begins by addressing a general audience "O ye that put your trust and confidence, In worldly joy and frayle prosperite," and when she meditates, speaking primarily to herself, on the bitter failure of "Worship," "wyt," and "money." But midpoint in the poem the tone changes significantly as she speaks to "myne owne dere spouse, my worthy lorde" with tenderness and respect, and then her children, her mother-in-law, her sisters, and finally, bidding farewell to her court and her English subjects, turns her address to God "Immortal god verely three and one / I me commende, they infinite mercy, / Shew to they servant, for lo now here I ly" (Ibid., 11. 82-84). The variations in tone caused by the changes of auditor contribute to the fullness of Elizabeth's character and to the reader's more intimate involvement with the drama of her salvation.

Elizabeth's wisdom and human affection are beautifully expressed throughout the poem. Each stanza gives evidence of her careful choice of words, her sense of irony, her economy of expression. In fact, she embodies the humanist values of eloquence and virtue described abstractly in "Candidus." She is also similar to More's portrayal of her mother, Elizabeth Woodville, in *Richard III*. She joins these other Morean portraits of women in representing the best of Renaissance humanism. As she moves from amazement at her fate, to bitterness, to profound affection for her family, to acceptance of her mortality, she achieves a living voice. She is admirable, yet vulnerable and wonderfully human.

In "A Ruful Lamentacion," as in the three Latin poems, More's imaginative energies seem to have been most fully and effectively engaged when he treated women positively. Just as readers of *Richard III* will long remember Shore's wife and the biting wit of Queen Elizabeth Woodville, readers of More's poetry are likely to be most moved by his memory of his lost love, his eloquently witty compliment of the French lady, his strikingly humanistic view of the ideal wife, and his sensitive and eloquent portrait of Elizabeth of York. On the other hand, More's satiric remarks about women, although often amusing, are, like the twenty short epigrams mentioned earlier,[21] nearly always forgettable.

Of course it would be surprising if attitudes towards women in More's art were not as complex, richly varied, occasionally even as contradictory as attitudes towards other important subjects. Evaluating the multiple shifts in tone of this master of jest and earnest is no easy task. But I hope to have shown here that some of More's finest work begins in an appreciation of women as intelligent and sensitive persons, and ends in moving and memorable art.

[21]See, p. 78, above.

Henry VIII, Thomas More, and the Bishop of Rome

Richard C. Marius

Henry VIII's *Assertio septem sacramentorum* of 1521 was only one of many handbooks that pounded the heresies of Martin Luther. Hardly anyone looks at any of these harsh little books today, yet Henry's work is like Ben Franklin's *Autobiography*; we have heard so much about it that we imagine that we have read it even if we have not.

For students of Thomas More, Henry's work is critical: willy-nilly, it provided a linchpin for More's own assaults on the heretics. He quoted the book again and again. And the events that unfolded from Henry's efforts helped lead More to a polemical career that in turn, led him to his death.

Two issues concern us here. What part did More have in doing the work? And what does the book say, especially about the papacy?

More has often been suspected of having a hand in the composition of the *Assertio*. Luther believed that Henry had only been a stooge, putting his royal name on a book done by others.[1] (He might have been provoked by Henry's insinuation that Luther had not really written the *Babylonian Captivity*!)[2] More himself said that he had only been a redactor.[3] And in his *Responsio ad Lutherum,* he stoutly defended Henry's authorship.[4]

But More would have had reason to conceal any part he may have had in shaping the thought of the *Assertio*. In those days, when royalty meant more than we can possibly imagine now, a book done by a king was a mighty weapon in polemics. Strange as it may seem to us, for More to have claimed much responsibility for the *Assertio* would have detracted from the work's reputation. Besides, Henry

---

[1]Martin Luther, *D. Martin Luthers Werke,* Kritische Gesammtausgabe (Weimar, 1883), vol. 10/2, p. 183. (Hereafter cited as *WA*.)

[2]Henry VIII, *Assertio septem sacramentorum aduersus Martin Lutherum* (London, 1521), sig. a4. (Hereafter cited as *Assertio.)*

[3]William Roper, *Life of St. Thomas More* in Richard S. Sylvester, ed., *Two Early Tudor Lives* (New Haven, 1962), p. 235.

[4]*The Complete Works of St. Thomas More,* vol. 5, *Responsio ad Lutherum,* ed. John M. Headley (New Haven, 1969), pp. 54-57. (Hereafter cited as *CW*.)

was so proud of being an author that for More to steal his glory would have been imprudent indeed. Thomas More was always a prudent man.

Later, in a letter to Thomas Cromwell written in March, 1534, More recalled a disagreement he had had with Henry concerning the power of the pope. When the king wrote his book against Luther, More had urged him not to mention that the papal primacy had been instituted by God. Or at least, he said, Henry should touch the matter only slightly. Popes and princes often fell into disrepute. If Henry praised the papal power too much, his words might prove embarrassing later on. "Whervnto," More wrote somewhat mysteriously, "his Highnes answered me, that he wold in no wise eny thing minishe of that mater, of which thing his Highnes shewed me a secrete cause whereof I neuer had eny thing herd byfore."[5]

And so, More told Cromwell, he found himself convinced both by the king's arguments then, and by what he read later in the fathers of the church, that the papal primacy came from God.

So we know that More was consulted when the *Assertio* was being written. I do not believe that he did any of the actual writing, for the Latin style of the *Assertio* is quite different from the style of More's own Latin works; the *Assertio* is much easier to read. But the fact that he was called on to write the *Responsio ad Lutherum* to reply to Luther's furious attacks on the *Assertio* would suggest that he had

---

[5]Sir Thomas More, *The Correspondence of Sir Thomas More,* ed. Elizabeth F. Rogers (Princeton, 1947), p. 498. (Hereafter cited as *Correspondence.*) Roper gives an expanded version of this discussion between Henry and More on the subject of the papacy. It is never wise to trust Roper when we have no other source to confirm him, but he may be plausible here. He has Henry declare, "Whatsoever impediment be to the contrary, we will set forth that authority to the uttermost. For we received from that See our crown imperial" (Roper, *Life,* p. 235). It is interesting that, if this statement is true, Henry was already thinking of England as an empire at the time he wrote the *Assertio.* That is, he was working towards a conception of sovereignty that was to become essential to what G.R. Elton has called "The Tudor Revolution in Government." See the book by that title (/Cambridge, 1953/, p. 302, n. 1), where Elton remarks, "Cromwell's political philosophy might be reduced to the words, 'empire' and 'commonwealth.' " Perhaps Henry was speaking only of papal recognition of the Tudor house. Certainly the legal claim of Henry VII was flimsy enough, and just as certain is the Tudor sense of a divine vocation to the throne of England. Perhaps Henry VII took papal recognition with much more seriousness than we have previously thought. All the way back to Pepin the Short popes had been called on to certify kings of doubtful legality, and Henry VII might well have accepted papal approval gladly, and passed his feelings onto his children. But all this is only conjecture. In the *Assertio* itself we find no declaration of gratitude to the pope for Henry's crown.

been involved in Henry's efforts.

Many things in the work find echo in More's later polemics—especially the sort of echo that slams back and forth among the mountains in endless repetition.

Henry saw the Catholic church as the infallible guardian of divine revelation, and he argued that if the church had done something for a long time, the practice must be correct.[6] Christ had promised to lead the church into all truth, and either the church was true or Christ was false. He did not go as far as Thomas More who held that if the church had venerated a certain relic for a long time, the relic must be authentic.[7]

Luther declared that he would believe only doctrines written in scripture.[8] Henry claimed that the church had authority over scripture, and to support this argument he quoted Augustine's statement that he would not have believed the Bible except by the church's authority.[9] So did More, time and again.[10]

Henry believed that Christ had taught his disciples doctrines and practices that were not written down in the New Testament. These things were handed on in the church by an oral tradition, and they remained as binding as the words of the Bible. As a prooftext Henry cited John 21:25: "*Sunt autem et alia multa, quae fecit Iesus: quae si scribantur per singula, nec ipsum arbitror mundum capere posse eos, qui scribendi sunt, libros.*"[11]

More repeatedly used the same text and the same argument. If we take theology to be the way we reconcile our divine authorities with our daily experience, we can understand why. The church was doing things that had no precedent in scripture. Luther claimed that these things were traditions of men and should be weeded out, thus changing the Christian experience to conform with his authority. The catholic church wanted to keep the experience, and to account for it, expanded the authority that justified it. What astonishes us in More

[6]*Assertio,* sigs. me, qiv, et al.
[7]Thomas More, *A Dialogue Concerning Heresies* (London, 1531), sig. o2v. This statement comes after a long discussion by More defending relics and explaining (among many other things) how so many churches possess the head of John the Baptist. (Hereafter cited as *DCH.*)
[8]Luther spoke at length in this regard, *WA,* 7, pp. 97-101.
[9]*Assertio,* sigs., m2v, p4-p4v.
[10]John M. Headley has an interesting note on the Catholic use of this text, *CW,* vol. 5, p. 743, n. 1.
[11]*Assertio,* sigs. m2v, qiv. Like More Henry held that if scripture had never been written, the gospel would remain in the church, written in the hearts of the faithful. *Assertio,* sigs. m2v, m3. Cf. *CW,* vol. 5, pp. 88-9.

is just how sweeping he made the oral tradition. He believed that even the gestures made by priests at the mass had been orally taught by Christ and handed down through the church.[12]

When Luther denied the oral tradition, Henry tried to prove that he observed it in spite of himself. How else could Luther accept the perpetual virginity of Mary, the mother of Jesus, or the mixing of water and wine in the mass?[13] These things, and many others, were not taught in the New Testament.

Henry vigorously defended both the doctrine of transubstantiation and its corollary, the belief that the mass is a sacrifice, an oblation renewed countless times, though Christ suffered and died only once.[14] Henry berated Luther for teaching that faith alone is necessary for salvation, and castigated him for writing in the *Babylonian Captivity* that no sin was damnable except unbelief.[15] Here he distorted Luther. He said that Luther was encouraging people to live in sin, in the confidence that they would not be damned as long as they believed that the Christian faith was true.

Here are staples of More's own polemics. Like Henry, More stressed the wickedness of justification by faith by listing heinous crimes, and claiming that the doctrine meant that anybody could commit these crimes and still be redeemed, if only he had faith.[16]

Henry, and later More, called up Jerome's metaphor of penance, the "second plank for the shipwrecked sailor."[17] (Baptism was the first.) And Henry, like More, lovingly cites the text, *De vera et falsa poenitentia,* ascribing it to St. Augustine and using it to prove that the Catholic form of penance was ancient.[18] The work was, in fact, written centuries after Augustine had died, and doubts were being raised about its authenticity before the Reformation began.[19]

Henry condemned Luther for his contradictions. In the *Babylonian Captivity* Luther said that the Church of Christ could discern the words of God from the words of men. Both Henry and More said

[12]*DCH,* sig. d2.
[13]*Assertio,* sigs. c4-m3.
[14]Ibid., sigs. c2-c4, nıv, et al.
[15]Ibid., sigs. i1v-i2.
[16]*CW,* vol. 8. *The Confutation of Tyndale's Answer,* ed. Louis A. Schuster, et al (New Haven, 1973).
[17]*Assertio,* sig. i2; Compare More, *CW,* vol. 8, p. 213 and note, pp. 213/18-19, 1543.
[18]*Assertio,* sigs. m2-m2v.
[19]See R. C. Marius, "The Pseudonymous Patristic Text in Thomas More's *Confutation,*" *Moreana,* 15-16 (1967): 253-266. See also *CW,* vol. 8, pp. 581, 867, 1542, 1613, 1682. Luther rejected the authority of this work as early as 1516. *WABr,* 1:65.

repeatedly that Luther's own words meant that the church was necessary to say what was scripture and what was not. And if that were the case, said they, Luther's principle of *sola scriptura* fell to earth.[20]

Henry, in the *Assertio,* and More after him, were troubled by the anarchy they saw bursting from Luther's books. The people were stirred up against the clergy and against all rulers. Sedition must inevitably result.[21]

But there are differences between the *Assertio* and More's later work. In these differences we hear other voices besides More's in the king's theological council.

For example, Henry, in the *Assertio,* demonstrated an interest in Hugh of St. Victor that More did not share.[22] Henry mentioned with appropriate horror Luther's teaching that priests should break their vows and marry.[23] But I do not find in Henry the deep and terrible loathing that More felt towards the breaking of vows of chastity. Of course we must recall that by the time More wrote polemics in his own name, Luther had married a nun. Oddly enough, Henry passed over in silence some of the radical comments that Luther made about marriage in the *Babylonian Captivity.* More would later pounce on these. They included Luther's advice that an impotent husband should provide a sexual partner to satisfy the needs of his wife, and raise children from such a union, and his rather biblical insistence that bigamy was better than divorce.[24]

Henry praised marriage lavishly, calling it the first of all sacraments to be observed among humankind.[25] Not surprisingly, More,

---

[20]*Assertio,* sigs. p4—s2;*CW,* vol. 5, pp. 71, 281; ibid., vol. 8, p. 690. Pointing out Luther's contradictions was a favorite indoor sport of his Catholic foes. The most notable effort in this regard was the work by John Dobneck, called Cochlaeus, *Septiceps Lutherus. Vbique sibi suis scriptis, contrarius, in visitationem Saxonicam,* (Leipzig, 1529). This is the work that has the famous woodcut of the seven-headed Luther as its frontispiece.

[21]*Assertio,* sigs. kl-klv; for More see *DCH* sigs. z2v, B3v-B4v *et passim* in all his polemical works.

[22]For Hugh of St. Victor see *Assertio,* sigs. 32v, i2v – i3, m4v, p2, n3, q1v.

[23]Ibid., sigs. p3-p3v.

[24]*WA,* 6: 558-9. Luther was not entirely sure that bigamy was legal, but he hated divorce so much, he said, that he would prefer bigamy. For More's response, see *DCH,* sig. y2v. The matter is quite difficult. It may be that Henry VIII was too prudish to discuss impotence, and that More thought the issue of bigamy was too dangerous because it naturally brought with it questions of how the Old Testament should be interpreted.

[25]*Assertio,* sig. n2.

whose ascetic tastes were extreme, rarely had anything good to say about marriage in his religious works. He was much more likely to praise the pure witness of chaste widows and undefiled virgins; and he said flatly that it was heresy to believe that the married state was as pleasing to God as virginity.[26]

In praise of marriage, Henry used a florid allegory. Christ by being at the wedding in Cana of Galilee, where he changed water into wine, shows how the ordinary water of fleshly lust is converted by the hidden grace of God into the most delicious wine.[27]

More seldom used allegory for anything. In fact it has often struck me that we are more likely to find allegories in the work of Luther than we are in More—in spite of Luther's furious denunciation of the allegorical method of interpreting the Bible. More was very much a literalist when he came to scripture, though he never felt any humanist fixation on original texts in Greek, which he knew, or Hebrew, which he did not.[28]

Henry used the little book called the *Celestial Hierarchies* to prove that holy orders should be a sacrament. Aquinas believed that this work had been written by the Dionysius converted by Paul with the sermon on Mars Hill recorded in Acts 17, and both he and other theologians of the high middle ages thought the book was almost as good as scripture itself. But Erasmus, and others, had correctly called the book a forgery over a decade before the Reformation began. Luther flatly rejected it, saying in the *Babylonian Captivity* that the *Celestial Hierarchies* had been done by a Platonist rather than a Christian.[29] Henry said that at the very least Luther must admit that Dionysius was an ancient authority, a witness to a practice centuries old.[30]

More hardly ever used pseudo-Dionysius for anything. In the *Responsio* he hastily cited Henry's argument that the works ascribed to Dionysius were an ancient witness to Catholic tradition no matter who had written them.[31] But never did he call the author of the *Celestial Hierarchies* a disciple of Paul, and never in the English works did he cite his authority.

---

[26]*DCH,* sig. t5.
[27]*Assertio,* sig. p1.
[28]R. C. Marius, "Thomas More and the Early Church Fathers," *Traditio,* 24 (1968): 386-9.
[29]*WA,* 6:561-2.
[30]*Assertio,* sig. q4.
[31]*CW,* vol. 5, p. 69. For More on Dionysius, see Marius, "Pseudonymous Text," pp. 256-9.

Other Catholic defenders were not so circumspect. In the Leipzig debate of 1519, John Eck flung Dionysius at Luther.[32] And John Fisher, seemingly uninterested in humanist squabbles over authorship, cited Dionysius continually and without qualification as a disciple of Paul.[33]

But the main difference between the *Assertio* and More's own works against the dissidents lay in just the point that More mentioned in his letter to Cromwell—the definition of the place of the papacy in the church.

It is startling to see just how little is made of papal authority in the huge body of More's work. Modern students have usually assumed that More suppressed his own views of the papal primacy only as a gesture to Henry VIII.[34] More himself said in the letter to Cromwell of March, 1534, that in the *Confutation* he deliberately muted some things that he had written about the pope. He said he did not want to meddle in the affair that had arisen between the pope and his king.[35]

But we must point out that More said very little about the papacy, not only in the *Confutation,* but in the *Responsio,* the *Dialogue Concerning Heresies,* and in his letter against Bugenhagen—all written before Henry's troubles with the pope became acute. Whatever the reasons for his silence, I do not see that it gives us license to suppose that he agreed with John Fisher, whose unstinting devotion to papal sovereignty clangs like a gong in nearly everything he wrote against Luther.[36] It seems much more plausible to me to suppose that More had his own reasons for this silence and that in his letter to Cromwell, when he was fighting for his life, he tried to interpret this silence in such a way that would win the king's favor. However that may be, it is clear that in the *Assertio* Henry VIII made much of papal authority and that Thomas More never did.

It may be argued that Henry's own pronouncements on the papacy were not nearly as sweeping as they have usually been said to be. If we recall that Henry wrote his book to win a title from the pope, we

---

[32] *WA,* 2: 255-6, 262, *et al.*

[33] For Fisher see his *De veritate corporis et sanguinis Christi in Eucharistia . . . aduersus Iohannem Oecolampadius* (Cologne, 1527), sigs. F3, Q2, and *Assertionis Lutheranae Confutatio* (Cologne, 1523), sigs. K4, I3v, L2v, *et al.*

[34] See John M. Headley, "More's Ecclesiology in the Revised *Responsio,*" in *CW,* vol. 5, p. 769.

[35] *The Correspondence of Sir Thomas More,* ed. Elizabeth Frances Rogers (Princeton, 1947), p. 500.

[36] See Headley, "More's Ecclesiology," in *CW,* vol. 5, pp. 766-7. And see Fisher, *ALC,* sigs I2v-L1-M3v *et passim.*

may be prepared for some regal syrup to be sloshed on the pope's head.

But just what did Henry say? He called the pope the Vicar of Christ.[37] He praised Leo X for his innocent life.[38] He begged the pope to correct anything in the *Assertio* that might be in error.[39] Luther, said Henry, served his own pride by attacking the pope in public. Had Luther been sincere, he would have written the pope a private letter, urging him to follow apostolic precepts, and the pope would have responded with kindness and thanks.[40] By withdrawing from the pope, Luther violated the commands of both love and obedience.[41] No one could deny that the church of all the faithful recognized the sacrosanct Roman See as mother and primate. Even in distant India, said Henry, people are obedient to the pope.[42] (Here he was beguiled by tales brought by Portuguese sailors who marveled that the images of saints in India had six arms.)[43]

Otherwise, Henry spilled a lot of ink arguing that papal indulgences applied to purgatory. This was the issue that had fired off the Reformation. Henry said that Christ granted the power of binding and loosing to Peter, and that this authority passed on to Peter's successors, the popes. The power extends to heaven and to hell, and it would be absurd to grant the pope power over the eternal and to deny him authority over purgatory, which was temporary.[44] Luther had said that the power of the keys extended to all priests and to all the church. Henry replied that it would be absurd then to deny that the pope, prince of all priests, possessed this power. Consequently, the pope could relieve souls of all temporal punishments, including those of purgatory.[45]

In fact, though popes had asserted their power over purgatory, the matter had been in dispute long before the outbreak of the Reformation.[46] But when Luther attacked indulgences and became a notor-

---

[37]*Assertio,* sigs. 23, v1v.

[38]Ibid., sig. b1v. Luther had remarked on Leo's innocent life *(WA,* 1:679). But in his answer to Henry's *Assertio* he held that Leo's personal goodness did not make the papacy a good thing *(WA,* 10/2, p. 196).

[39]*Assertio,* sig. a3.

[40]Ibid., sigs. t4-t4v.

[41]Ibid., sigs. b4v-c1.

[42]Ibid., sigs. b3v-b4.

[43]J.H. Parry, ed., *The European Reconnasiance* (New York, 1968), pp. 84-5.

[44]*Assertio,* sigs. b2-b2v.

[45]Ibid., sig. b2v.

[46]See Et. Magnin, "Indulgences," *Dictionnaire de théologie catholique,* 7/2, cols. 1614-9.

ious heretic, it was natural that Catholics should defend what Luther denied. They could not defend indulgences without also defending the power of the pope. Henry VIII did his bit along with many others in this regard. But never once in all his polemical works—not even in his *Supplication of Souls*—did Thomas More argue that papal indulgences had any effect in Purgatory.

But we wander from the point at hand—Henry's thoughts on the papacy.

By what authority does the pope exercise his power? Henry turned rather naturally to the story of Peter's confession and Christ's gift of the keys in Matt. 16:15-19. (Here was a text that More rarely used at all.) Here was the great scriptural bulwark of all papal claims. "Thou art Peter, and on this rock I will build my church," said Christ. Did he mean the church would rest on Peter and on his successors the popes? No, said Luther and his epigoni.[47] The rock was Peter's faith, not Peter himself, and faith was the foundation of the church.

Henry replied with an appeal to infallible tradition. Catholics had so long received papal indulgences that if the pope had no power to grant them, the church had erred. All nations agree, he said, that it is not right to change things that have remained unchanged for a long time. And since the conversion of the world, all churches have been obedient to Rome.[48] If Luther says that the pope's church is not the church of Christ, he must also say that none of the countries that obey the pope could belong to the true church. And if he does such a thing, he must either declare that Christ's church is no place to all or else, like the Donatists, reduce the Catholic church to two or three heretics whispering in a corner.[49]

On the surface we have a ringing affirmation of papal power. But if we look a little more closely, we find a haze of ambiguity that makes Henry's exact thoughts on the subject difficult to know. Important questions are not posed. Just how far does papal power extend? Can the pope err in doctrine? Is a pope supreme over a general council? Can a pope be deposed for any reason other than heresy?

The clearest thing Henry said was that the pope has authority to issue indulgences that will release souls from purgatory. He did not

[47] *WA*, 1: 655; ibid., 2: 632-4, ibid., 6: 312. And see William Tyndale, *The Obedience of a Christen Man* (Antwerp, 1528), sig. S6v.
[48] *Assertio*, sig. b4.
[49] Ibid., sig. p. 4.

tell us if that release is instantaneous—a matter of some debate before Luther came on the scene.

The question of conciliarism was probably the most serious theological issue facing the church before Luther. Henry said little about it, though John Fisher hardly ever mentioned the general council without asserting the pope's superiority over it.[50] Henry mentioned the general council only to denounce Luther for making a frivolous appeal to such a body. He said that Luther promised to listen not to the next council that was called but to the next one called in the Holy Spirit. And Luther proposed to judge for himself whether the council met his standard. Henry, mentioning with scorn Luther's attitude, passed over in silence an obvious chance to flaunt papal power.

Henry did say that the pope should be obeyed. But in what does this obedience consist? Does it mean that kings should obey popes in temporal matters? Certainly not. England was already being thought of as an empire in the *Morte d'Arthur* of Thomas Malory, published by Caxton within a decade of More's birth. Henry VIII and his great minister Thomas Cromwell were to make the notion of empire fundamental to the schism from Rome that they together engineered. But already in the early years of his reign Henry VIII had blocked publication of a papal bull in England, because the bull did not suit his interest.[51] Of course, he was by no means original here.

What of the role of the pope in defining doctrine? Henry made some gestures in this direction. He quoted Jerome who said that even if his faith were not approved by others, it was enough for him if it was approved by the Bishop of Rome.[52] But Henry did not make a more precise statement. "I shall not wrong the pope," he said, "by anxiously and carefully sitting as umpire on his law as if it were a doubtful thing."[53] Considering how other Catholic polemicists delighted in expounding on the pope's authority, I find Henry's comment evasive.

---

[50]Edward J. Surtz, *The Works and Days of John Fisher*, (Cambridge, Mass., 1967), p. 67. For Henry's comment on Luther's frivolous appeal to the council, see *Assertio*, sigs. t4v-v1.

[51]See J. J. Scarisbrick, *Henry VIII* (Berkeley and Los Angeles, 1968), pp. 46-7, for a brief discussion of the carelessness with which Henry and Wolsey treated the pope. We should also remember the story Roper tells of the pope's great ship confiscated by Henry at Southampton. Thomas More defended the pope's case and won it, but the important thing here is Henry's decided lack of servility to the pope in a legal case involving temporal affairs.

[52]*Assertio*, sigs. b4-b4v.

There is an attitude in both the *Assertio* and in More's work that would tend to erode any thought that the pope had any special divine inspiration concerning doctrine. More always justified himself, a layman writing theology, by saying that Catholic doctrines are so well known, and the errors of the dissidents so manifest, that he was quite competent to refute heresy.[54]

Henry VIII began the *Assertio* by contemplating the astonishment of the pope when the supreme pontif learned that a king who had devoted his life to martial pursuits and affairs of state now turned to theology.[55] But, he said, the menace of heresy was such that every Christian must do what he could to oppose it. He would count on the grace of God to help his own weakness, he said as humbly as he could, and he modestly mentioned his earlier theological studies.[56] He also, as I have noted, submitted his work to the judgment of the pope.[57]

But in the work itself his attitude was always that Luther was contradicting doctrines well known to all the church. If we compare the *Assertio* to John Fisher, to John Eck, to Cochlaeus, or to the common run of Catholic apologists, we find Henry truly reticent on any indispensable role of the pope in defining doctrine.[58]

Henry, believing that doctrines necessary for salvation were evident to all good Christians, was in some sense leaving himself room to hold that if popes should ever command something other than evident truth, they should not be obeyed. I do not think for a moment that he was imagining such a case when he wrote the *Assertio,* for he did make some sort of obedience to the pope an essential part of Catholic tradition. But Henry's mind—like all minds—was an odd mixture of flexibility and rigidity. If he became convinced that the pope had erred in doctrine, he could (like Luther) easily convince himself that the pope was being malicious. Only a malicious person

---

[53]Ibid., sig. b4v.

[54]*DCH.* sigs. b3, b5.

[55]*Assertio,* sig. à2.

[56]Ibid., sig. a2v.

[57]Ibid., sig. a3.

[58]See among many examples, Eck's *Enchiridion locorum communum aduersus Lutteranos* (Ingolstadt, 1525), sigs. B4-D1v, and see also the importance Eck grants to papal approval of images in his *De non tollendis Christi et sanctorum imaginibus contra haeresim Faelicianam sub carolo magno damnatum, & iam sub carolo .v. renascentem dicisio* (Ingolstadt, 1522), sigs. b3v-c2. And see the concern of Cochlaeus for the pope in his book devoted to the subject, *Ob Sant Peter zu Rom sey gewessen* (Strasbourg, 1524). See also his *Canones Apostolorum* (Mainz, 1525), and his *De Petro et Roma, adversus velenum Lutheranum* (Cologne, 1525).

could fail to perceive truths that were so clear to other Christians that no good man could doubt them. By failing to believe—as so many did—that the pope was the source of the church's hold on truth, Henry was in effect leaving room for the thought that the pope was only head of the church when he proclaimed what all the church believed. As I have said, Henry assumed in the *Assertio* that all good Christians know what the church believes. So we might say that the seeds of Henry's own later disobedience lie germinating in the very vagueness of his stern summons to Luther to obey the pope.

Henry obviously accepted some sort of papal jurisdictional authority. When a rule of the canon law required the relief of equity in a special case, a long-standing tradition allowed the pope to issue a dispensation that lifted the legal restraints. The pope acted as chief justice in a high court that decided how the canon law applied to cases. To enforce his judgments, especially in cases of notorious heresy, the pope could issue edicts of excommunication and interdict.

Henry married Catherine of Aragon on the authority of a papal dispensation, and in the process accepted the pope's judicial authority. Later he was to seek to nullify the marriage on the authority of another pronouncement he tried to wrest from another pope. In effect, he wanted Clement VII to say that the legal dispensation granted by Julius II had violated the clear doctrine of the church and should be cancelled. The pope refused to grant his request, and in the process refused to make a distinction between judicial authority and doctrinal authority. With the papacy under fierce attack, no one could really expect that one pope could dare declare another in flagrant error in anything.[59]

I believe that I have already conveyed my opinion (which is not very original) that the reformation was a godsend to the papacy. Luther and his motley crew did more to build the power of the papacy within the church than anyone or anything since the Investiture Controversy and the first crusade. The papacy was the Verdun of the Reformation, and the more the dissidents attacked it, the more Catholics were compelled to defend it. In the process, the distinction between judicial authority and doctrinal authority was swept away.

Luther's fiery reaction to the *Assertio* is well known. The fact that he published versions of his reply in both German and Latin is a

---

[59]The details of Henry's suit have been recounted again and again. The best work I have seen is Henry Ansgar Kelly, *The Matrimonial Trials of Henry VIII* (Stanford, 1976). See especially his chapter "The Attack on the Dispensations," pp. 101-131.

measure of how agitated he was by Henry's book.[60] He had expected princes everywhere to rise up with him against papal tyranny. And yet, by the time he read the *Assertio* in the spring of 1522, he had been condemned by the Emperor Charles V, declared an outlaw of the empire by the Diet of Worms, and secluded for months in the Wartburg Castle as a fugitive and an exile. He was a passionate man with a genius for obscenity and vituperation when he was contradicted, and in his answer to Henry, he made the most of his considerable talents.

Henry was left in a dilemma. His temperament was such that he could never allow any challenge to his authority to go unanswered and, if he could help it, unpunished. But if he debated with Luther, "a mean and base little friar," he would lower his own dignity by granting that Luther was worth the effort.

His first step was to send a letter to the Saxon princes, the Elector Frederick the Wise and Duke George of Leipzig.[61] Frederick was Luther's own prince. George had sponsored the Leipzig debate between Luther and Eck, and hated Luther ever afterwards.

More probably helped the king write this letter. He was now close to Henry, often writing to Wolsey to convey the king's wishes. Since he had helped put the *Assertio* together, he might be expected to give advice on how Luther should be pummeled.

Many things in this letter remind us of More's later polemics against the heretics. Luther is called insane; his arguments are mad and malicious.[62] He writes in such a way that the people may be seduced by him.[63] The book that Luther has written against Henry is so offensive that Henry could not respond to it. Though David did

[60]For the best account of the controversy and the books engendered by it, see John Headley's introduction to *CW,* vol. 5, pp. 715-731. Also see the modest little book by Erwin Doernberg, *Henry VIII and Luther* (Stanford, 1961).

[61]A printed edition of the letter is to be found bound in the back of the volume entitled *Libello huic regio haec insunt* (STC 13083). The *Libello* contains the *Assertio* with the notation at the back that it was printed in June, 1521. Since Henry's letter could not have been done before 1523, we must assume that Pynson had a great many copies of the *Assertio,* probably unbound, lying around his shop, and that he saw the exchange with Luther as a chance to help the sales of the king's book. We may assume that the *Assertio did not* make Pynson's fortune. I am citing an edition of the letter that includes a reply from Duke George, *Serenissimi ac potentissimi regis Angliae Christianae fidei defensoris invictissimi ad illustrissimos ac clarissimos Saxoniae principis, de coercenda abigendaque Lutherana factione & luthero ipso Epistola. Item Illustrissimi principis Ducis Georgii ad eundem Regem rescripto,* Anno MDXXIII. The *Assertio* to which this version was attached was printed in Strasbourg in 1522 and the exchange of correspondence added later on (The British Library shelfmark to the volume containing both works is 475.a.22).

[62]Ibid., sig. A2.

[63]Ibid., sigs. A3-A3v.

not think it indecorous to dance naked before the Lord, Henry was not accustomed to fight in an undignified way for religious faith. Though Luther might have hated Henry personally, Luther might yet have respected the king's royal office. This disrespect was the heart of the matter. For this little friar in effect damned not only Henry but the German emperor as well, and all German princes.[64]

The consequence of this irreverence could only be sedition. All religion would be smashed, all laws overwhelmed, good customs corrupted, governments ruined, all things sacred profaned, the sacraments of Christ trampled underfoot, the freedom of the will destroyed, faith extolled so that good works might be abased and license granted to sin. Mercy is taken away and justice suppressed, and the cause of all these horrors is not located in some evil god as at least the Manichees taught, but goodness is removed from the one good God Christians are supposed to worship. It is as if a poisonous serpent, expelled from heaven, had fallen out on the earth, moving the church to division, abrogating laws, enfeebling magistrates, and inciting the laity against the clergy.[65]

We have here a rag-bag of evils interesting both for what is included and for what is omitted. Luther's teaching of predestination, unmentioned in the *Assertio,* here becomes the mark of the beast, and it is understood in the way that More was always to view it. In this letter, and in More's works, Luther's doctrine of predestination is said to make God unjust. It raises the ordinary man to rebellion and license by freeing him from the restraining belief that he has some responsibility for his own acts. Neither More nor Henry cared to perceive the immense moral power in Luther's concept of predestination. Rather they insisted that Luther's teaching must lead to the license and abandon that make orderly government impossible.

In this letter the Lutheran matter is seen as a revolution, not merely in religious doctrine or in the way Christians view the sacraments, but in the way that Europeans understand themselves and live together. No part of Luther's heresy can be detached from the rest. One part of Luther's teachings brings everything else with it, and this totality threatens the totality of Christian civilization. This was always to be More's dark way of seeing the Lutheran danger.

Yet, in this long catalogue of Luther's crimes, there is no mention of his attacks on the papacy! I find this omission remarkable, and I think it testifies to Thomas More's hand in the composition of the letter. Again, I say that one must look at other examples of Catholic polemical literature with their cacophonous chorus in praise of papal

⁶⁴Ibid., sigs. A2v-A3.
⁶⁵Ibid., sigs. A3-A3v.

power to see just how rare it is to find attacks on Luther that do not mention his assaults on the pope.[66]

I wish I had time to discuss More's *Responsio ad Lutherum* that has been so splendidly edited by my colleague, John M. Headly of the University of North Carolina at Chapel Hill. Here again I find the discussion of the papacy fascinating because of its ambivalence.[67]

But I want to close with a consideration of Henry's letter to Luther written in 1526.

Sometime in the late summer of 1525 a rumor blew into Wittenberg that Henry had begun to lean towards the Gospel and that Cardinal Wolsey was about to fall from power. The Peasants' War was just over. It was a bad time for both Luther and the court of Electoral Saxony that had become his protector. They needed friends. And so Luther was persuaded with some difficulty to write a meek letter offering apology to Henry for his part in their late unpleasantness. After several false starts, Luther got a proper letter off late in September. It seems to have taken until the following spring to arrive in England.[68]

Luther was never very apt in his diplomacy with princes, and his

[66]See Friedrich Lauchert, *Die italieneschen literarischen* (Niewkoop, 1972). This book is interesting because it is one of the rare summaries of the thought of a group of Luther's early Catholic foes. The thinkers in question are not household names, and with the exception of Ambrosius Catharinus, Gasparo Contarini, and Jacopo Sadoleto, they are not very interesting. But it is remarkable to see with what unanimity they consider denial of the papal power to be a damnable sin. They were Italians, and they might be presumed to have a special interest in the papacy. But my own study of northern Catholics who opposed Luther confirms my opinion that nearly everybody who defended the Catholic church began where Luther began attacking it—at the papacy.

[67]Among many things that might be mentioned is the fact that the only mention More/Rosseus makes in the *Responsio* of Matt. 16:19 and the power of the keys is a quotation from Henry's *Assertio* (*CW*, vol. 5, p. 273). More, who was always ready to refute the heretics down to the last jot, has nothing very strong to say about papal power. Even where he is speaking of the papacy, he speaks more often of the *sedem petri* than he does of *papatum* (*Responsio*, ibid., pp. 195 *et passim*). With regard to the papacy, More makes only three points in the *Responsio*, and any of them might easily have been made by a conciliarist such as Jean Gerson. The popes are the successors of Peter. A solitary rebel like Luther has no right to dispute the legitimate commands of a pope. Obedience to the papacy is one of the signs of a church well known to common sense. What More carefully avoids is any definition of the nature of the pope's authority or the precise requirements of Christian obedience to the Bishop of Rome.

[68]*L & P Hen. VIII*, 4, 2420, 2445. *Correspondence*, p. 368. For an analysis of the exchange of letters between Henry and Luther, see William A. Clebsch, *England's Earliest Protestants* (New Haven and London, 1964), pp. 36-41. Clebsch says, "there is not a word in the royal letter that might not have flowed from the knight's pen."

approach to Henry was not of a sort to soften the hard, blunt edge
of Henry's wrath. He began by declaring that he had not earlier
understood that the *Assertio* had not been written by the king
himself. But now that he knew the king's true mind, he was willing
to do his part in a reconcilation. There followed a number of self-
effacing remarks accompanied by a little fulsome praise for Henry's
grandeur.[69]

But this was a fit of humility that would have done credit to Uriah
Heep, since, in effect, what Luther offered was to certify Henry as a
worthy king and good fellow if Henry would only renounce the previous errors published in his royal name, and agree that Luther's
teachings were just and righteous altogether.

Henry—or someone delegated to write in his name—replied with a
broadside blast against Luther intended to show that the royal mind
was as unchanging as granite, and that Luther had been, was now,
and ever would be a heretical dog.[70]

Anyone acquainted with the polemics of Thomas More is bound to
hear a certain familiar rhythm in Henry's reply. Among other things,
Henry pounded Luther for his marriage to a nun, an offense that
according to the canon law made Luther guilty of incest.[71] Henry
also pointed out that among the Romans, Luther would have been
buried alive for violating a virgin consecrated to religion.[72] The pope
and the cardinals had justly and impartially condemned Luther for
his sins.[73] Luther's affair, writes Henry, began with envy and presumption, proceeds with rancor and malice, is blown forth with
pride and vainglory, and ends in lechery.[74] And what Luther calls
"Christian liberty" was interpreted to mean insatiable license to all.

What is most interesting here is an enumeration of Luther's heresies. These include writing against the sacraments, condemning chastity in priests, denying holy orders, joining bread with the body of
Christ, taking away from all men the benefit of the mass, railing
against the canon of the mass, making women confessors and minis-

---

[69] A modern translation of the letter from Luther is found in Doernberg, *Henry VIII and Luther,* pp. 50-53. The original text is in *WABr,* 3, 562-5.

[70] The letter appeared in two Latin and two English editions. The first Latin edition (STC 13084) was *Literarum, quibus Henricus octavus respondit ad quandam episto-lam M. Lutheri et ipsius Lutheranae quoque epistolae exemplum* (Pynson, 1526). I cite the first English edition (STC 13086), *A Copyof the ltters wherein kyng Henry the eight made answere vnto a certayn letter of Martyn Luther* (Pynson, 1526).

[71] Ibid., sig. A4.

[72] Ibid., sig. B8.

[73] Ibid., sig. B8.

[74] Ibid, sigs. A4, B8.

ters of all sacraments and allowing them to consecrate the body of Christ, teaching little difference between the Virgin Mary and the nun Luther had made his whore, blaspheming the holy cross, and finally, teaching that there is no purgatory, but rather that all souls sleep till the day of doom.[75] There is no mention of Luther's attacks on the papacy. I was unable to find any other Catholic writer who catalogues Luther's heresies in such detail, and yet does not mention his offences against the papacy—any other, that is, except Thomas More. In fact, this list might serve as a sort of introduction to More's *Dialogue Concerning Heresies,* for these were the things that raised More's ire. In that larger work, More treated every one of these points at great length. Like Henry, he neglected to spend much time on the papacy.

In one of the introductory essays to our edition of the *Confutation,* I argued that More was not a papalist in the way that we may use that term for most other Catholic apologists during the early years of the Reformation.[76] Of course, I did not mean to suggest that More thought the papacy should be abolished. No one with his deep sense of tradition could have imagined that the church could get rid of the papacy altogether. We have his own statement to Cromwell that he believed in the divine institution of the papal primacy. But primacy is not the same as supremacy or sovereignty, and I believe

---

[75]Ibid., sigs. C2-C2v. Henry did respond to Luther's ridicule of the *Assertio* by saying that the Holy See Apostolic approved of it, "of whom St. Jerome reckoned it sufficient that his faith were approved" (ibid., sig. B4). One may compare the list of Luther's heresies in this letter with a list More made in his letter to Bugenhagen done about the same time though it was not published until long after More's death.

> *Nam quaeso te, quae mendacia feruntur de vobis? Aut quomodo Euangelium profitemini? An mendacium esse contendes, si quis factionem vestram dicat bonam Germaniae partem tumultu, caede, rapinis, incendio deuastasse? Audebis eos mendaces dicere, qui vestram doctrinam impiam, tot scelerum, tot damnorum, tot vastitatum causam esse testantur? An seditiones mouere, laicos in Clerum concitare, plebem in Magistratus armare, populos aduersus Principes incitare, pugnas, ruinas, bella, strages procurare, idem esse probabis, quod Euangelium profiteri? Dic, obsecro, nobis, egregie professor Euangelii, destruere Sacramenta Christi, Sanctos Christi spernere, Matrem Christi blasphemare, Crucem Christi contemnere, vota Christo facta vilipendere, dicatum Christo caelibatum soluere, virginitatem Christo consecratam polluere, monachos ac velatas Christo virgines ad coniugium, hoc est, ad perpetuum stuprum hortari, nec hortari solum verbis improbis, sed exemplo quoque foedissimo prouocare: Dic, inquam, praeclare professor Euangelii, vel tu Euangelista Lutheri, vel Christus tuus Lutherus ipse, an haec flagitia facere et docete, id demum sit Euangelium profiteri?*

[76]*CW*, vol. 8, pp. 1294-1315.

that he wanted a pope with very limited authority in the church. I think he was heart and soul a conciliarist.

Many reviewers took exception to my remarks, though no one presented a text to refute them.[77] The nature of More's polemical works does indeed make the matter difficult. If More was a conciliarist, he would hardly have been able to argue the point while he defended the Catholic church against the heretics. He simply could not say to Luther and Tyndale, "Yes, the pope should have his wings clipped and be caged by the general council." He was lawyer enough to understand how damaging such an admission would have been in a trial that would decide the church's very existence in the world. As he himself said when he evaded a discussion of the papacy, once the question of the church was settled, another question might be raised about the place of the pope in the church.[78]

[77]See especially the rebuttal by John M. Headley, "On More and the Papacy," *Moreana,* 41 (1974): 5-10. I was especially annoyed by the review by Dom Hubert Dauphin, *Revue d'Histoire Ecclésiastique,* 70 (1975): 140-144. Dom Dauphin appears unable to understand either Thomas More or me: "Cette position de More sur la question de "Eglise est longuement étudiée par Richard C. Marius dans la deuxième partie de l'introduction . . . et généralement le problème est bien posé. Il arrive a l'A. de differer de J. M. Headley, l'éditeur dans la même collection, de la *Responsio ad Lutherum;* en particulier sur le pape et ses prerogatives. Il y aurait tendance a faire de More un partisan du conciliarisme, car il est plus réservé que S. John Fisher sur le pouvoir du pape. Cependant, s'il répugne a déclarer très nettement ses vues en une époque où la prudence était necessaire, il en a dit assez pour montrer que sa position est catholique: et s'il cite explicitement les paroles de Fisher sur ce point, n'est-ce pas parce qu'il y souscrit et qu'elles représentent aussi sa propre pensée? Quoi qu'il en soit, la constitution des Etats-Unis ne semble pas un terme de comparaison très heureux pour définir une position prise an XVIes. De même rien ne prouve que More ait accepté la position d'un Gerson ou d'un Pierre d'Ailly. N'allon pas trop loin dans le domaine de la spéculation!"

I could easily write a long essay on the vacuity of these remarks. I shall limit myself to saying only that More was always prudent, but he was also a martyr to his faith, and I cannot imagine that he would have been so reserved about the papacy if he really believed that it was a mortal sin not to accept the papal supremacy. Of course his position was Catholic! The first Vatican Council was not held in the sixteenth century. One has only to read volume one of Hubert Jedin's *A History of the Council of Trent* to know that a great many Catholics in More's time and during the century before believed that primacy was not the same thing as supremacy, and that popes should be controlled by councils. I agree with Dom Dauphin that we should not go too far in the domain of speculation. But the greatest speculation of all is to make Thomas More an ardent partisan of the papal supremacy when we have not a shred of textual evidence to support such a thing.

[78]*CW,* vol. 5, pp. 139, 143. In the light of Dom Dauphin's remarks about the necessity for prudence, we should note that More's reluctance to say anything about the papacy is visible in 1523, long before anyone imagined that Henry VIII would fall out with the pope.

I think that the evidence that I have presented is in harmony with my earlier conclusions. We may ruminate a final moment about some wider consequences of More's thought concerning the papacy.

People have frequently remarked on the paltry resistance that Henry VIII met when he began his schism from Rome. Some have argued that he met with more popular resistance than earlier generations had supposed.[79] But the fact remains that only John Fisher among the bishops became a martyr. Among the monastic orders the Carthusians made a noble witness to their faith. From the laity we have the spectacular martyrdom of Thomas More. We cannot denigrate the glory of these heroic men. But neither can we say that they were typical of the English nation.

I believe that the reason for Henry's success is the obvious one. The English people had come to think that loyalty to the pope was not really the same thing as loyalty to the Catholic church. Henry was able to convince the men who held the commanding heights of his realm that he meant no more than to end the slavery of the good English people from a papacy that had gone astray.

We all know that once Henry made his break, the English church had to turn for theological support to men who believed that much more was involved in reformation than a mere schism with Rome. Thomas More probably foresaw such a result at the very beginning, and so he died.

Yet it would seem that his own hesitations about the papacy were a part of the English mentality that made the break with Rome so easy. I believe that he had much to do with the *Assertio,* with Henry's letter to the Saxon princes, and with Henry's later letter to Luther himself. And very clearly in these letters we see Henry's mind turning away from preoccupation with the papacy as the centerpiece of Catholic orthodoxy.

There are ironies in history. One may be that Thomas More contributed to a detachment from the papacy that led England to schism and himself to the scaffold.

[79]See especially C. H. Smyth, *Cranmer & The Reformation Under Edward VI* (Westport, Conn., 1970), pp. 1-15.

The Heart of the Final Struggle: More's Commentary on The Agony in The Garden

Clarence H. Miller

One of the most priceless objects featured in the 1977-78 Thomas More exhibition at the National Portrait Gallery in London is More's own manuscript of the last work he wrote. In the Tower of London, on June 12, 1535, less than a month before his martyrdom, More's long and varied literary career came to an end. On that day, when his last worldly comfort, his books and writing materials, were removed from his cell in the Tower, More had almost finished his last major work: *De tristitia, tedio, pavore, et oratione Christi ante captionem eius* (the Sadness, Weariness, Fear, and Prayer of Christ before his Capture). It is an exegetical commentary, sometimes brief and quite traditional, sometimes unfolding into long and more personal essays, on the gospel accounts of Christ's agony in the garden of Gethsemani, ending with the words *manus injectas in jesum* (they laid hands on Jesus). Apart from one, or perhaps two, short letters, this is the last work we have from More's hand.

Unlike any of his other long works, we have this one from his hand in a very literal sense. We have his own draft, written and heavily revised by his own hand, the so-called Valencia holograph. Some fifteen years ago, by a fine combination of alertness and good luck, Geoffrey Bullough rediscovered this invaluable manuscript at the Royal College and Seminary of Corpus Christi in Valencia, an institution usually called the Patriarca after its founder San Juan de Ribera, who was the Patriarch of Antioch, as well as the Archbishop and Viceroy of Valencia.

During the two decades before his death in 1611, San Juan devoted considerable time, energy, and money to establishing this liturgical center where the worship of God, and especially the Blessed Sacrament, was to be conducted with great reverence and solemnity according to his own detailed regulations. The noble church and cloister, which have the grandeur of the Escorial without its chilling immensity, are still splendidly preserved, as in San Juan's liturgy, so that the Patriarca provides an unparalleled example, not merely in stone but in living ceremony, of the intensity fostered by the Council of Trent. Hidden away behind the apse of the main church is the

Chapel of the Relics, one whole wall of which is covered by an immense reliquary closet. Locked behind the two huge, gilded doors of the closet, reposing in a tortoise-shell box side by side with a volume of sermons thought to be in the hand of the Valencian saint, Vincent Ferrer, Mr. Bullough found a small volume bound in rich cloth, once bright red and blue, but now faded and frayed. When he read San Juan's note on the inside cover identifying the manuscript as written by the hand of Thomas More, this "hidden treasure" (as San Juan called it) which had made its way from More's gloomy cell in the Tower to the sunny splendors of Spain only to become hidden for almost 400 years, once more became known to the friends and admirers of More.

Thanks mainly to San Juan's note, we can trace the history of the manuscript in considerable detail. His Spanish note may be translated:

> This book was sent to me by the Count of Oropesa, who told me that it belonged to Senor don Fernando de Toledo, to whom it had been given by the friar Father Pedro de Soto, Confessor to the Emperor, King, and Lord Charles V, because it was by Thomas More and written with his own hand.

Father Pedro de Soto, an eminent Dominican theologian, who died in 1563 at the Council of Trent, was in England for about sixteen months in 1555-1556, at the invitation of his friend Cardinal Pole, whom he assisted in the task of restoring the English Church to union with Rome. While he was teaching at Oxford, de Soto wrote a polemical work, the *Defensio Catholicae Confessionis,* which he had printed at Antwerp in 1557 on his way back to Spain. In this work he tells us that he took the greatest pleasure in conversations about More with those who had known him well. They told him of More's words and deeds, and even presented him with some of More's writings. Savoring these reminiscences, de Soto wrote, he found more ease and refreshment for his weary spirit than in the lovely English gardens. While de Soto was in England, More's granddaughter Mary Bassett was a lady in waiting, and her husband James was a gentleman of the chamber, at the court of King Philip and Queen Mary. Mary Bassett translated the *De Tristitia Christi* for Rastell's edition of More's English Works, published in 1557; and, though she did not translate directly from the manuscript, some of her marginal remarks make it clear that she had seen it. In all likelihood she had inherited it from her mother Margaret Roper, More's beloved daughter Meg, who died in 1544. When de Soto was recalled to the Low Countries by the Emperor in the fall of 1556, he received (according to the Venetian ambassador) handsome presents from

Queen Mary and Cardinal Pole, who were very sorry to see him go. Perhaps the Queen or Pole, himself a professed admirer of More, was instrumental in procuring the holograph for de Soto. Certainly it would have been a handsome present for a theologian who had taken a vow of poverty, and who was a loyal servant of Charles V, the nephew of Katherine of Aragon.

The manuscript almost surely came into the possession of Mary Bassett's mother Margaret after being smuggled out of the Tower by More's servant John à Wood, or one of his visitors. If the work had fallen into the hands of More's persecutors, it seems unlikely that they would have wished it to be published. It contains no opinion punishable under the statute by which More was convicted, but its profound and pointed discussion of martyrdom might have been embarrassing to the party in power. The physical make-up of the manuscript shows that the leaves of the eight individual gatherings were stitched together when More wrote, but the gatherings themselves had not yet been bound together. They are of an unusually, perhaps designedly, compact size.

Another feature of the manuscript, the stiff piece of parchment used to make its cover, shows that it was bound in or near Louvain, probably after Pedro de Soto had acquired it, and before he returned with it to Spain in 1558. The parchment is part of a discarded legal document which, from its mention of a Cardinal of Tortosa, can be dated between 1517 and 1534, and which concerns persons and places in Louvain.

Sometime before 1561, when he left Spain for the last time to journey to Rome and the final sessions of the Council of Trent, Pedro de Soto gave the manuscript to Don Fernando de Toledo. From my point of view, he could hardly have made a worse choice. The mystical mazes of the sixteenth-century Spanish nobility, which no one should ever enter unless he has a taste for such things as modern mathmatics or blindfold chess, are profusely decorated with a nobleman named Don Fernando de Toledo. Fortunately, an early biographer of San Juan de Ribera mentions a certain Don Fernando de Toledo, a brother of the Count of Oropesa, as one of San Juan's closest friends from the time of his university days at Salamanca. This Don Fernando became a priest and refused Gregory XIII's offer of a cardinalate in order to devote himself to serving the poor. He also sent San Juan a collection of his own sermons written by his own hand. Unfortunately, among the known progeny of the first six counts of Oropesa, some of whom were sufficiently polyphilopro-genitive, no count has a brother named Don Fernando. In the light of the evidence we have, the best hypothesis is that San Juan's friend, Don Fernando de Toledo, who probably had the manuscript for at least ten years, was an illegitimate son of the fourth count, over-looked by the genealogists because of his bastardy and obscurity. Thus he would be the brother of Don Juan Garcia Alvarez de Toledo, who became the fifth Count of Oropesa in 1571, and is almost surely the count mentioned in San Juan's note.

In 1626, two distinguished visitors to Valencia, the papal legate Cardinal Francesco Barberini and Cardinal Giulio Sacchetti, were escorted to the Chapel of the Relics, where they were shown the More manuscript, together with other precious relics. In 1697 it was mentioned as one of the notable sights of Valenica. In 1904 it was mentioned in passing in a little known Spanish book about the Patriarca. The official lists of the relics in the reliquary closet do not mention it until 1947, after More's canonization. The official biography of San Juan de Ribera, which appeared for his canonization in 1960, also mentions it in a brief footnote. But for all practical purposes the treasure remained hidden until Geoffrey Bullough brought it to light in 1963.

These historical facts and conjectures about the transmission of the manuscript may allay some of our surprise at finding a holograph of More so far from home. But external evidence is merely useful to confirm, not at all necessary to prove, the authenticity of the manu-script. There is ample evidence that More was the author of the *De Tristitia*: besides his granddaughter's translation, two sixteenth-century manuscripts, and the 1565 edition of his Latin works, reliably attribute the work to More. And the Valencia manuscript is clearly authorial: no one but the author could have written it because the writer revised during the very process of composition, pruning, shap-ing, changing constructions in mid-sentence. It is doubtful that any scribe could have reproduced the complex cancellations and revi-sions; it is all but certain that none ever would have done so. And the physical make-up of the manuscript rules out the faintest possibility that it is the work of some incredibly clever modern forger. The Val-encia manuscript authenticates itself, and the few other pieces written in More's italic hand must be authenticated by comparison with it.

Certainly the Valencia manuscript is the most noble relic of Thomas More, as Fr. Marc'hadour has called it. Beginning in 1965, I worked with the manuscript (or a microfilm of it) for over ten years, deciphering, transcribing, peering, prying, puzzling, wondering, speculating, imagining, sometimes cursing, praying, or waiting for some secret inspiration. In the spring of 1967, I spent three intense weeks with the manuscript itself, all but oblivious to the subtropical splendors—the flowers, fruit, and fish—of Valencia. Perhaps it was no accident that I finished on Thursday, the octave of the feast of Corpus Christi, and emerged from the dim archive room into the sunny cloister just as the eucharistic procession was beginning, performed exactly according to the directives of San Juan himself, complete with strewn rose petals and sixteenth-century polyphony. At any rate, the results of my labors have been preserved, not to say embalmed, in two volumes of the Yale edition which appeared in 1976.[1] I would like to touch on three points elaborated in considerable detail in my edition. The manuscript is especially valuable for three reasons: (1) it provides an absolutely authoritative text for the work itself; (2) it gives an unparalleled view of More in the actual process of shaping his thought and language; and (3) it brings into prominence a somewhat neglected work which reveals, perhaps better than anything else he wrote, the ultimate grounds of his martyrdom.

But first, if I may be allowed a brief digression, I would like to reflect for a moment on a topic not discussed in my edition, though the raw material for it is there in the second commentary—I mean More's way of interpreting scripture, his exegetical method. Naturally, More was writing for an educated audience, since he wrote in Latin, but he was not writing for professional theologians or expert exegetes, as his friend Erasmus had done in his edition of the Greek New Testament. He does not fragment his discussion into numerous logical questions and subdivisions like the medieval exegetes, nor has he abandoned Erasmian, humanistic principles of biblical interpretation and translation.[2] He is aware of Erasmus' work and occasionally makes use of it. His main purpose is not academic or theoretical, but practical and moral. But the text and the cancelled jottings show that he knows of some difficulties and problems which he deliberately ignores, because they are not closely applicable to his own immediate circumstances and those of his family, friends, and fellow countrymen.

The range of his sources is extremely broad—from Origen to Theophylactus, from Tetullian to Jerome, Augustine, and Bede.

[1] *The Complete Works of Sir Thomas More,* vol. 14, *De Tristitia Christi,* ed. Clarence Miller (New Haven, 1976).
[2] Louis Martz, "Thomas More: The Sacramental Life," *Thought,* 52 (September, 1977):300-318, and Heinz Holeczek, *Humanistiche Bibelphilogie als Reformproblem bei Erasmus von Roterdam, Thomas More, und William Tyndale* (Leiden, 1975).

Most, but not all of them, were ready-to-hand in medieval compendia like the *Glossa ordinaria* or the *Catena aurea* of Aquinas. Nor does More neglect the medieval commentators, including Nicolas de Lyra, and his "corrector" Paul of Santa Maria. Surveying 1200 years of biblical commentary, More shapes and focuses it on contemporary and immediate issues. One reason that More was infuriated by Protestant reformers like Tyndale was that they insisted on consigning *in toto* eight hundred years of Western Christendom and Western Christians to outer darkness and eternal perdition. Indeed, in one place More went out of his way to add a passage updating a standard interpretation of the first two words of the Lord's Prayer by applying it to reformers who claim private inspiration instead of sharing in the common inspiration of the church. By the words "Our Father," says More, "we acknowledge that we are all brothers who have one Father in common, whereas Christ Himself is the only one who can rightfully, because of His divinity, address the Father as he does here, 'My Father.'"

But More does not intend simply to give an objective cross-section of biblical scholarship like the modern Jerome commentary. On some points he disagrees, modestly but firmly, with such luminaries as Jerome and even with his favorite among the fathers, Augustine. On a few points his interpretations are, so far as I can tell, original extensions of traditional interpretations, or else entirely original. More believed that scripture must be approached by considering the mind of the church throughout the ages, but he also held that the inspired pages are so rich that there is always something left for each age and each reader to discover through diligent and devout scrutiny. God's word must continually be brought home to the business and bosoms of men. Hence, some of his original interpretations concern the burning issues of his time, such as heresies about the eucharist, and the sinful failure of bishops to stand up against heresy. They also concern a most urgent question for More himself: should a person be reluctant to die a martyr's death or eager to seek it out?— a question to which we shall return. But now back to our three points.

First, the text. Since More was executed less than a month after his work on the Valencia manuscript was interrupted, it is very unlikely that he had any opportunity to make further revisions, and the Valencia manuscript has full and absolute authority in establishing the text. The real value of such an authoritative source can perhaps be fully appreciated only by those who have had to struggle with the snarled and difficult textual problems of such works as *Richard III*, the *Utopia,* and the *Dialogue of Comfort against Tribulation.* For no other long work of More can we be absolutely certain that we have all of the text in all its details exactly as More intended it.

But the Valencia manuscript is far more important for what it reveals about More's own habits of composition and the qualities he strove to achieve in his thinking and writing. First, it shows that More wrote very quickly. Though his hand, even in his illness, is bold, clear, and swift, his mind frequently outran his pen so that he sometimes began a word too soon and had to cancel it, or omitted a word, or part of a word, and had to go back and interline it, or hastily anticipated part of a following word. He worked so quickly that he often plunged into a sentence before he was completely certain about the construction of the whole sentence. Usually he swept through quite triumphantly, making a few necessary adjustments as he went, but occasionally he wrote himself into such a corner that he had to go back and reshape the sentence.

If he wrote quickly, he also strove to write clearly. We cannot say from the manuscript whether More thought this work might eventually be printed, but he certainly made copy so legible and unambiguous as to furnish a reliable basis for a fair copy. In such a heavily revised work, it is remarkable how few of the errors in the succeeding manuscripts and editions are due to peculiarities or difficulties in the holograph. I can find only four instances: More's *"olim"* was misread as *"diu,"* his *"uultum"* as *"multum,"* his *"nisus"* as *"uisus,"* and his *"agit animus"* as *"agitauimus."* More sometimes cancels and rewrites a word simply because a letter or two was badly formed. He carefully avoids dividing words at the end of a line, even when it means cancelling part of a word he has already begun. He sometimes draws framing lines to avoid confusion between the main body of the text and additions in the margin or at the bottom of the page. He is very careful to place a caret-mark before interlined words, and a matching mark beneath the place where the addition is to be inserted. Where there is a chance of confusion, he even distinguishes pairs of carets by placing one, or sometimes two, dots within the carets. He is sparing and careful in his use of abbreviations, except in a few places where he is extremely pressed for space. In fact, it is remarkably easy to produce the final version of the text as More intended it. The trouble comes in deciphering heavily cancelled words or preliminary jottings that More intended only for his own use.

This clarity should serve to correct any tendency to overstress the purely personal and biographical significance of the work, however valid and poignant that may be. If there has been some attempt to emphasize the personal and biographical import of such a formally structured, dramatic work as the *Dialogue of Comfort,* the danger is even greater with the *De Tristitia,* which more nearly resembles a collection of essays. When More said he intended to devote himself to meditation on the Passion during his imprisonment, no one need doubt that he had quite personal reasons for undertaking these spiritual exercises, entirely apart from his desire to avoid any incriminating topics in his conversation and writing. Nevertheless, to find relief from his emotional distress, to control and channel his fear, to find meaning and even fruit in his weariness, More needed not merely to realize his feelings in ordered literary composition, not even merely to assimilate them to the sufferings of Christ, except insofar as that also included imparting his meditations, his comfort, to the suffering members of Christ's body, to his family and friends, to the pastors and bishops of England, and to all those who would face martyrdom (of whatever sort) in his own and later times. However emergent his occasions, More never became as self-absorbed in his devotions as his great grand-nephew John Donne.

The clarity of the Valencia manuscript is especially evident when the final text is contrasted with the telegraphic jottings More made for his own use. These notes, which are usually only fragments of sentences, are uniformly difficult to decipher, though it is almost always possible to discover their relevance to the finished work. Both sides of the first leaf were wholly given over to such notes, but the others were squeezed in at the bottom of pages More had already finished. Since the binder cut away the first and last leaves of the gatherings whenever he could do so without removing any of the final text, we may well have lost other leaves containing preliminary notes.

Among these notes, the ones More rejected and omitted are often as interesting as the ones he expanded and incorporated into the final text. For example, some of the omitted ideas were intended as arguments to be assigned to More's imaginary opponent, who insists that he cannot understand why Christ chose to feel fear in the face of death, since this would surely set a bad example for future Christian martyrs, who ought to rejoice at the prospect of their future reward. One item in the cluster of jottings connected with the opponent's arguments, and More's answers, was never used. It runs *"et maiora hijs facient sed non suis uiribus"* (and they shall do greater things than these, but not by their own power), and alludes to Christ's words at the last supper in the 14th chapter of John's gospel: *"Amen*

*amen dico vobis qui credit in me opera quae ego facio et ipse faciet:
et maiora horum faciet: quia ego ad patrem vado"* (Amen amen I
say to you whoever believes in me will do the deeds that I do; and he
will do even greater ones than these, because I go to the father). The
idea that Christ's followers would do greater things than Christ
Himself has relevance to the question whether Christ's martyrs com-
ported themselves better, by their fearlessness, than Christ Himself,
who was afraid; and hence it supports the opponent's assertion—
emphatically denied by More—that no Christian ought to be afraid
of a martyr's death. More did not incorporate the text into his opponent's arguments, perhaps because it is a very difficult saying that
requires much explanation. More's own addition *"sed non suis
uiribus"* (but not by their own power)—which has ample precedent
in the *Glossa ordinaria* and Nicolas de Lyra—is a basic step in
resolving the difficulties, but Augustine gives four possible explana-
tions of the text. At any rate, when we see More here tempted to
strengthen his opponent's arguments, we may remember his mild
boast in one of his polemical works, that he had sometimes presented
the heretics' case more fully and subtly than did they themselves.

More's revisions, as distinct from his cancelled jottings, tend to
center on single sentences or small groups of sentences, rather than
on whole paragraphs or long sections. He usually revised as he
wrote, interlining often in two or three stages, sometimes interlining
within the interlineations until he was forced into the margin or the
bottom of the page. The larger structural plan of the work was partly
predetermined by the progression of the biblical passage on which
More was commenting, even though More creates a different sort of
pattern by the space and emphasis he devotes to various texts, and
sometimes by explicitly contrasting one section with another. Within
the sections More seems to have had his main points fairly well lined
up before he began writing. Only once do the revisions show him
hesitating and vacillating about the order in which to present the
main points of one of the longer sections.

Judging from the writing and pen-strokes, keeping in mind that a
writer may well sharpen his pen during the actual course of writing, I
would say that the *De Tristitia*, which is almost as long as the
Utopia, was written in about twenty-five sittings, averaging about six
manuscript pages and ranging in length from hardly a page to over
twenty pages—this longest sitting being the last. These sittings were
usually broken off in the middle of a section—once even in the
middle of a sentence—so that More had to keep the progression of
his ideas in mind in spite of interruptions. When he began writing

afresh, he sometimes read over the last few pages he had written, making a few additional revisions. But the Valencia manuscript provides only the slightest evidence that he read over and further revised whole sections. It is impossible to say whether some revisions were made during actual composition or at a later time, but many, perhaps most, of them had to be made at the actual time of writing. In a couple of places More left a blank, intending to return and supply a name or fill in a biblical quotation. In one or two places we can be fairly sure that a slight revision was made sometime after a page was originally written and revised, because a word or two interlined at the top of the page was still wet enough, when the page was turned, to leave a mirror-image on the facing page. And twice More made additions of some length by inserting a pair of pages into a finished gathering. But on the whole, More seems to have been the sort of writer who has his main points pretty firmly and fully outlined before he begins to write, and who then revises his sentences rather thoroughly as he writes, not shifting or shaping large units, but producing a near-final version without the need for a further stage of thorough-going revision.

The frequent revisions in the Valencia holograph also give us a rare opportunity to analyze More's style as it reflects the movements of his mind and feelings. We can examine the choices and changes he made in diction and sentence structure as he strove to express his meaning and tone with the greatest accuracy and intensity. Such an examination can also reveal something about the ebb and flow of his mind as he struggled to achieve equipoise between conflicting opinions and impulses.

In diction and phrasing More's revisions show him striving for precision and accuracy, weighing one word against another, exercising a lawyerlike caution to avoid any possible misunderstanding or misconstruction. At the same time, they often reveal a tendency seemingly at odds with such restraint: an effort to achieve persuasive force by amplifying his clauses, packing them with additional details, adding the momentum of repetitive phrasing or sound. Similarly, in the framing of his sentences, More often moves toward balanced and parallel constructions, but he also sometimes seems deliberately to eliminate balance in favor of asymmetry and to introduce sudden, not quite logical, shifts in point of view.

In his pursuit of accuracy More occasionally found it necessary to correct mere errors of fact: hence the change from *"apostoli"* to *"euangeliste"* because Mark, one of the persons referred to, was an evangelist, but not an apostle. Usually, such revisions depend on more subtle distinctions, whether literary, legal, or theological. He refined a few comparisons to make them more logical and consistent. More often the changes reveal a legal mind at work, refining and qualifying absolute judgments to take account of the necessary conditions and exceptions. One example of lawyerlike caution concerns a primary question discussed in the *De Tristitia:* should a candidate for martyrdom willingly offer himself to his persecutors? Granting part of his imaginary opponent's position, More originally wrote: "To expose one's self to death for Christ's sake is, I admit, a work of extraordinary virtue."³ The final version is not only softened by litotes ("I do not deny"), but also qualified by two important conditions: "To expose one's self to death for Christ's sake when the case clearly demands it or when God gives a secret prompting to do so, this, I do not deny, is a deed of pre-eminent virtue."

More is especially cautious when he is dealing with theological matters, moral or doctrinal. His insistence that when the church is persecuted bishops must not allow their sadness to prevent them from acting for the salvation of their flock, was very carefully phrased to begin with, and was rendered even more precise by his revisions. His revisions show his exactitude about such doctrinal points as the difference between the interior and exterior acts of the Trinity, God the Father's free decision as the source of what is possible or impossible, the hierarchical ranking of saints in heaven, and the degree to which prophets know the content of each other's prophecies. But he took the greatest pains when he tried to express precisely the union of divinity and humanity in the person of Christ.

The cancellations and substitutions in the autograph show More exercising more care in his choice of diction than we might otherwise have suspected. He very often substituted one word for another when the use of a doublet would have saved him the trouble of choosing between them. Nor were the choices always easy: in four places, having interlined a synonym above a word, he was unable to make up his mind and left both uncancelled, not resorting to a doublet but reserving the decision till later. Refinements of diction, slight added strokes of the brush, sometimes create or intensify nuances and crosslights of irony, particularly concerning Judas. More almost never mentions the traitor without stressing the irony of his position, deeds, and death. In sentences as taut as those of *Richard III,* More particularly pinpoints the irony that Judas rejoices in his power to cause Christ's death, completely unaware that his own death will precede that of his victim:

³Here, and in the following selections I have translated More's Latin.

For though a man may send someone else to his death, he himself is sure
to follow him there. Even more, since the hour of death is uncertain, he
himself may precede the very person he arrogantly imagines he has sent
to death ahead of him.

In a lighter vein, More sometimes changed or added words that
created a tone of wry, self-depreciatory irony. Arguing with an imaginary opponent who insists that eager martyrs receive a greater reward in heaven than do fearful ones, More answers that how the
various degrees of reward are granted in heaven is, in our present
state of earthly darkness, not quite crystal clear. Anticipating that his
opponent might legitimately cite the text "God loves a cheerful
giver," More replies that God also loved Tobias and Job, neither of
whom was particularly cheerful in his affliction: "For, though I
grant that God loves a cheerful giver, still I have no doubt that he
loved Tobias, and holy Job too. Now it is true that both of them
bore their calamities bravely and patiently, but neither of them, so
far as I know, was exactly jumping with joy or clapping his hands
out of happiness." "So far as I know," which heightens the tongue-
in-cheek tone, was entirely missing in the original version.

Thus More's revisions throughout the autograph show a constant
pursuit of precision and refinement, both of thought and style. On
the other hand, they also reveal, especially in passages of intense
feeling and persuasive energy, a tendency to double synonyms, to
pile up details, to load, pack, and weigh down clauses and phrases
far beyond the requirements of accuracy, clarity, or logic. Sometimes, when words flood in upon him, More seems loathe to let any
of them go. Heaping obloquy on Christ's persecutors, More seems
unwilling to omit and eager to add. He is especially willing to multi-
ply vivid details in his exhortation to mental concentration and
reverent deportment in prayer. It is not surprising that such intensive
amplification should also be associated not only with prayer but also
with More's second major preoccupation: the fear and mental
anguish of Christ and His martyrs. In his discussion of the contrast
between fearless and fearful martyrs, More grants that fearless
martyrs may animate others to similar bravery, but he insists that
many may find help in the example of fearful martyrs who gained
heaven by conquering their fear. Originally, his vindication of those
"who have held up shaking hands in the fire, and humanely contend-
ed for glory," was rather direct and straightforward:

Who can know how many have also been helped by those whom we see
face death with fear and trembling but nevertheless bravely break
through such great obstacles.

In the final version, the last clause is stretched out almost unendurably to give the feeling of enormous difficulty triumphantly overcome:

> Who can know how many have also been helped by those whom we see
> face death with fear and trembling but whom we also observe as they
> break bravely through the hindrances blocking their path, the obstacles
> barring their way with barriers harder than steel, that is, their own weariness, fear, and anguish, and by bursting these iron bars and triumphing
> over death take heaven by storm?

Thus far we have traced opposite tendencies revealed by More's revisions of diction and clauses: on the one hand, caution, accuracy, precision, refinement; on the other, enthusiasm, intensification, expansion, amplification. A similar contrast appears in the structure of phrases, clauses, and whole sentences: a movement toward balanced, parallel constructions, expressing either similarity or contrast; and a countermovement toward deliberate asymmetry, imbalance, and sudden shifts in point of view. The balanced elements are often clauses or even whole sentences, but words and phrases within the large frames are frequently drawn into such patterns of comparison and contrast. The parallelism introduced by More through his revisions sometimes touches directly on such dominant polarities in the *De Tristitia* as body and soul, Christ's divinity and humanity, and eager and fearful martyrs.

Such balanced parallels and contrasts are also dominant features of the larger structural patterns of the *De Tristitia*. Though the progression of More's reflections is fixed by the sequence of biblical verses, and though he feels compelled, at least, to mention the traditional questions and answers about each text, he was still free to emphasize certain points above others and to focus on subjects especially applicable to himself and his contemporaries: martyrdom, prayer, the dangers of modern heresies (especially those concerning the eucharist), and—pervading all of these—the union of suffering humanity with omnipotent divinity in the person of Christ. On these points, and others, the movement of his thoughts reveals the flux and reflux of a mind considering and reconciling opposite views. Reading the *De Tristitia* reminds us how pervasively such a dialectic of contrasting viewpoints is woven into the fabric of More's writings. The ironical cross-lights of *Richard III*, the give-and-take of the dialogues (whether between More and Hythloday, More and the Messenger, or Antony and Vincent), the statement and counterstatement of the polemical works emanated from a mind habitually accustomed to debating both sides of an issue, whether in an academic exercise on tyrannicide or an actual legal case. A group of polarities, most of them related to each other and to the united duality of Christ, pervades the *De Tristitia:* humanity and divinity, body and soul, passion and reason, the literal and figurative meanings of scriptures, fearful martyrs and brave ones. Two lengthy sections on prayer are conceived as weight and counterweight: in the first More insists on mental concentration, which ought to be reflected, and even intensified, by a reverent deportment of body; in the second he offers consolations (drawn from Gerson) for those who may be too scrupulous about distractions during prayer. Feelings such as sadness may be salutary or fatal according to whether reason brings them into a right relationship with Christ. The literal sense of scripture teems with figurative meanings just as the soul permeates all parts of the body. Body and soul are joined in Christ no more completely than humanity and divinity. Christ felt fear, but He offered Himself bravely to His enemies. To the brave martyr Christ's fear offers a check against presumption; to the fearful martyr it offers consolation and comfort.

Nevertheless, in spite of his deliberate use of parallel, balanced, and contrasting structures, More's Latin style in the *De Tristitia* is not at all reminiscent of Isocratean balance or Ciceronian roundness. It is so restless, nervous, and muscular (sometimes even muscle-bound) that Monsuez was quite right in suggesting an affinity with the anti-Ciceronianism which can be found in the Latin writings of some of More's comtemporaries and immediate predecessors, buɩ which finally triumphed and flourished, in both Latin and English, in the first half of the seventeenth century. In a series of pioneering essays, Morris Croll first mapped out this new territory of stylistic criticism, naming the style "baroque," subdividing it into "curt," and "grand," and identifying it with such qualities as parataxis, asymmetry, and shifts in point of view, which give the impression of a mind thinking rather than thought already found and formulated.[4]

The baroque character of More's sentences in the *De Tristitia* suggests that the parallel dichotomies I have already described (reason and passion, body and soul, fearful and eager martyrs) are not finally allowed to stand in a merely static balance, but are finally resolved by a deep awareness of God's providential love in the person of Christ. Just as More's style is not only precise and careful, but also exuberent and exultant, not only balanced but also baroque, so too his was a mind that weighed questions carefully, precisely, pru-

[4]R. Monsuez, "Le Latin de Thomas More dans 'Utopia,'" *Annales publiées par la Faculté des Lettres et Sciences Humaines de Toulouse,* Nouvelle Série, Tome II, Fasc. 1 (January, 1966), *Caliban 3,* 35-78, and *Style, Rhetoric, and Rhythm: Essays by Morris W. Croll,* ed. J. Max Patrick, et al. (Princeton, N.J., 1966).

dently, even ironically, but which also resolved all oppositions and conflicts by fervent response to Christ, who reconciles all contrarieties and unites all things in Himself. The style bespeaks a man who had the patience and skill to avoid, during many months, and under importunate inquisition, giving his opinion on the oath of supremacy. It also bespeaks a man who, after he was finally condemned, spoke out eloquently and lovingly in defense of Christ's church, and with forgiveness for those who condemned him.

Indeed, the *De Tristitia* gives us the fullest and deepest explanation of why More strove so intently to save himself from death by hiding behind the law, and it tells us better than anything else why More died, the motive of his martyrdom. Hence, it may serve to correct (or perhaps better, to complete) the two best known modern portrayals of More – that is, R.W. Chambers' biography, and Robert Bolt's *A Man for All Seasons.*[5] More hid behind the law not merely because he was afraid (though he was that), and not merely because the law represented the shelter society offers against the terrifying cosmos, as Bolt would have it. He hid out of a humble awareness that if he exerted all his strength to save himself and was unable to do so, he would be sure that it was God's will for him to die a martyr's death. He admitted that some men might be inspired by God to seek out martyrdom, but he thought it safer to exhaust every legitimate means to escape; for then he could be certain not only that he was not deceived by presumptuous pride, not only that it was God's will that he should die, but also that God would give him the strength to do so. In fact, More strongly suspected that the way he chose, the humble and surer way, might indeed be more difficult than the eager pursuit of a martyr's death. Of the eager martyr he comments:

> Besides is it not possible that God in His goodness removes fear from some persons not because He approves of or intends to reward their boldness, but rather because He is aware of their weakness and knows that they would not be equal to facing fear. For some have yielded to fear, even though they won out later when the actual tortures were inflicted. . . . And so God proportions the temperaments of His martyrs according to His own providence in such a way that one rushes forth eagerly to his death, another creeps out hesitantly and fearfully, but for all that bears his death none the less bravely—unless someone perhaps imagines he ought to be thought less brave for having fought down not only his other enemies but also his own weariness, sadness, and fear— most strong feelings and mighty enemies indeed.

[5] R.W. Chambers, *Thomas More* (Ann Arbor, Mich., 1958), Robert Bolt, *A Man For All Seasons: a play in two acts* (London, 1960; New York, 1962).

Bolt and Chambers give varying grounds for More's martyrdom: the integrity of the self as witnessed by an oath, the irreducible freedom of the individual conscience in the face of an authoritarian state, papal supremacy as a sign of the supranational unity of Western Christendom, past and present. All of these are true as far as they go. But in the last analysis, More did not die for any principle, or idea, or tradition, or even doctrine, but for a person, for Christ. As Bolt himself makes More say in the play: "Well . . . finally . . . it isn't a matter of reason; finally it's a matter of love." If for More that love was love of the church, it was so only insofar as the church is made up of Christian persons in whom Christ is present and who constitute the mystical body of Christ. It is not easy to cite short passages from the *De Tristitia* which reveal this final motive of More's martyrdom, though I think the fact will be clear to anyone who reads the whole work. Perhaps we come closest to realizing the martyr's loving dependence on Christ as a person when More imagines Christ's speech to those who are afraid to die:

> O faint of heart, take courage and do not despair. You are afraid, you are sad, you are stricken with weariness and dread of the torments with which you have been cruelly threatened. Trust me. I conquered the world, and yet I suffered immeasurably more from fear, I was sadder, more afflicted with weariness, more horrified at the prospect of such cruel suffering drawing eagerly nearer and nearer. Let the brave man have his high-spirited martyrs, let him rejoice in imitating a thousand of them. But you, my timorous and feeble little sheep, be content to have me alone as your shepherd, follow me as your leader; if you do not trust yourself, place your trust in me. See, I am walking ahead of you along this fearful road.

Indeed the real presence of the suffering Christ is the core of all three of the long Tower works. The English *Treatise on the Passion* culminates in a subtle theoretical discussion of Christ's presence in the eucharist, signifying both His suffering body on the cross and the mystical body of His church. *A Dialogue of Comfort against Tribulation* reaches its climax in a meditation on the physical sufferings of Christ on the cross. And one of the major concerns of the *De Tristitia* is a psychological analysis of Christ's mental suffering, His fear and weariness, His victory over them through prayer, in the Garden of Olives.

The Ironic and the Prophetic: Towards Reading More's *Utopia* as a Multidisciplinary Work

Richard J. Schoeck

Let me offer a text for my paper. A king should take history as his mistress (echoing the Ciceronian *historia magistra vitae*), for in this way, as that most learned of More's contemporaries, Guillaume Budé, wrote: "A wise prince can resemble Janus, who is represented with two faces seeing equally well forwards and backwards."[1] When one looks both forwards and backwards, the ironic and the prophetic may both be generated and brought into play, especially where there is the dissimulation of pretended ignorance and the semblance of inspired utterance. With clearer understanding of the ironic and the prophetic, we can move away from the purely biographical, or the still-current notion that *Utopia* is only a *jeu d' esprit* (what I would term the synecdochical fallacy: seeing a part for the whole), or reading the work as only political, or philosophical, or rhetorical, or whatever. Readers have rarely tried to look at *Utopia* as a whole, as a structure of relationships.

I want to stress More's book as it appeared in 1516, considering it as both a visual and a verbal production, and then move to some of the parerga and Budé's letter in particular. I shall conclude by offering additional possibilities that may enable us to look more fully, more clearly at More's multidisciplinary work as a whole.

---

[1] *De Philologia*, p. 81, quoted in Donald R. Kelley, *Foundations of Modern Historical Scholarship* (New York, 1970), p. 65. Pictor's *Theologia mythologica* (Antwerp, 1532), began with Janus: see Don C. Allen, *Mysteriously Meant: the Rediscovery of Pagan Symbolism and Allegorical Interpretation in the Renaissance* (Baltimore, 1970), pp. 219-20. Later, Guillaume Du Choul in *Discours de la religion des Anciens Romains* (1556) – "apparently the first student of ancient cult to use the reverse of coins as illustrative documents"—expands the symbolism of Janus, drawing from some coins which gave him a double face to signify man's progress from savagery to civility, and from other coins in which his double head may be read as peace or as prudence; on coins of Hadrian, Janus has four faces to represent the four climates of the world (ibid., pp. 257-8). Janus was known to both Dante and Chaucer, and More has an epigram which speaks of "the two-faced god, Janus *[who]* saw everything in front of him and behind him," no. 143 in *The Latin Epigrams of Thomas More*, ed. Leicester Bradner and Charles A. Lynch (Chicago, 1953), p. 190.

Not until 1579, with the publication of Spenser's *Shepheardes Calender* and its elaborate glosses, would there be another such attempt to launch an instant classic: to establish a text with the fullest measure of authority, to give it all the visual apparatus of tradition, as there was in 1516 with the publication of More's *Utopia*. Consider what was given, and how it was given, to the first readers: (1) the title-page, with the original title: *Libellus vere aureus nec minus slautaris quam festivus de optimo reipublicae statu deque nova insula Utopia* (the word *Utopia* not appearing until the end of the third line); (2) on the reverse of the title-page, a rough woodcut of the island (to which I shall return); (3) then the Utopian alphabet with a *Tetrastichon vernacula Utopiensium lingua,* and on the reverse a *Hexastichon Anemoli* (containing the pun of Utopia/Eutopia); (4) the letter from Peter Giles to Busleyden, with one from Paludanus to Giles; which is followed by (5) Elegiac verses; and (6) the letter of Busleyden to More, and More's prefatory letter to Giles. The printing in Roman letter is "close and unattractive to the eye, and full of contractions"—in short, as much like a medieval manuscript in appearance as possible.[2] The marginal notes or glosses are in blackletter; this feature not only sets them apart from the text even more, it was supposed to give them greater authority.

Let us return to the map of the island. It is entitled: *Utopiae Insulae Figura.* We are given a tract of land shaped like a horseshoe, with the opening at the bottom, and the sea all around it; a large ship in the foreground, trees and buildings on the mainland in the background. In the middle of the entrance there is a large ship, and a fort has been erected there. A river follows the line of the curve on the island, its source at the left labelled *fons anydri,* and its mouth on the right *ostium anydri.* Temples or public buildings appear at intervals, on the uppermost the inscription *civitas amaurautum.* Despite the text in Book II which speaks of the homogeneity of buildings in Utopia, those pictured are all different. There is a slightly different woodcut in the 1518 edition, which reduces the number of buildings, adds figures in the foreground, changes the inscription from *civitas* to *Amaurotum urbs,* and adds plant-like chains connecting the island to the mainland —interesting changes which bespeak attention to the visual. The title of the sketch in 1516 (slightly modified in 1518) is *Utopiae Insulae Figura,* and I take *figura* here as significant: literally it is a form or shape, or, a sketch or map, but rhetorically it is a figure of speech, especially one which contains hints or allusions—thus the *Figura* of

[2]Quoted in J.H. Lupton, *Introduction to "Utopia"* (Oxford, 1895), p. lxvi.

Erich Auerbach.[3] In an age which we sometimes are asked to think was totally literal, Budé, we must observe, suggested even in his textual criticism the superiority of the figurative to the literal sense (*vagina est historia, gladius est litteraturae spiritus*).[4]

To elucidate still further the kind of impact *Utopia* as book had at its first appearance let us go back to More's own efforts. Before September 20, 1516, More had sent Erasmus his *Nusquam* (as he called it), and on that date he wrote Erasmus:

> I am most anxious to have it published soon and also that it be handsomely set off with the highest of recommendations, if possible, from several people, both intellectuals and distinguished statesmen.[5]

This was done, as we have been reminded by Peter Allen, and by Warren Wooden.[6] Rogers thinks that More alluded to Busleyden as one who "regrets that the work is being published before the lapse of nine years," but that is not supported by Busleyden's letter; and with Allen I think that the allusion is more likely to Colet, who was a notoriously slow publisher.[7] Thus, the first edition of December 1516 contained letters or verses from five literary friends (certainly friends of Erasmus, perhaps all also friends of More himself), and one of them was from Jerome Busleyden, who was also a statesman. We need not comment again on the excellence of Busleyden's library, house, and coin collection, all of which impressed More, but I do want to dwell for a moment on the letter from Peter Giles to Busleyden. For it speaks of the *Utopia* as far exceeding Plato's commonwealth, of the eloquence of the setting forth, and in general continues the spoof. Next there is a letter from Desmarais to Giles, which declares that "whatever pertains to the good constitution of a commonwealth may be seen in it as in a mirror (*velut in speculo*)."[8] Prof. Nauwelaerts of

---

[3]See E. Auerbach, "Figura" (1944), translated and reprinted in *Scenes from the Drama of European Literature* (New York, 1959), pp. 11-76. Auerbach notes (p. 23) that in Vitruvius "often *figura* means 'ground plan'. . . ." See further his discussion of figura in the phenomenal prophecy of the Church Fathers (pp. 29 ff.); in Alexandria, "not only texts and events, but also natural phenomena, stars, animals, stones, were stripped of their concrete reality and interpreted allegorically or on occasion somewhat figurally" (p. 55).

[4]Thus in *De Transitu*, p. 715 (see Kelley, *Foundations*, p. 61).

[5]Thomas More, *Selected Letters*, ed. Elizabeth F. Rogers (2nd printing with corrections; New Haven, 1961), p. 76. (Hereafter cited as *Letters*.)

[6]Peter Allen, "*Utopia* and European Humanism: The Function of the Prefatory Letters and Verses," *Studies in the Renaissance*, 10 (1963):91-107. Wooden's paper appears in this volume, see p. 151.

[7]*Letters*, p. 76; but see P.S. Allen, ed., *Opis Epistolarum Des. Erasmi Roterdami* (Oxford, 1906-47), II:346 (note to Ep. 467): "Can Colet be intended?"

[8]*The Complete Works of St. Thomas More*, vol. 4, *Utopia*, ed. Edward Surtz, S.J. and J. H. Hexter (New Haven, 1965), p. 27. (Hereafter cited as *CW*.)

Belgium tells me that the house of Peter Giles in Antwerp had as its name *in speculo*—having stayed there for some time, More would have relished this play of wit. The notion of the mirror is echoed in Busleyden's letter to More, where Busleyden speaks of Utopia as holding up before reasonable mortals, as by a mirror,

> that ideal of a commonweal, that pattern and perfect model of morality, whose equal has never been seen anywhere in the world for the soundness of its constitution, for its perfection, and for its desirability.

A mirror is one thing, a pattern and perfect model is something else, and the author of the *Utopia* might well have murmured that the sentiments expressed were not necessarily those of the author himself. But then Busleyden wrote that,

> every object and every action . . . is totally directed to the maintenance of one uniform justice, equality, and communion. . . .'

Here we should note the stress on "one uniform justice," (we may wish to modulate the absolutes of *every* and *totally*, characteristic of Busleyden's rhetoric). Here is one holistic, and contemporary, reading of *Utopia* which looks to the unifying idea of, and concern for, justice; 20th century students need, of course, to be reminded that the 16th-century study of law subsumed what is now found in economics, social science, and other modern departments.

At this point let us turn to the colophon of the 1516 edition, which closes Book Two, and the entire work, with these words: "The end of the afternoon discourse of Raphael Hythlodaeus on the laws and customs of the Island of Utopia. . . ." *Laws and customs (de legibus et institutis)*: an English lawyer could not but think of the title of Bracton's great work *De legibus et consuetudinibus Angliae,* or of other works with like titles such as St. German's *Dialogue de fundamentis legum,* or the *Tractatus de legibus et consuetudinibus regni Anglie.*[10]

The letter of Budé to Lupset (added in the second edition at Basel of March 1518) seems to me to have been too much neglected in the study of the *Utopia* and its *parerga,* and in our efforts towards a fuller understanding of the work. Like More, Giles, and Busleyden, Budé was a lawyer. Giles and Busleyden were the two with whom More spent so much of his leisure in 1515, and their ideas likely had an impact upon More during the period of gestation of the *Utopia;* but I would suggest that the influence of Budé was deeper. First, Peter Giles (Pieter Gillis), whom Erasmus had met as early as 1504 and who was More's host in Antwerp. Giles had been appointed chief secretary of the town of Antwerp, but he continued to work as an editor for

'Ibid., p. 35.
'ºCf. *STC* 3475, 10023, 1197.

Martens for some time. At the time of More's visit, Giles was himself working on Roman law, and he published *Summae . . . legum diversorum imperatorum* (a study of the sources of Justinian) in 1517.[11] Next, Jerome Busleyden, who died rather elderly in 1517, having been a provost of a nearby town, a canon of Brussels, a Master of Requests, and a Councillor of young King Charles, then king of the Netherlands. It was he who gave the foundation for the Collegium Trilingue in the University of Louvain for teaching Hebrew, Greek, and Latin.[12] The third of the trio of friends was Guillaume Budé (born c. 1467 and died 1540), who had studied law at Orleans, which was for law the great center in France at the end of the 15th century. If Busleyden had the larger public reputation, particularly in the Low Countries, Budé had by far the greatest reputation among humanists, and not least in France. Hence the value of his letter to Lupset. I do not know whether More and Budé ever met (perhaps they did in 1520), but it is clear from a letter that they had not met before 1517. They did exchange gifts in 1518.[13]

Yet More knew the work of Budé, and knew it thoroughly. In 1508 Budé published his *Annotations on the Pandects,* which applied to the Roman Law the methodology of Valla on the New Testament, and as Kelley summarizes in his excellent book on lawyers, historians, and humanists in France: "It did for Roman law what eight years later Erasmus' New Testament was to do for Biblical studies; it introduced a new method of criticism into one of the major professional domains in order to begin a reformation."[14] Budé's most celebrated work before 1517 was the *De Asse* (1514), which studied Roman coinage in full context, and also commented on contemporary problems, More praised the work in his correspondence.[15] Indeed, while there are

[11]On Giles, see *CW*, vol. 4, p. 299.

[12]On Busleyden, ibid., pp. 279-80.

[13]On Budé, see *Letters*, p. 197. For a fuller discussion of the correspondence of More and Budé, see M-M. de la Garanderie, "Correspondence de Budé et de More," *Moreana,* 19-20 (1968): 39-70, and *La Correspondence D'Erasme et de Guillaume Budé* (Paris, 1967). Budé's remarkable *De Transitu* appeared in the spring of 1535, while More was in the Tower, and it is not likely that he knew of it: see *De Transitu Hellenismi ad Christianismum,* ed. Maurice Lebel (Sherbrooke, 1973).

[14]Kelley, *Foundations,* p. 57. This judgment is echoed by Lebel: "Budé créa une véritable révolution dans les études juridiques en appliquant la philologie, l'histoire et la philosophie à l'intelligence du droit romain" (*De Transitu,* p. xviii).

[15]*Letters,* p. 108. As well as the detailed study of weights and measures, and of values, observe the immense learning to be found in the digressions of *De Asse,* and above all the extraordinary similarity between the ideas of Budé in *De Asse* and those of More in *Utopia.* Mme. de la Garanderie writes ("Budé et de More," p. 51): "Mais l'étude technique n'occupe en fait que les sept-dixiéme de l'ouvrages; le rest, auquel Budé

many extraordinary letters in the correspondence of Thomas More, one of the most extraordinary, surely, is this letter from More to Budé (probably August 1518):

> I never skim any of your works, but study them seriously as works of the first importance. To your treatise, however, on Roman Measure (*De Asse*) I gave a very special attention such as I have given to no ancient author. . . . But yet if anyone will turn his eyes to what you have written and give it careful and continued attention, he will find that the light you have thrown upon your subject brings the dead past to life again. Whilst he ponders your words, he will live in imagination through all the past ages, and will be able to gaze upon, to count and almost to take into his hands, the hoarded wealth of all kings, tyrants, and nations, which is almost more than any misers have been able to do.[16]

The importance of Budé's writings to More could not be made more explicit, but More was also attracted by other qualities: "Your temperament," More wrote him, "hardly differs from mine." And More must have loved Budé's punning on his name: "*et pro Moro Oxymorum te vocem.*"[17]

The letter of Budé to young Thomas Lupset deserves far more attention than it has received. Lupset had "handed" Budé More's *Utopia,* and Budé took the book with him into the country:

> As I learned and weighed the customs and laws *[Utopianorum moribus et institutis],* the reading of the book impressed me so much. . . .[18]

Almost as a great legal scholar speaking frankly about the question of law, which he took to be central to all else, Budé wrote that the object of legal and civil arts and sciences is stealing, cheating, and conniving:

> This condition prevails all the more in those countries where the so-called civil law and canonical law *[iura, quae civilia et pontificia vocantur]* have greater authority in both forums.[19]

A rather astonishing admission from a civilian in France to be writing to an Englishman with his unique common law tradition. Then Budé made a Morean turn:

> But suppose we were to estimate laws by the standard of truth and by the command of the Gospel to be simple. . . .[20]

---

lui'même donne le nom de *digressions*—et en particulier un *epilogue* qui est comme un livre accroché au livre—est consacré à la crituque des scandales contemporains (cupidité et ambition du clergé, mauvaise politique ou mauvaise administration des princes et des grands), ou à des reflexions philosophiques, morales ou religiouses . . . ."

[16]*Letters,* p. 108.

[17]*The Correspondence of Sir Thomas More,* ed. Elizabeth F. Rogers (Princeton, N.J., 1947), p. 126. Mme de la Garanderie glosses: "sage sous une apparance de folie" (Budé et de More," p. 56).

[18]*CW,* vol. 4, p. 5.

[19]Ibid., p. 7.

[20]Ibid.

We would have to admit, if pressed, he said, that there is a vast difference between true equity and law, both in canonical censures and in civil statues, and in royal decrees. Hence, he went on,

> if you should now wish to explain justice according to the definition acceptable to ancient writers, namely, as the virtue which gives his due to every man, either you would find it nowhere in evidence or . . . treated . . . like a scullery maid. . . .[21]

The virtue which gives his due to every man (*quae ius suum uniquique tribuat*). There are echoes of the Circeronian *De Finibus,* but the definition is even more closely drawn from the opening sentence of the Institutes of Justinian: "Justice is the set and constant purpose which gives to every man his due."[22] About the lamentable contemporary condition, Budé went on,

> This situation obtains unless you admit their contention that the real and world-old justice which is called the natural law has been the source of that law of theirs.[23]

I must comment on the translation, which misses the full force of Budé's irony. Budé was challenging the appeal to what they call the natural law *(quod ius naturale vocant)* on the part of those who feel that all wealth is justified by that law. According to that law and such interpretation, then, Budé argued,

> The stronger a man is the more he should possess, and the more he does possess the more eminent among his fellow citizens he ought to be. The result is that we see it accepted by the law of nations (*iure gentium*) that persons who cannot help their fellow citizens by any art or practice worth mentioning . . . should each have an income equal to that of a thousand of his fellow citizens and often of individual states, or even more than that, and that these same persons should be hailed by the honorable titles of wealthy men, honest men, magnificent fortune-builders.[24]

This happens, of course, Budé commented, in institutions and nations which have "pronounced it lawful that every man should have reputation and power in proportion to the resources by which he has built up his own family furtunes . . . ." Here is a critique of contemporary society that makes its point clearly enough, provided that we see how it rests four-square upon an ironic statement about the so-called natural law—for Budé has, in effect, accused the whole tradition of teaching as well as of administering the law of falsifying its own principles of justice and equity. Budé ended his critique by this hyperbole:

---

[21]Ibid., pp. 7-9.

[22]*Institutes of Justinian,* trans. J.B. Moyle, (5th ed. reprint 1967; 1913), Book I Title 1.

[23]*CW*, vol. 4, p. 9.

[24]Ibid. Note the irony of *"tum locupletes, tum frugi, homines, tum magnifici conquisitores honorifice vocitentur"* (p. 8).

> This process snowballs as great-great-great-grandchildren and their great-great-grandchildren vie in increasing by splendid additions the patrimonies received from their forefathers—which amounts to saying that it snowballs as they oust, far and wide, their neighbors, their kindred by marriage, their relations by blood, and even their brothers and sisters!

By contrast, Budé then wrote, Christ

> seems to me to have abolished, among His own at least, the whole arrangement set up by the civil and canonical law of fairly recent date in contentious volumes. This law we see today holding the highest position in jurisprudence and controlling our destinies.[25]

Pace Aratus and the ancient poets, Budé concluded, Justice after her flight from earth was not stationed in the zodiac: *si Hythlodaeo credimus*, "she must have remained behind on the island of Utopia."[26] *Si Hythlodaeo credimus:* Richard Sylvester has argued well for our believing Hythloday on the fiction of Utopia; I would also follow Budé in insisting upon the centrality of our believing in justice on the island of Utopia.[27] For justice loomed large in the furniture of More's mind in 1515.

Believing in Hythloday runs hand in glove with larger problems of reading and interpretation. It is not idle to conjecture whether some of More's contemporaries who were locked into scholastic habits of mind and scholastic terminology might not have looked at the *Utopia* in scholastic terms. This conjecture has yet to be fully developed and I want to return to it another place.[28] My plea to read *Utopia* as dialogue, which demands seeing it in the fullness of the rhetorical tradition, likewise has yet to be fully responded to, although in a recent graduate seminar I explored something of the Ciceronian requirements for the dialogue, and then examined More's mode of establishing his dialogue. A great deal of further study is needed in the areas of More's control and employment of traditional logic and rhetoric. Traditional rhetoric will help to understand More's irony (which can be explained by Quintilian's terminology), and rhetoric will also account for the form of the work, which I take to be a *declamatio* in Book II, enclosed by the multiple dialogues of Book I and the work as a whole (including the parerga).

Yet another alternative possibility for understanding the *Utopia* as a

---

[25]Ibid., pp. 9-11.
[26]Ibid., pp. 11-13.
[27]"'Si Hythlodaeo credimus': *Vision and Revision in Thomas More's "Utopia,"* in Richard S. Sylvester and G.P. Marc'hadour, eds., *Essential Articles for the Study of Thomas More* (Hamden, Conn., 1977), pp. 290-301.
[28]First put forward in my "On Reading More's *Utopia* as Dialogue," in ibid., pp. 281-8, 621-30.

whole is to be found in the schemes to which Dante alluded. Dante spoke of the ten terms for the treatment of the treatise, and we should have another R.P. Blackmur to apply his ten terms, in a provisional and heuristic way (but as fruitfully as he did for the *Commedia*) to so complex a work as the *Utopia*. Let me remind you of those ten terms:

> The form or method of treatment is poetic, fictive, descriptive, digressive, transumptive; and likewise proceeding by definition, division, proof, refutation, and setting forth of examples.[29]

Too much time has been spent upon the merely descriptive in our teaching and discussions of the *Utopia,* and we have not fully understood the role of the fictive under form or method of treatment, or the proceeding by division, proof, etc. Let me remind you simply of Blackmur's pointing up of the fictive: "Imitative as feigned or inventive, using devices irrespective of truth. A convenient assumption by which to get over a disputed point or a field of ignorance . . . ."[30] Or, in other terms, and from another point of view, a monk of the 11th century had asked Anselm the question, how would you go about proving to someone that a fictive island did exist?[31] Dante's fictive and the problem of proof are intimately related.

The point to stress—that I would wish to stress in bringing forth Dante's two quintets of terms—is that the first five have to do with qualities of movement, and the second five with manipulation, logic, order, adjustment—as Blackmur has summarized. We may not need the rhetorical schemes of Dante (though he got along pretty well with

---

[29]Dante, *Epistolae* X, 9, *ad fin* noted in R.P. Blackmur, "Dante's Ten Terms for the Treatment of the Treatise," in *The Lion and The Honeycomb* (New York, 1955), p. 227.

[30]Ibid., p. 235. Cf. Blackmur on Proof: "the effect of evidence which convinces the mind by its urgency, that is, its adherence to recognized manipulative habits of thought: a test. (From *probare,* with over-notions of right and good and proper.)"

I refer to Gaunilan's remarkable objections to Anselm's argument for the existence of God, contained in the essay or appendix "In Behalf of the Fool": "It is said that somewhere in the ocean is an island, which, because of the difficulty, or rather the impossibility, of discovering what does not exist, is called the lost island. . . . If a man should try to prove to me by such reasoning that this island truly exists, and that its existence should be no longer doubted, either I should believe that he is jesting, or I know not which I ought to regard as the greater fool. . . ." Translated (sometimes inaccurately) by S. M. Deane, *St. Anselm* (Chicago, 1903), pp. 151, 158, 244-47.

[31]See E. Gilson, *La Philosophie au Moyen Age* (2d ed.; Paris, 1947), p. 241, and *History of Christian Philosophy* (London, 1955), pp. 133, 618; and A.A. Maurer, *Medieval Philosophy* (New York, 1962), pp. 52-3.

[32]Paul Valéry, "Paradoxe sur l'Architecte," in *Dialogues,* tr. William McCausland Steward, Boilingen Series XLV, 4 (New York, 1956), p. 178: "Il naîtra, peut-être, pour élever les premiers tabernacles et les sanctuaries imprévus où le Credo futur, à travers l'encens, retentira."

them), and we may not need the new semiotics (though Jonathan Culler and others have argued pretty persuasively for their fittingness today), what we do need is a methodology for seeing the relationships of sub-systems within the work (philosophy *and* economics *and* arts of war *and* history *and* so on): if not the old rhetoric, then a new rhetoric for seeing the whole of the work.

Our undergraduates are quick to tell us that society in More's *Utopia* is static, and that it might be a good place to visit, but they wouldn't want to live there. But that is to mistake the role of the fictive with the dynamics of the work as a whole; we need to stress the movements, rhetorical and otherwise, within the work. Take the houses in Utopia which are demonstrably like row-housing at worst, and early Tudor town-houses at best. Architecture is building, and architectonics is the systematic arrangement of knowledge. One might speak of Utopus as the architector of the kingdom, which by his design and building was so ordered that it became in time a commonwealth (though we are not told of the process). But then one thinks of Valery on "Paradoxe sur l'Architecte": "He will perhaps be born to raise the first tabernacles and unforeseen sanctuaries where the future Credo will resound across the incense."[32] Is this not like Utopus, who so built the first temple within the structure of his kingdom that unforeseen sanctuaries might be born in a commonwealth that he surely prophesied, in which the Credo of the future—including, in this case, Christianity—would resound?

I have glanced at the authority of the text, at the force of some of the parerga, at controls of irony from those statements, and at the interrelatedness of very diverse activities and categories within the work, especially that of justice, which seems to me most central, yet most neglected. For in the time of More and Budé, most of what we now call the social sciences (political science and economics especially) would have been subsumed in the study of law; and law, we must again recall, was generally the largest faculty, and often the dominant one, in the continental universities. Not the least important fact is that for many decades during the Renaissance thousands of young men spent their formative years studying the law (as Brian Tierney has commented).[33] This suggested reading—and it is sketchy and fragmentary indeed—explicitly denies any notion that Utopia can be

---

[33]See my article "Recent Scholarship in the History of Law," *Renaissance Quarterly,* 20 (1967): 274-291, and "Neo-Latin Legal Literature," in *Acta Conventus Neo-Latini Lovaniensis/Proceedings of the First International Congress of Neo-Latin Studies, Louvain 1971* (Leuven and München, 1973), pp. 577-88.

meaningfully read only as a literary, political, educational, or polemical treatise, or, least of all, simply as *jeu d'esprit* or spoof. For *Utopia* is a multi-disciplinary work, and it requires a critical theory, whether semiotic or that of Dante's ten terms, that allows for such an adductive, but holistic, reading.[34]

[34]'For amplification of my views of Thomas More and the Law, see my paper on this subject presented at the More Symposium, Washington, D.C. (June 1978), to be published later. In *The Achievement of Thomas More* (Victoria, B.C., 1976) I have endeavored to place the question of More's legal studies and legal career within the larger context of More's life, writings and public career.

Festivitas, Utilitas, et Opes: The Concluding Irony and Philosophical Purpose of Thomas More's *Utopia**

Thomas I. White

The question most frequently asked about Thomas More's *Utopia* is, of course, what does the author seriously intend in the book? As is well known, the work is so rich that this question has been answered by a number of interpretations, ranging from the view that *Utopia* is a blueprint for an ideal society to the idea that it is simply a literary *jeu d'esprit*. Relatively little, however, has been offered from the perspectives of social and political philosophy and ethics (which are concerned with general principles based on such concepts as equity, justice, moral goodness, the source of authority, the common good, and the nature of the state), and it is my hope to somewhat redress this situation. This essay will discuss the conclusion of *Utopia*, a part of the book that has in recent years received a fair amount of attention, and address the question of whether Thomas More seriously intended the reservations expressed by the persona More about Utopian communism.[1] This essay will argue for an ironic interpreta-

---

*The conference title of this paper was *"Festivitas, Utilitas, et Opes: Utopia's Concluding Irony."*

[1]The passage in question reads: "When Raphael had finished his story, many things came to my mind which seemed very absurdly established in the customs and laws of the people described—not only in their method of waging war, their ceremonies and religion, as well as their other institutions, but most of all in that feature which is the principal foundation of their whole structure. I mean their common life and subsistence—without any exchange of money. This latter alone utterly overthrows all the nobility, magnificence, splendor, and majesty which are, in the estimation of the common people, the true glories and ornaments of the commonwealth" (*The Complete Works of St. Thomas More*, vol. 4, *Utopia*, ed. Edward Surtz, S.J., and J. H. Hexter [New Haven, 1965], p. 245). (Hereafter cited as *CW*.) The most recent exchange of views about *Utopia's* conclusion was between J.H. Hexter and Ward Allen: Hexter, "Intention, Words, and Meaning: The Case of More's *Utopia*," *New Literary History*, 6 (1975): 529-41, and Allen, "The Tone of More's Farewell to *Utopia*: A Reply to J.H. Hexter," *Moreana*, 51 (September 1976): 108-18. Hexter argues for irony, while Allen supports a verbatim reading. See Charles Doyle's note in *Moreana* immediately preceding Allen's paper for a review of the dispute. In its main lines, this paper supports the generally satisfactory interpretation found in J.H. Hexter's *More's "Utopia": The Biography of an Idea* (Princeton, N.J., 1952).

tion by reference both to *Utopia* and to some of More's other works in that same "humanistic," or "pre-polemical," stage of his life. It is my contention that at this point in his career, More's attitudes on such matters as wealth and public opinion made it impossible for him to intend seriously the criticisms of the persona More, and that *Utopia* is most appropriately read as a book of ultimately serious moral, social, and political purpose.

The passage in question appears at the end of Book II when the character Thomas More asserts that the Utopians' "common life and subsistence—without any exchange of money . . . alone utterly overthrows all the nobility, magnificence, splendor, and majesty which are, in the estimation of the common people, the true glories and ornaments of the commonwealth."[2] By these words, the persona More accepts qualities which flow from wealth as good things, and a straightforward interpretation attributes this attitude to Thomas More the author.[3]

An ironic reading of the passage maintains that this is Thomas More's criticism of conventional ideas of worldly riches, and this interpretation is more consistent with the general thrust of *Utopia* than is a straightforward reading. Throughout Books I and II More clearly argues that the selfishness, greed, and (especially) pride of men have so distorted their thinking that they regard money, power, and material finery as worthwhile ends; and an ironic conclusion underscores this theme. In Book I, for example, Raphael criticizes the wealth which sustains a class of idle and useless nobles; he excoriates the landowners for their greed; and he condemns unjust policies designed to fill the royal coffers. Similarly, in Book II we are told that the Utopians attribute the prizing of gold and silver to human folly. Further, the Utopians think that those "who think themselves better men, the better the coat they wear," those who "dote on jewels and gems," and "those who keep superfluous wealth to please themselves" experience only *false* pleasures from their material goods.[4] The persona More's objections not only embody the materialistic attitudes that More criticizes throughout

---

[2]Ibid., p. 245.
[3]For example, Allen writes, "More means what he says about Tunstal /at the beginning of *Utopia/* and, it seems likely, about the public satisfaction at Tunstal's appointment. There are, then, places in *Utopia* where More offers unironic statements. He is speaking in his own voice at the opening of *Utopia.* And so he is in the conclusion. If he is plain and direct in one place, there are grounds for assuming that he is in the other" ("Tone of More's Farewell," p. 117).
[4]*CW*, vol. 4, pp. 167, 169.

Utopia, but because they are offered by this particular character, they show how conventional materialism has become. If More seriously intends these objections, he is disavowing one of *Utopia's* major themes.

It will no doubt be objected that all I have shown is that Raphael Hythloday and the Utopians do not approve of materialism. How do we know, it might be asked, which of Raphael's ideas, if any, Thomas More endorses? A good indication that *Utopia's* criticism of wealth is serious is that the theme of the proper use of wealth and material goods is echoed in other writings from the same period of More's career. In the prefatory letter to Thomas Ruthall in More's translations of Lucian, More cites St. John Chrysostom's approval of Lucian's *Cynicus,* describing the dialogue's appeal as follows:

> For what should have pleased that grave and truly Christian man more than this dialogue in which, while the severe life of Cynics, satisfied with little, is defended and the soft, enervating luxury of voluptuaries denounced, by the same token Christian simplicity, temperance, and frulity, and finally that strait and narrow path which leads to Life eternal, are praised?[5]

In the epigrams, there are twelve cases in which More's targets are misers, greed, and useless wealth.[6] And in More's epistle to William Gonell, he charges the tutor "to warn my children . . . not to be dazzled at the sight of gold; . . . not to think more of themselves for gaudy trappings, nor less for the want of them."[7] Thus we find clear indications that More is seriously critical of material wealth as an important goal of human behavior.

In *Utopia,* Thomas More is not simply lamenting a conventional infatuation with wealth. Instead, he is arguing against the European practice of valuing objects because of their scarcity, and he is proposing instead as morally superior the diametrically opposed conception of worth which depends on how useful something is. The most obvious economic application of this idea is that gold and silver

---

[5]Ibid., vol. 3, *Translations of Lucian,* ed. Craig R. Thompson (New Haven, 1974), pp. 3-5.

[6]Epigrams 1,2,3,4,5,23,53,58,81,116,117, and 121, in *The Latin Epigrams of Thomas More,* ed. Leicester Bradner and Charles A. Lynch (Chicago, 1953). (Hereafter cited as *Epigrams.*)

[7]"To William Gonell" in Thomas More, *Selected Letters,* ed. Elizabeth F. Rogers (New Haven, 1961), pp. 104-5. (Hereafter cited as *Letters.*) The most significant non-Utopian source. More is instructing his children's tutor, so there is no reason to question the sincerity of his statements. Also, the letter was written about two years after *Utopia,* it too has pride as a major theme.

have "no use that we cannot dispense with, if the folly of men had not made them valuable because they are rare," but this principle pervades More's work.[8] Raphael responds to the claim that hanging thieves is just by charging, "Such justice is more showy than really just or useful *[utilis]*"; and he recommends that farming and cloth-working be restored so that "there may be honest jobs to employ usefully *[utiliter]*" those who are idle.[9] More writes that the Utopians "are all busied with useful trades *[utiles artes]*"; the Utopian policy that combines travel and work has the effect that the traveler is "no less useful *[non minus utilis]*" to his city than if he were at home; and when the syphogrants prepare to elect the governor, they swear to choose the man "whom they judge most useful *[maxime utilis]*." Usefulness is the rationale for Utopian ideas about clothing;[11] the Utopians "consider it a most just cause for war when a people which does not use *[non utitur]* its soil but keeps it idle and waste, nevertheless forbids the use and possession of it to others who by the rule of nature ought to be maintained by it"; and they do not usually require payment of debts owed by other nations because, "They think it hardly fair *[haud aequum]* to take away a thing useful to other people *[quibus usui est]* when it is useless *[nullum habet usum]* to themselves."[12] The theme is stressed throughout *Utopia* that articles and institutions should be valued according to how useful they are to the common welfare, and the moral force of this concept is illustrated by More's linking utility with justice and fairness. A major theme of *Utopia* is that in order for a society to be just and virtuous, it must base its institutions on a principle of social usefulness.[13]

[8]*CW*, vol. 4, p. 151.

[9]Ibid., p. 71.

[10]Ibid., pp. 135, 147, 123.

[11]Ibid., pp. 133, 167.

[12]Ibid., pp. 137,149.

[13]There are other examples of the principle of usefulness in *Utopia*. Raphael endorses the Roman practice of putting criminals to work as a *via utilis* (ibid., p. 75); Cardinal Morton says of the plan, "if success proved its usefulness *[utilis]*, it would be right to make the system law" (p. 81); both rich men and gold are called *inutilis* (pp. 104, 157); the senate debates nothing on the same day it is first proposed so that all will have ample time to decide what will be *ex reipublicae usu* (p. 125); Raphael explains that "the Utopians, just as they seek good men to use *[utor]* them, so enlist *[*the Zapoletans*]* to abuse *[abutor]* them" (p. 209); and the priests "take the greatest pains to instill into children's minds . . . good opinions which are also useful *[utilis]* for the preservation of the commonwealth" (p. 229). There should be no question about More's seriousness. He writes to Gonell, "Among all the benefits that learning bestows on men, I think there is none more excellent than that by study we are taught to seek in that very study not praise, but utility *[usum]*. Such has been the teaching of

A conception of worth based on scarcity underlies the persona More's objections at the end of Book II, but it is the moral implications of this position which are so significant. When the persona More states that the Utopians' "common life and subsistence—without any exchange of money . . . alone utterly overthrows all the nobility, magnificence, splendor, and majesty which are, in the estimation of the common people, the true glories and ornaments of the commonwealth," he is referring not to *genuine* nobility, magnificence, splendor, and majesty, but to *counterfeit* varieties of these four qualities which are symbols of an immoral social order.[14] That is, the persona More explicitly refers to qualities which depend on wealth, and since the picture we are given in *Utopia* is that this wealth is obtained generally through greed, avarice, and pride, since it is misused at the expense of the common good, and since it leads only to "false pleasure," there should be little doubt that More regarded such wealth as immoral, and any qualities which proceed from it as corrupt.[15]

Thomas More no doubt believed that there were such virtues as nobility, magnificence, splendor, and majesty, but he surely thought that the genuine versions of these qualities, inasmuch as they could be attributed to a political society, would depend on goodness and justice.[16] However, by appealing to a species of these qualities which

---

the most learned men, especially of philosophers, who are the guides of human life" (*Letters,* p. 104). Also see note 31. More's emphasis on *utile* could very well be part of his debt to Cicero. The Roman denied that the good and the useful could be opposed: *numquam posset utilitas cum honestate pugnare* (*De Officiis,* III, ii, 9, also see II, iii, 9). On More and Cicero also see notes 17 and 46.

[14]*CW,* vol. 4, p. 245.

[15]Ibid., p. 169. The Utopians consider "false" pleasures to be "spurious," (p. 167) "counterfeit," (p. 169) "empty," (p. 241) "base," (p. 177) and "against nature" (p. 167).

[16]There are some honorific uses of these qualities in *Utopia.* The Utopian priests are said to have acquired majesty because of their humanitarian conduct during battles (ibid., p. 231), and, as Allen notes, Utopians who oversee estates in countries which have been defeated by the Utopians live *magnifice* and the Utopian city-states are all "spacious and magnificent" ("Tone of More's Farewell," pp. 113-15). More's idea that nobility and honor depend upon virtue can be seen from his remarks at the beginning of his translation of the life of Pico: "*/L*earning and virtue*/* be the things which we may account for our own, of which every man is more properly to be commended than of the nobleness of his ancestors, whose honour maketh us not honourable . . ., for honour is the reward of virtue" ("The Life of John Picus, Earl of Mirandula," in *The English Works of Sir Thomas More,* ed. W. E. Campbell */*London, 1931*/,* I:349). A. W. Reed points out that "the passage on honour and ancestry which occupies the greater part of the long opening paragraph" was

depends upon wealth, the persona More speaks as though the genuine virtues could somehow exist apart from an equitable social and economic order, and the point of this speech is probably to show just how perverse sixteenth century Europe had become. That is to say, public opinion esteems highly the counterfeit, rather than the genuine versions, which would require a good and just society. What greater perversity could there be than that the people of a society should feel that their commonwealth's "true glories" *(vera decora)* are those things which have been won precisely at their expense—their exploitation, inequity, and the loss of justice?[17]

In this connection, the persona More's reference to public opinion (*ut publica est opinio*) is especially revealing about the author's intentions.[18] First of all, this phrase offers the specific contrast between the good sense of Utopia and the folly of Europe. As Hexter has noted, "But in the passage whose sense we are trying to winkle out, the public opinion which, according to More, finds nobility, magnificence, splendor, and majesty the glories and ornaments of the commonwealth is the perverse, depraved, false, and mad opinion of

added by More ("Introduction," ibid., p. 19). In his "Tone of More's Farewell," Ward Allen tries to show that *Utopia's* conclusion is not ironic by arguing from concrete illustrations of nobility, magnificence, splendor, and majesty which are in the notes to the Yale *Utopia.* Allen's argument is convincing, however, because he does show that More, his contemporaries, and the ancients believed that genuine versions of these qualities are good things. He does not explain why we must assume that the persona More is referring to genuine, and not counterfeit, qualities.

[17]More's choice of *vera decora atque oblectamenta* suggests some possible connections with Cicero. Cicero used the phrase ironically in his *Oratio pro A. Caecina* when he described Fidiculanius Falcula as: *senator populi Romani, splendor ordinis, decus atque ornamentum judiciorum* (X:28). More may have deliberately echoed Cicero to underscore his own irony. Cicero used *decorum* to render πρέπων, a term with moral connections, and More may have employed *decora* in that sense: *Huius [decori] vis ea est, ut ab honesto non queat separari; nam et, quod decet, honestum est et, quod honestum est, decet; . . . et iusta omnia decora sunt, iniusta contra, ut turpia, sic indecora (De Officiis,* I, xxvii, 93-94). It is possible, then, that "true glories" is not the best translation of *vera decora* since it lacks any moral force. Perhaps one could say "true virtues." Therefore, the persona More would be explicitly identifying the nobility, magnificence, splendor, and majesty which depend upon money as the essential moral attributes of a commonwealth, and this would make the irony even clearer. Concerning decorum, also see note 46.

[18]The Yale edition translates *ut publica est opinio* by "in the estimation of the common people" (245). Hexter changes this to "such is public opinion" ("Intention, p. 535) and Allen concurs ("The Tone of More's Farewell," p. 116). This translation is supported by the renderings of Ralph Robinson ("as the common opinion is" *[The Utopia of Sir Thomas More,* ed. J. H. Lupton, (Oxford, 1895), p. 308*]*), and Robert Adams ("in the popular view" *[Utopia,* New York, 1975), p. 91*]*). While this does broaden the point, it does not, as Allen claims, substantially alter it ("Tone of More's Farewell," p. 117).

Europeans."[19] More significant, however, is that More consistently condemns common or public opinion as a guide to one's beliefs and actions. Erasmus praises More to Hutten saying, "There is no one less guided by the opinion of the multitude."[20] In More's epigram "On Fame and Popular Opinion" *(De Gloria et Populi Iudicio)* he writes, "Why do you derive satisfaction from the comments of the populace *(vox populi)?* In their blindness they often interpret what is best as a failing and thoughtlessly approve what is very reprehensible."[21] In his prefatory letter to Peter Giles, More makes some acidulous remarks about the reading public: "So varied are the tastes of mortals," he laments, "so peevish the characters of some, so ungrateful their dispositions, so wrongheaded their judgments," and later he comments, "Most men are ignorant of learning, many despise it"[22] And he forcefully condemns public opinion in his letter to Gonell: "A mind must be uneasy which ever wavers between joy and sadness because of other men's opinions"; he hopes that his children "will neither be puffed up by the empty praise of men, nor dejected by evil tongues"; he chides those who have "abused learning, like other good things, simply to court empty glory and popular renown"; he notes that "almost all mortals, through ignorance of truth, greedily snatch at /shadows of good things/ as if they were true goods"; and he warns that pride can be encouraged so much in children that they will constantly seek more and more praise, and will end up trying to please "the greater number, that is, the worse."[23] More's fundamental objection is that common opinion is not shaped by reason and virtue, and it is therefore an unreliable guide to morality. The virtuous man does not care about public opinion; indeed, his virtue usually flies in the face of public opinion.[24]

[19]Hexter, "Intention," p. 540.

[20]"To Ulrich Hutten," in *Opus Epistolarum Des. Erasmi Roterodami,* ed. P.S. Allen and H.M. Allen (Oxford, 1922), IV, Ep. 999.

[21]*Epigrams,* pp. 55, 178.

[22]*CW,* vol. 4, pp. 43, 55. It translates *Plurimi literas nesciunt* (44) as "Very many men are ignorant of learning" (45), but I think that translating *plurimi* by "most" is preferable here, given the context in which the word occurs.

[23]*Letters,* pp. 105, 106. More's reference to "those shadows of good things" echoes the allegory of the cave in Plato's *Republic (The Correspondence of Sir Thomas More,* ed. Elizabeth F. Rogers /Princeton, N.J., 1947/). Socrates explains that the prisoners of the cave would recognize as real only shadows of objects. Ficino's translation reads, *Omnino igitur, inquam, tales nihil verum esse arbitrarentur, nisi fabricatarum rerum umbras (Republic,* VII, 515 c).

[24]It is true that the concept of *consensus* plays an important role in More's polemical writings, and that this might appear to limit the extent to which one can push his anti-

Finally, it must be remembered that Thomas More was well trained in philosophy and knew that from a philosophical viewpoint an argument from public opinion is one of the weakest that can be offered.[25] If he wanted to defend a materialistic variety of nobility, magnificence, splendor, and majesty, More would have given a more persuasive argument than an appeal to common opinion. He at least would have said that doing away with money would endanger the public order, because the people could never recognize true virtue, and so it would be better that they respect qualities dependent on money than nothing at all. (This would be a variation on one of the Aristotelian objections to communism used in Book I.) At the end of *Utopia*, however, the persona More offers only the extremely weak argument from public opinion, and this is about as clear a signal as our author could give to the irony.

Therefore, More's criticisms of wealth, his endorsement of a principle of social usefulness, and his distrust of public opinion strongly argue an ironic reading of the passage.

The dispute about whether this passage is ironic may seem trivial, but actually the whole point of *Utopia* effectively rests on the tone of More's conclusion.[26] That is, if at the end of *Utopia* Thomas More

---

democratic tendencies. However, when More defines the validity of law in terms of *consensus*, he speaks of "the judgment of all learned men . . ., the judgment of all good men . . ., the public agreement of the whole world" *(Responsio ad Lutheram, p. 281, see below).* Therefore, in his criticism of popular opinion, More no doubt has in mind foolish judgments by the many which contradict the wisdom of the learned, the good, and legitimate authority, and which thus prevent *consensus,* see John M. Headley, "Introduction," in *CW,* vol. 5, *Responsio ad Lutherum [*New Haven, 1969*],* pp. 743-45, and Richard C. Marius, "Thomas More's view of the Church," in ibid., vol. 8, *The Confutation of Tyndale's Answer [*New Haven, 1973*],* pp. 1294-97.) On public opinion also see the note to p. 244 in ibid., vol. 4, p. 568.

[25]While there is a slight possibility that More was introduced to philosophy at Oxford, it is more likely that it was after his return to London that, as Erasmus writes to Hutton, "*[*More*]* applied himself to Greek letters and the study of philosophy." More's friends (Grocyn, Linacre, Erasmus, and Colet) were interested in philosophy, and throughout More's writings there are references to a variety of thinkers, e.g., Plato, Aristotle, Cicero, Seneca, Epictetus, Augustine, Boethius, and Aquinas.

[26]Hexter nicely summarizes the importance of this passage: "For our understanding of *Utopia* it does matter how we read that last passage about the jeopardy into which community of living and subsistence put nobility, magnificence, splendor, and majesty. If we take it seriously, we will take the condemnation of private property elsewhere in *Utopia* satirically or trivially—as a mere *jeu d'esprit.* If we take the passage satirically, we will take the condemnation seriously. So the determination of More's intention in this passage affects our entire sense of what *Utopia* means—whether it was directed against the abuses of the European world like Erasmus' *Praise of Folly,* or against its uses like—in a different sphere—Luther's *Babylonian Captivity.* " ("Intention," p. 541).

disavows his critique of the abuse of wealth and his condemnation of nominally Christian sixteenth century Europe, this means the book is primarily a play of wit, or literary tour de force—more interesting for how More writes than for what positions he advocates. Since arguments have been made for these interpretations, it is important that we address their claims as one final defense for *Utopia's* philosophical seriousness.

The *locus classicus* for the idea that *Utopia* is a *jeu d'esprit*, of course, is C.S. Lewis's statement that

> as long as we take the *Utopia* for a philosophical treatise it will 'give' wherever we lean our weight. It is, to begin with, a dialogue: and we cannot be certain which of our speakers, if any, represents More's considered opinion. . . . It becomes intelligible and delightful as soon as we take it for what it is—a holiday work, a spontaneous overflow of intellectual high spirits, a revel of debate, paradox, comedy and (above all) of invention, which starts many hares and kills none. It is written by More the translator of Lucian and friend of Erasmus, not More the chancellor or the ascetic.[27]

Lewis's interpretation, however, is not at all persuasive. First, *Utopia's* dialogue form poses insurmountable problems only to the individual who would read *Utopia* apart from both its milieu and its author, ignoring the humanists' desire to imitate classical writings, More's considerable knowledge of classical philosophy, and More's role as social critic. Furthermore, not only is there no reason to assume that any one character in the book consistently reflects More's serious thoughts, but at the very least we can conclude that opinons expressed in *Utopia* should be taken seriously when found in More's other writings from the same period—especially in something like the epistle to Gonell.

Lewis is correct in maintaining that there is a good deal of humor, invention, and folly in *Utopia,* but he confuses means and ends when he concludes that "It all sounds as if we had to do with a book whose real place is not the history of political thought so much as that of fiction and satire."[28] While More does write fiction and satire in *Utopia,* implicit in the book is a program of reform not generally present in satire. Lewis is right to see the author of *Utopia* as "More the translator of Lucian and friend of Erasmus," but he fails to see that this put More squarely in the tradition of reform represented by

---

[27]C. S. Lewis, "Thomas More," in Richard S. Sylvester and G.P. Marc'hadour, eds., *Essential Articles for the Study of Thomas More* (Hamden, Conn., 1977), pp. 390-91. (Hereafter cited as *Essential Articles.)*
[28]Ibid., p. 390.

the Dutch humanist. Both More and Erasmus employ much wit in their writings, but it is usually to some social, political, or religious purpose. One need only think of *The Praise of Folly, Julius Excluded,* or the *Colloquies* for examples of the marriage of high humor and very serious social or religious criticism.[30] That the play of wit in *Utopia* is similarly didactic can be seen from its title, because More describes his book as "no less beneficial than entertaining."[31] More, like Erasmus, used fiction and satire in the hope of reforming men's morals, so his play of wit is more accurately described as a *jeu d'esprit sérieux.*

It should be noted that this directing of "intellectual high spirits" to serious ends is also characteristic of More at this time in his career. In the prefatory epistle to his translations of Lucian, More gives high praise to the way in which the Greek satirist "combined

[29]For this view of More and Erasmus, see, for example, Robert P. Adams, *The Better Part of Valor: More, Erasmus, Colet, and Vives on Humanism, War, and Peace, 1496-1535* (Seattle, 1962).

[30]In his defense of *Folly* to Dorp, Erasmus writes, "In the *Enchiridion* I laid down quite simply the pattern of a Christian life. . . . And the *Folly* is concerned in a playful spirit with the same subject as the *Enchiridion.* My purpose was guidance and not satire; to help, not to hurt; to show men how to become better and not to stand in their way . . . I had often observed that this cheerful and humorous style of putting people right is with many of them most successful" *(The Correspondence of Erasmus: Letters 298 to 445,* tr. R.A.B. Mynors and D.F.S. Thomson [Toronto, 1976], pp. 114-115).

[31]*CW,* vol. 4, p. 1, *Nec minus salutaris quam festivus.* More conjoins profit and pleasure three other times in *Utopia.* In his unfriendly remarks on the "varied tastes of mortals," he speaks of the plight of "those who torment themselves with anxiety in order to publish something that may bring profit *[utilitas]* or pleasure *[voluptas]* to others" (p. 43); Raphael praises the Utopians' fondness for gardens by saying, "Certainly you cannot readily find anything in the whole city more productive of profit *[usum?]* and pleasure *[voluptas]* to the citizens" (p. 121); and some Utopians are not entrusted with the care of a fool because they "would find in him neither use *[usus]* nor even amusement *[oblectamentum]*" (p. 193). This combination was especially characteristic of the humanists: Paul Kristeller writes, "The synthesis of philosophy and rhetoric in [Cicero's] work provided the humanists with a favorite ideal, namely the combination of eloquence and wisdom, an ideal which pervades so much of Renaissance literature" *(Renaissance Thought* [New York, 1961], p. 19). Furthermore, not only is the title's sentiment characteristic of More, but so is its form. Elizabeth McCutcheon notes that "one of More's favorite litotic constructions . . . [is] some combination of a negative with *minus* or *minus quam"* (Denying the Contrary: More's Use of Litotes in the *Utopia,"* in *Essential Articles,* p. 273). Erasmus testifies to the joining of wit and sagacity in *Utopia* when he tells William Cop to read the book "if you ever want to laugh, or rather if you ever want to observe the sources from which arise nearly all the evils of the commonwealth" *(Opus Epistolarum,* II, 483, 11. 17-19).

delight with instruction" in reprimanding and censuring human frailties.[32] A similar spirit inhabits More's Latin epigrams.[33] This further supports the idea that the comedy, paradox, and invention in *Utopia* ultimately has a serious purpose.

An interpretation more difficult to counter than that of Lewis, however, is one which regards *Utopia* not so much as a play of wit, but as serious literature; an interpretation which asserts the primacy of literary form, paradox, characterization, and deliberate ambiguity on the author's part. Richard Sylvester, for example, does not question More's seriousness in writing *Utopia,* but he speaks of it as a "new type of mental exploration," and "as posing a question rather than offering a solution." Recalling that More wrote Book II before Book 1, Sylvester observes:

> Thus the order in which we read the work, which represents More's final intention, reverses the order in which he conceived it; the genetics of composition have been displaced by a measured rethinking and reassessment; what was once an autonomous monologue has been set in a dialogic framework. Perhaps our own interpretations of the work as a whole should be modelled on this process. *Utopia,* as we have it, begs us to continue the discussion, to confront Hythlodaeus for ourselves so that, as Thomas More puts it at the end of Book II, we may have another chance "to think about these matters more deeply and to talk them over with him more fully."[34]

In a similar vein, Ward Allen writes,

> More's literary devices are, to my mind, a means for making the experience of visiting Utopia real. The visitor comes away from the experience, as he does from most experiences, with an ambivalent and puzzled view. More encourages just such a view when he steps into his work to have a last word about the strange experience.[35]

Claims for studied ambiguity through literary method, however, must first be limited by the clarity and strength of the major positions More does take in *Utopia.* Book I criticizes a number of institutions which do not serve the public interest: an idle nobility, standing armies, the evils of enclosure, the practice of hanging thieves, useless and non-didactic punishment, the unfair distribution of a society's wealth, ambitious and greedy monarchs, and the councilors who are only too willing to suggest unjust policies. Book II is more theoreti-

---

[32]*CW,* vol. 3, p. 3. *Voluptatem cum utilitate coniunxerit* (p. 2).

[33]In his prefatory letter, Beatus Rhenanus lauds Mcre by noting how rare it is that epigrams should be learned as well as witty, and by describing them as more profitable than those of Pontanus and Marullus. *(Epigrams,* pp. 3-4).

[34]Richard S. Sylvester, " *'Si Hythlodaeo credimus' ":* Vision and Revision in Thomas More's *Utopia,"* in *Essential Articles,* p. 292-93.

[35]Allen, "Tone of More's Farewell," p. 118.

cal, but More generally advocates social and political principles oriented towards the common good and human happiness: for example, useful labor and universal diligence, rule by the most competent, political authority based on a measure of consent, the proper use of material goods, the principle of usefulness, open-mindedness to social change, the necessity of moral virtue, the efficacy of reason, its compatibility with true religion, and the danger of human pride. In many cases, More appears simply to criticize the status quo without offering any practical solution (the betrothed Utopians' premarital viewing of one another is probably the best example), and so he at times seems to be deliberately ambiguous, challenging the reader to think about these issues. But in such cases, More usually endorses a principle (in this case, that marriage should be entered into seriously, carefully, without deception, and /possibly/ without shame about being concerned with physical attraction), and so any ambiguity is only in terms of the practical implementation of this principle. Throughout *Utopia,* More offers more answers than questions, although the answers are usually conceptual ones.

More important, however, is that claims about the primacy of *Utopia* as literature must also be qualified by the significance of the circumstances under which *Utopia* was written. The very beginning of Book I and the bulk of Book II were composed somewhat at leisure, but most of Book I and the end of Book II were produced in stolen moments while More was again actively engaged in his legal career.[36] This is important for two reasons. First, it is not unreasonable to assume that these conditions could have left *Utopia* with a number of rough edges; More simply did not have the time to worry about the fine points, and some aspects of the book are probably attributed to this than More's literary intention, for example, the breakdown of organization in Book II and the lack of formal unity between the two books.[37] Second, if we believe this order of *Utopia's* composition, we must see that most of the evidence cited by literary critics about characterization in *Utopia* was written back in London after the description of the island was completed. Thus, while Book II is, in a sense, given through Raphael's eyes, at the time it was written Hythloday was a relatively tame fellow, lacking the passion he later acquired, and more interested in

---

[36]See Hexter, *More's "Utopia,"* pt. 1.
[37]R. S. Sylvester, for example, seems to suggest that the structure of Book II was deliberate ('" 'Si Hythlodaeo credimus,' "' in *Essential Articles,* p. 300).

describing than in endorsing Utopia.[38] In fact, if we take Raphael at his word, he criticizes a number of Utopian institutions. For example, in a very important criticism of Utopia's philosophical underpinnings, he charges that the Utopians "lean more than they should to the school which espouses pleasure as the object by which they define either the whole or the chief part of human happiness";[39] Raphael finds the Utopians' achievements in logic wanting,[40] although More is obviously ironic here; and Hythloday remarks that the premarital viewings seemed to him "very foolish and extremely ridiculous."[41] And since More seems to have told Peter Giles that he would send the manuscript within a month or so, obviously too short a time to make major changes or additions, I see no reason to think that More wrote Book II through the eyes of the Raphael of Book I.[42] Therefore, Sylvester makes a critical error when he writes that

[38]Edward Surtz notes, "Except for occasional flashes, only toward the end of Book II does Hythlodaeus the zealous idealist reappear in all the glow and color which is his in Book I" (*CW*, vol. 4, p. cxxxix). While Surtz attributes this to the fact that Book II is a monologue, I think it more likely stems from More's not having fully developed the character of Raphael Hythloday when he wrote Book II. Raphael does criticize: European idleness and luxury (129-131); fashion (135); wineshops, brothels, alehouses, and any other "opportunity for corruption" (147); the belief that honor is deserved for rich clothing, ancestry, or superfluous wealth (167-171); and hunting (171). Raphael explains, "Whether /the Utopians' views of virtue and pleasure/ are right or wrong, time does not permit us to examine—nor is it necessary. We have taken upon ourselves only to describe their principles, and not to defend them" (179).
[39]Ibid., p. 161.
[40]Ibid., p. 159.
[41]Ibid., p. 189. Sylvester writes that when Raphael "seems to be criticizing Utopian customs, we find that he quickly rights himself and launches into a vigorous defense of the very thing he had just cast doubt on. Utopian pre-marital inspection, for example, which 'seems to us very foolish and ridiculous,' is wittily rationalized in the next paragraph so that it seems suddenly to be the *only* sensible procedure" (" '*Si Hythlodaeo credimus,*' " in *Essential Articles*, p. 299). Actually, Raphael's description shows only that the Utopians have a reason for their practice. That is, the explanation shows that the practice is in some way sensible, but surely not that it is the only sensible procedure. There are other examples of Hythloday's misgivings about Utopia. Raphael's description of how the Utopians store their gold begins very apologetically (*CW*, vol. 4, p. 151); he explains that if instead gold were locked in a tower, "the foolish imagination of the /Utopian/ common folk" would conclude that the people were somehow being deceived (ibid.); he criticizes those Utopians who worship as the chief divinity the sun, moon, a planet, or some deceased person (p. 217); and he also maintains that those who believe that animals have immortal souls are in error (p. 223).
[42]Ibid., p. 39. While some students of *Utopia*, e.g., Sylvester and Allen, find the moral passion and single-mindedness of Raphael a flaw in his character and a matter of crucial importance, I do not share their views.

"the distinction *[of Giles and Budé]* between what Hythlodaeus sees
in the new land and what More's narrative reveals to us about both
the ideal country and Hythlodaeus' view of it is crucial," and again
when he writes,

> We do not go wrong if we see Book II as an extended image of Hythlo-
> daeus' own personality. Utopia enshrines his ideal and virtues, but it
> also—and he himself is completely unaware of this—hints at the defects
> in his thinking and at the moral flaws in his character. Utopia is made
> like all famous creations, in the image and likeness of its creator.[43]

Sylvester's Raphael, however, is not the creator of Utopia, for he did
not exist when Book II was written. To claim that More changed the
nature of Book II when he added Book I, and created the character
of Raphael the visionary, seems unpersuasive. It suggests no reason
why More would want to change a relatively straightforward description of the "philosophical city" to a biased one. That is, it does not
explain the character of More's so-called "reassessment" of Book II.
More importantly, even Sylvester's description of Raphael as a
self-absorbed visionary idealist with serious flaws cannot be sustained. For not only are the main ideas of Book II found in More's other
writings of the same period, but Raphael, ostensibly at his most visionary (in the peroration on pride), is offering a theme which More
stresses in his letter to Gonell. Thus, Raphael is not offering his own
vision, he is offering More's.

There is certainly no denying that the literary element looms large
in *Utopia,* and that More occupies an important place in the study of
sixteenth century literature; *Utopia* is, after all, both *festivus* and *salutaris.* Nonetheless, the second of these two qualities must be given
more weight, since what is festive in *Utopia* is generally offered for
a salutary purpose. That is, the entire book is an exhortation to
moral reform. The jest about the premarital viewings has already
been mentioned; similarly, the high comedy of the Utopians' use of
gold and the Anemolian ambassadors' visit is a lesson on wealth and
pride; and the point of the wryly ironic remarks about the holy and
inviolable treaties of Europe is quite clear. Furthermore, More's seriousness of purpose is supported by the very similar testimony by
the two men who would have best known More's mind on *Utopia*:
Peter Giles and Erasmus. Giles praises More's sagacity in noting
"the sources from which all evils of the commonwealth arise or from
which all blessings possible could arise," and Erasmus echoes this
when he recommends that William Cop read *Utopia* "if you ever
want to observe the sources from which arise nearly all the evils of

⁴³Sylvester, " 'Si Hythlodaeo credimus,' " in *Essential Articles,* pp. 296, 298-99.

the commonwealth."[44] Such close agreement is surely more than coincidence, and probably stems directly from their contact with More while he was composing the book.[45]

Therefore, while the fiction has a number of purposes, pride of place must ultimately be given to the philosophical. *Utopia* is informed by a philosophical approach lacking in such a satirist as Swift, the work is a philosophical critique of contemporary society, and it argues that an equitable and virtuous society is possible if only man would be led by reason.[46] To assert the primacy of dialogue and structure in *Utopia*, and to say that the book must be read as a work of literature before it can be considered as a philosophical treatise or a plea for reform, is to misrepresent the seriousness of More's intentions, and thus to misread the book. *Utopia* is a masterpiece of literature, but it must ultimately be seen as a serious philosophical examination of the fundamental problems of human society in general, and of the dominant social, political, religious, and economic order of sixteenth century Europe, and as a treatise which proposes a series of social, political, and ethical principles on which the just society is based.

[44]*CW*, vol. 4, p. 23. Giles refers to *fontes, unde omnia reipublicae vel oriuntur mala, vel oriri possent bona* (ibid., p. 22); Erasmus echoes this when he writes, *fontes ipsos intueri unde omnia fere reipublicae mala oriuntur (Opus Epistolarum,* II, Ep. 539, p. 483). Similarly, Erasmus writes to Hutten that More "published his *Utopia* for the purpose of showing what are the things that occasion mischief in commonwealths."

[45]The seriousness of More's intention is also emphasized in Edward Surtz, S.J., *The Praise of Pleasure: Philosophy, Education, and Communism in More's "Utopia"* (Cambridge, Mass., 1957), and J.H. Hexter, *More's "Utopia".*

[46]The philosophical character of *Utopia* is evidenced in a number of ways. Raphael is described as having "devoted himself unreservedly to philosophy" (*CW*, vol. 4, p. 51). Book I criticizes certain European practices by appealing to ethics and social philosophy, and Book II describes a society whose institutions are based primarily on reason. It is usually overlooked, however, that the Dialogue of Counsel in which Raphael's uncompromising approach *(philosophia scholastica* [ibid., p. 98]) is opposed by the persona More's more accommodating attitude *(philosophia civilior* [ibid.]) is at base a dispute between two schools of philosophy—roughly between the Epicurean's decision to shun the world and Cicero's conviction that "that duty which is connected with the social obligation is the most important duty, and service is better than mere theoretical knowledge, for the study and knowledge of the universe would somehow be lame and defective, were no practical results to follow *(De Officiis,* tr. Walter Miller [Cambridge, Mass., 1913] xliii, 153).

Especially significant is More's use of Cicero's concept of *decorum* (propriety), for this is at the heart of the persona More's argument. Responding to Raphael, the More of the dialogue states, "But there is another more civic philosophy which knows its stage, adapts itself to the play in hand, and performs its role neatly and appropriately *[cum decoro]*" (*CW*, vol. 4, p. 99, trans. adapted); he expands the idea saying that even if your /desired/ contribution would have been superior in itself /, w/hatever play is being performed, perform it as best you can, and do not upset it simply because you think of another which has more interest" (ibid.); and he concludes by saying, "What you cannot turn to good you must at least make as little bad as you can" (p. 101). The similarity with Cicero's appeal to *decorum* is striking. Beginning his discussion about how one should conduct one's life with the remark that "everybody, however, must resolutely hold fast to his own peculiar gifts . . . in order that propriety *[decorum]* . . . may the more easily be secured *(De Off.,* I, xxxi:110), Cicero invokes the example of actors: "Everyone, therefore, should make a proper estimate of his own natural ability and show himself a critical judge of his own merits and defects; in this respect we should not let actors display more practical wisdom than we have. They select, not the best plays, but the ones best suited to their talents. . . . Shall a player have regard to this in choosing his role upon the stage, and a wise man fail to do so in selecting his part in life?" (ibid., p. 114). While the ideas of More and Cicero are not exactly the same, it is clear that they are very close.

Most interesting, however, is Cicero's conclusion that "We shall, therefore, work to the best advantage in that role to which we are best adapted. But if at some time stress of circumstances shall thrust us aside into some uncongenial part, we must devote to it all possible thought, practice, and pains, that we may be able to perform it, if not with propriety *[si non decore],* at least with as little impropriety *[minime indecore]* as possible" (ibid.). When one recalls that *decorum* is a moral concept *(quod decet, honestum est et, quod honestum est, decet* /I, xxvii: 94/), the similarity between this last passage and the persona More's recommendation at *CW,* vol. 4, p. 101/1-2, becomes even clearer. I am currently studying the influence of classical philosophy on *Utopia,* which will treat the connection between More and Cicero. Concerning *decorum,* also see note 17.

A Reconsideration of the Parerga of Thomas More's *Utopia*

Warren W. Wooden

Through its early publication history Thomas More's *Utopia* resembled nothing so much as an edition de luxe of a Latin classic. The work featured an extensive apparatus, or parerga (R.S. Sylvester's apt title for this material),[1] consisting of six letters of commendation from prominent European humanists, two letters from More himself, several commendatory poems, a map of Utopia, a chart of the Utopian alphabet, some verses by the Utopian poet laureate, and a running editorial gloss, appended, with various additions and deletions, to the editions of *Utopia* which appeared between 1516 and 1518. Although recently reprinted in full only in the standard Yale edition of *Utopia,* these letters, and indeed the entire prefatory apparatus, are a potentially vital guide to More's meaning in his most controversial work.

Students of *Utopia* who have considered the parerga tend to adopt one of two relatively extreme views of it. One group, eager to disassociate More the saint from the often unorthodox practices of the Utopians, points to such devices as the ironic tinge of the prefatory letters and the manifest fooling of the alphabet to argue that *Utopia* is only "a phantasy after the ancient model . . ., a learned diversion of a learned world," according to Claude Jenkins—at most, writes Christopher Hollis, "a felicitious trifle."[2] At the other extreme, some modern critics regard the prefatory letters, in particular, without notice of irony, reading them as a balanced and judicious assessment by his humanist colleagues of More's thought and achievement in *Utopia.* Thus, for example, J.H. Hexter entitles a section of his pioneering study, "The Orthodox View: What More's Friends Believe," and quotes from the prefatory letters to establish a consensus of how the early sixteenth century viewed More's communistic theories in *Utopia.* In fact, however, a reconsideration of the parerga prepares the reader for a work more serious than the classi-

---

[1] " 'Si Hythlodaeo credimus': Vision and Revision in Thomas More's *Utopia,* " *Soundings,* 51 (1968): 277.

[2] Jenkins, *Sir Thomas More* (Canterbury, 1935) pp. 19-20; Hollis, *Sir Thomas More* (London, 1934), p. 112.

cal Lucianic prototype suggests, yet featuring a broad and pervasive vein of humor and satire which extends from the parerga itself deep into the discourse of Raphael Hythloday. If this is true, then, such a reconsideration will re-emphasize both the crucial importance of humor and the central serious core of *Utopia,* thus bringing us closer to the meaning of More's "little golden book," a work more apparently controversial today than at any time since its original publication.

The chief item in the parerga of 1516 is a group of commendatory letters from eminent humanists, rounded up for the early editions by Erasmus in accord with More's instructions in a letter of September, 1516. Subsequently, for the editions of 1517 and 1518, also supervised by More, his English friend Thomas Lupset and others helped secure additional items for the apparatus. A review of these letters reveals several common threads. All of the letters, for example, lavish indiscriminate praise on Hythloday, the putative author, More, the reporter of Hythloday's tale, and the new island of Utopia. Similarly, each letter specifically reinforces the ruse that *Utopia* is a genuine traveler's memoir, that Hythloday is a real person, and that More's function is simply that of amanuensis. Although the proportionate amount of space devoted to each of these points differs from letter to letter, all the prefatory epistles reflect these primary emphases.

The uncritical, exaggerated enthusiasm for both Hythloday and for all things Utopian is particularly remarkable; the humanists were a very diverse lot, united in their enthusiasm for the classics and their distaste for scholasticism and scholastic pedagogy, but distinctly individualistic in their political, economic, social, and even pedagogical thinking. That the members of the humanist fraternity who contributed prefatory letters offer a blanket endorsement of Utopian mores is extraordinary. Yet this is the case. Peter Giles avers that More's Utopia is "superior to Plato's Republic,"[4] and John Desmarais wishes a delegation of distinguished theologians would visit Utopia, encourage Christianity there, and "at the same time bring home to us the customs and laws of the Utopian people."[5] Finally, Jerome Busleyden is sure that Utopia contains the cure for all the diseases that afflict Europe. Thus, he writes, "Such notable disasters,

[3] *More's Utopia: The Biography of an Idea* (New York, 1965), pp. 43-47.
[4] *The Complete Works of St. Thomas More,* vol. 4, *Utopia,* ed. Edward Surtz and J.H. Hexter (New Haven, 1965), p. 21. (Hereafter cited as *CW.*)
[5] Ibid., p. 29.

devastations, destructions, and calamities of war our common-wealths one and all will easily escape provided that they organize themselves exactly on the one pattern of the Utopian commonwealth and do not depart from it, as they say, by a hair's breadth."[6] Nor does the humanists' praise for Utopia's leading exponent lag behind. Of Hythloday Peter Giles writes that "to my mind he was a man superior even to Ulysses himself in his knowledge of countries, men, and affairs. I think he has no equal anywhere in the last eight hundred years; in comparison with him Vespucci himself may be thought to have seen nothing."[7]

What are we to make of these hyperbolic endorsements? Are we to agree that Europeans should copy without deviation the polity and social mores of a fictional country based on communism, a frankly imperialistic policy abroad and a strict domestic curtailment of the rights of its citizens to speak or move about freely, and featuring such approved social practices as slavery, euthanasia, and divorce? And do we concur that a character whose name means "Mr. Speaker of Nonsense," who functions as chief barker for this new society, is likely to be the wisest man the past eight centuries have produced? I think not. Instead of wondering how these humanists could blithely endorse such a mixed bag of propositions as the *Utopia* represents, we should rather recognize the consistent irony of their superpraise of Utopian mores. R.C. Elliott has aptly advised us that "one must read the *Utopia* with an eye—and an ear—to complexities of the kind one finds in Horace and Alexander Pope, testing the voices of the speakers against the norms of the work, weighing each shift of tone for possible moral implications. The meaning of the work as a whole is a function of the way those voices work with and against each other: a function of the pattern they form."[8] I believe a no less sensitive reading of the parerga is also needed. For in both the *Utopia* and its parerga there is a serious center ringed by humorous snares for the unwary. The hyperbolic praise of Hythloday and Utopianism is such a snare, a trap for the reader who is encouraged to believe that he is about to receive a detailed blueprint for social perfection.

The humor of the lavish praise of Utopia is complemented by the emphasis on the reality of More's narrator, Hythloday. All the letters accept and support this fictive premise. Peter Giles relates how

---

[6]Ibid., p. 37.
[7]Ibid., p. 21.
[8]*The Shape of Utopia: Studies in a Literary Genre* (Chicago, 1970), pp. 31-32.

a cough from one of the auditors at a crucial moment caused him to miss Hythloday's discussion of the exact geographical position of the island; More himself writes Giles to check on the exact length of the bridge over the river Anydrus for, More says, "I shall take great pains to have nothing incorrect in the book"[9]; and William Budé notes that "I personally, however, have made an investigation and discerned for certain that Utopia lies outside the limits of the known world. Undoubtably it is one of the Fortunate Isles . . . ." Or, in approving of More's function as Hythloday's recording secretary, Budé, explains that "manifestly it was a point of conscience with him not to arrogate to himself the major part of the work. Otherwise Hythlodaeus could rightly complain that, if he ever would have decided to commit his own experiences to paper, More had left him a prematurely plucked and deflowered glory."[10] Indeed, even the appended Utopian verses by their poet laureate Anemolius, or "Mr. Windbag," serve this function, for we are told that Anemolius is Hythloday's nephew by his sister. It is a suggestive blood bond.

The heavy stress in the letters on the fictive premise of the *Utopia,* along with the alacrity and enthusiasm with which the commentators insist that Hythloday is a real person, suggests that the element of play in the work is much more important than generally recognized, and that the fictional scaffolding of a returned traveler's fantastic tale is much more than a simple device for launching a political, sociological, or philosophical treatise. As in *The Epistles of Obscure Men,* Ulrich Von Hutten's satire which More reports enjoying immensely in a letter of October, 1516, the humorous entrapment of the unwary and the uninitiated was a source of great delight, almost rivalling the high seriousness of the work. For example, More reports with scarcely concealed delight, of "a devout man and a theologian by profession, who is burning with an extraordinary desire to visit Utopia" to help foster religion, and, presumably, as Busleyden had suggested, to bring back a pattern of their laws.[11] Beatus Rhenanus, another member of the humanist fraternity, reported in 1518 one instance where he witnessed the deception work:

> When the *Utopia* was mentioned here recently at a certain gathering of a few responsible men and when I praised it, a certain dolt insisted that no more thanks were due to More than to any recording secretary who merely records the opinions of others at a council, sitting in after the

---

[9] *CW*, vol. 4, p. 41.
[10] Ibid., p. 13.
[11] Ibid., p. 43.

fashion of an "extra" as they say, and without expressing any opinions of his own, in that all More said was taken from the mouth of Hythlodaeus and merely written down by More. Therefore, he said, More deserved praise for no reason other than that he had recorded these matters well—and there were some present who approved the fellow's opinion as that of a man of very sound perception. *Do you not, then, welcome this elegant wit of More, who can impose upon such men as these, no ordinary men but widely respected and theologians at that.*[12]

On the level of a literary hoax, *Utopia* apparently was successful.

The parerga then advances several appealing, but untrue propositions: that Utopia is a real place and Hythloday a real person, and that the society described is an ideal model for Europe, and the narrator is a wise and dependable observer. The humanists, whose knowledge of Greek made them privy to the game of the Utopian nomenclature, would have perceived this comic deception immediately. Other readers, however, had to learn this lesson on their own. As every reader comes to realize, Utopian society, when Hythloday finally does describe it in Book II, is such a mixed bag of good and bad institutions that blanket endorsements like Busleyden's are impossible outside an ironic context. The reader is forced to pull back from uncritical acceptance of *Utopia* and Hythloday to determine for himself just how far Hythloday is to be believed, or Utopian manners copied. As in Erasmus's *Praise of Folly,* the road to wisdom must pass through folly, through a recognition of our own gullibility. The reader who begins with the expectation created by the parerga of a blueprint for a perfect society as drawn from a functioning model learns his expectations are false. Instead of a perfect model served up on a platter, he receives a fascinating portrait of a strange society with customs of all kinds for his study and amusement, guided by the discussion in Book I of the bases of justice and happiness in the commonwealth. The *Utopia* first entices the reader by fostering one set of assumptions, and then teaches him by substituting another more challenging set. More offers the guidelines and the means, but he trusts his readers to find the answers *Utopia* offers.

The humanists who contributed to the parerga, under the tutelage and guidance of Erasmus, entered wholeheartedly into the spirit of play which informs the surface of More's book. The letters echo a pattern of comic deception complementary to that in *Utopia* itself. It is not necessary here to retrace the contradictions, fumbles, and misfires that punctuate Hythloday's discourse. A.R. Heiserman, Harry

---

[12]Ibid., p. 253, italicized portions originally in Greek.

Berger, Jr., R.S. Johnson, and others have illustrated what Sylvester aptly calls Hythloday's "misreading of his own story."[13] It is enough to note that the lavish praise bestowed on Hythloday in the parerga contributes to an inflated estimate of Hythloday's sagacity which the reader must subsequently revise in accord with his own experience of More's narrative.

Other items in the parerga also contribute to the pattern of humorous deception. The early editions of *Utopia,* for example, contained a map of the new land, supposedly drawn according to Hythloday's report. But the maps (the original in the 1516 edition was revised for the edition of 1518) hardly correspond to the description of the island provided by Hythloday at the beginning of Book II. There, Hythloday reports the following:

> The island of the Utopians extends in the center (where it is broadest) for two hundred miles and is not much narrower for the greater part of the island, but toward both ends it begins gradually to taper. These ends form a circle five hundred miles in circumference *[circunducti]* and so make the island look like a new moon, the horns of which are divided by straits about eleven miles across. The straits then unfold into a wide expanse. As the winds are kept off by the land which everywhere surrounds it, the bay is like a huge lake, smooth rather than rough, and thus converts almost the whole center of the country into a harbor which lets ships cross in every direction to the great convenience of the inhabitants.[14]

The reader who comes to this description from viewing the prefatory maps is hardly likely to see a correspondence between them. Hythloday describes an island resembling an atoll with a distinctive new moon shape and an enormous bay filling its center. In the original sketch of the 1516 edition drawn by one "N.O.," however, there is apparently a bay indicated, although it is far too small to correspond with Hythloday's figures. In fact, the "great crag" Hythloday mentions at its mouth almost obscures the bay entirely on the map. In Ambrosius Holbein's re-making of the map which appeared in the 1518 and subsequent editions, the small bay disappeared altogether along with the distinctive half-moon shape of the island. What appeared to be the fortified "great crag" of the 1516 map has become in the 1518 map the chief cathedral of Utopia situated on the mainland. Thus the readers of early editions of *Utopia,* especially

[13]R.S. Sylvester, " '*Si Hythlodaeo credimus,*' " pp. 285-286. For Heiserman, see "Satire in the *Utopia,*" *PMLA,* 78 (1963): 163-174; Berger, "The Renaissance Imagination: Second World and Green World," *Centennial Review,* 9 (1965): 36-78; Johnson, *More's Utopia: Ideal and Illusion* (New Haven, 1969).

[14]*CW,* vol. 4, p. 111.

those of 1518 and later, containing the polished Holbein rendition of the map, are caught off-balance by a map which they learn, half-way through the text, is manifestly and grossly incorrect, a direct contradiction of the geographical description furnished by Hythloday.

There is additional humor in Hythloday's juggling of figures in his description of Utopia.[15] The island is, he tells us, 500 miles in circumference and 200 miles in width at its broadest point. It takes mathematical expertise to ascertain that these are nonsense figures since a circular island 500 miles in circumference cannot possibly be 200 miles wide at any point, even leaving out the distinctive bay as Holbein does. Thus, while the reader may or may not pick up the game of the inflated figures, he cannot miss the discrepancy between the solid chunks of real estate in the two early maps of Utopia and Hythloday's description of an island with an enormous bay as its center. In brief, the physical representation of the island of Nowhere keeps changing, from Hythloday's new moon to N.O.'s three-quarter moon to Holbein's full moon. The reader trying to reconcile these phases may feel moon-struck indeed.

The parerga, then, are a part of a humanist game, a trap for the unwary, especially those ignorant of Greek. But the prefatory apparatus is more than a frivolous contribution to a learned joke. It teaches both by indirection, since we learn most surely from our mistakes, and directly through the serious passages in the prefatory letters, several of which go beyond play to point the reader to a way of reading More's enigmatic masterpiece. An examination of the prefatory letter from the great French humanist William Budé, whom J.H. Hexter calls "the shrewdest and most perceptive commentator on the book at its time of publication," will illustrate this facet of the parerga's function.[16]

Budé's letter to the English humanist Thomas Lupset begins with thanks for the loan of the Latin translation of Galen's *The Preservation of Health* by another member of the humanist brotherhood, Thomas Linacre. With this easy cameraderie and discussion of mutual projects the reader is introduced into the world of early sixteenth century humanism. Here, as Peter Allen observes, "every one knows every one else; the names in the group recur through-

---

[15]Alan F. Nagel, "Lies and the Limitable Inane: Contradiction in More's *Utopia*," *Renaissance Quarterly*, 26 (1973): 173-180, notices the mathematical fooling and geographical discrepancy in Hythloday's description of Utopia.
[16]*CW*, vol. 4, p. xlviii.

out.''[17] The bonds of friendship and common interest united the humanists in England with those on the continent through a web of shared epistles and messengers. Indeed, H.A. Mason reminds us that "these scholars constituted a *vast mutual-admiration society,* and . . . one of their principal activities was self-praise. These scholars were conscious of belonging to a clique and they industriously puffed themselves as a body.''[18] Thus, first Erasmus and then Lupset were able to call forth the kinds of letters wanted for the parerga including several, like Budé's, from men who had never met More. In such an atmosphere of learned familiarity, the shared joke of the Greek nomenclature, or the lavish praise of Mr. Speaker of Nonsense, were not out of place.

After a humorous discussion of the context in which he read *Utopia*—Budé says he read the attack on private property, the privileges of the rich, and the like, while overseeing the construction of a lavish country estate to complement his city one—Budé moves not to praise of Utopia but to an attack on European vice prompted by, and complementary to, that in More's book. Here the parerga emphasize through imitation, the sincerest of compliments, one of the most important facets of *Utopia*: its value as an indictment of corrupt European practices. Like Budé's, most of the prefatory letters prefer the straight-forward attack we associate with Book I over the indirect protest which is dominant in Book II; certainly they testify to the humanists' appreciation of *Utopia* as a document of social protest.

When Budé does arrive at a consideration of positive values in *Utopia,* his emphases are most instructive. Rather than embarking on a discussion of specific Utopian customs, Budé drives straight for the heart of the Utopian ethic, the principles upon which the state is founded, spiritual principles not civil laws. This ethic is the result, Budé affirms, "of holding in close con. :at (as they say) to three divine principles: (1) the equality of all things, good and bad, among fellow-citizens, or if you prefer, their civic sharing of them, absolute on all counts; (2) the resolute and tenacious love of peace and quiet; and (3) the contempt of gold and silver. These are the three over-throwers, I may say, of all frauds, impostures, swindles, rogueries, and wicked deceptions.''[19] These great principles are not the exclu-

---

[17] *"Utopia* and European Humanism: The Function of the Prefatory Letters and Verses," *Studies in the Renaissance,* 10 (1963): 99.
[18] *Humanism and Poetry in the Early Tudor Period* (2nd ed.; London, 1966), p. 28.
[19] *CW,* vol. 4, p. 11.

sive property of Christians, Budé reminds us. If they were to be adopted as the philosophy of European societies, "avarice, the vice which perverts and ruins so many minds otherwise extraordinary and lofty, would depart hence once for all, and the golden age of Saturn would return."[20] In invoking another purified abstraction of reality, the vision of human harmony embodied by classical pastoral poets in the myth of the Golden Age, Budé reminds us that the Utopian ethic is indebted not only to the Christian ideas of charity and community, but also to the pastoral virtues of *pietas, gravitas,* and *virtus.* Indeed, Budé's comment suggests that *Utopia* might profitably be approached much as we approach Golden Age literature, as a metaphoric repository of positive principles and ideals contained within a fictional social paradigm. But just as the eternal leisure and absolute commonality of the Golden World are not a concrete program for institutional reform in Europe, neither may be Utopian society, despite its greater degree of surface realism.

The relationship between the Golden Age and *Utopia* is the subject for another paper. Here it is enough to note that it is the principles, the spirit, of Utopia that are of primary value to Budé, not the particular social and institutional forms through which these principles are realized in the state. Significantly, Budé concludes his letter with the prediction that "our age and succeeding ages will hold his account as a nursery of correct and useful institutions from which every man may introduce and adapt transplanted customs to his own city."[21] The concept of adaptation is the key to this passage. Budé praises the Utopian ethic unreservedly, but he holds back from praise or endorsement of specific Utopian institutions, which represent the translation of ideal theory into human practice, observing instead that selection and adaptation may be required in the importation of Utopian customs into Europe. Finally, while offering us a viable method for reading *Utopia,* stressing the work's censure of European vice and advocacy of healthy spiritual principles, Budé also furthers the literary ruse through comments on the location of Utopia and the relationship between Hythloday's narration and More's reporting of it.

In conclusion, this reconsideration has emphasized the constant element of play in the parerga. The contributors all join enthusiastically in the literary hoax which sought to establish *Utopia* as the authentic memoir of a returned traveler. This view of the parerga as

[20]Ibid.
[21]Ibid., p. 15.

in some respects a game, taken with the prefatory comments of the humanists on Utopia, suggests that More engaged in an art of pleasant deceit in *Utopia,* tricking the reader into thought while piquing his interest with a portrait of a strange new society. Thus, in the parerga we are led to expect a pattern of a perfect society delivered to us by a wise expositor. Instead, in *Utopia* proper, we are treated to a new country with customs which range from the absurd, the oppressive, and the totalitarian, to the enlightened, the practical, and the judicious, all of which are enthusiastically commended to us by a tour guide who frequently exemplifies the meaning of his name. As the reader revises his initial set of assumptions through his experience of *Utopia,* he finds himself continually challenged and intellectually stimulated by the debates of Book I and the marvellous new society of Book II to sift for himself the constituents of "the best state of the commonwealth." More provides ample aids for the reader in this task, as does the parerga, which point to the essential serious element in Utopian society, the shared values of community, harmony, and love. The parerga, then, are both an introduction and a guide to More's method and meaning in *Utopia.*

INDEX